LATIN AMERICA

By Edwin A. Roberts, Jr.

NEWSBOOK

The National Observer
Silver Spring, Md.

Published by The National Observer
11501 Columbia Pike, Silver Spring, Md.

Library of Congress Catalog Number: 64-8569

Printed in the United States of America
By Danner Press of Canton, Inc., Canton, Ohio

Contents

One and Twenty

A WORLD order which was preserved for hundreds of years by the powers of Europe has, since World War II, given way to a new and diffuse arrangement of nations. Continents that a generation ago were only curiosities to the busy inhabitants of the Northern Hemisphere are now inextricably involved in the most fateful questions before mankind.

It is difficult to argue with the late President Kennedy's statement that no region on earth is more important to the United States than Latin America. A continent and a half in mass, stretching more than 7,000 miles from the Rio Grande to Cape Horn (about the distance from London to Calcutta), Latin America is divided into 20 countries and assorted islands and territories. It accounts for 14 per cent of the land area of the earth and its population of 230,000,000 is 8 per cent of the world total.

Now in the process of difficult change, Latin America has already seen one of its countries adopt a Communist dictatorship instead of freedom. Should Castroism spread to South or Central America—and Cuba is working on it—the security of the entire hemisphere would be in extreme jeopardy. Thus it is that Uncle Sam is supporting the Alliance for Progress to give the people of Latin America the alternative of freedom.

But the importance of Latin America to the United States transcends the Communist threat. The nations of the Western Hemisphere share a common revolutionary heritage as well as geographical proximity. From Latin America comes one-third of all United States imports, to it goes one-fifth of all United States exports. And American private investment in the area is responsible for one-third of all the exports of all the Latin countries.

Most significant of all, perhaps, are the implications of Latin America's 2.9 per cent population growth rate—the highest of any world area—which in 35 years will expand the number of the region's inhabitants to 600,000,000. The republics south of the border promise to influence the life of the United States in an increasingly greater measure.

This Newsbook explains what is happening in the area today. Included is a detailed examination of Castro's Cuba and the Communist movement in South and Central America, a study of the development and structure of the Alliance for Progress and a report of its activities, and analyses of Latin America's peculiar approach to politics and economics.

In addition, this Newsbook includes situation reports on all the countries and key territories of the area, as well as special reports on commodities that typically determine the area's economic fortunes.

More than 100 pictures, along with many charts, have been used to help tell the story.

Latin America, the third Newsbook in a series dealing with vital topics of our times, was preceded by *Elections 1964* and *Barry Goldwater, A New Look at a Presidential Candidate.* More than half a million copies of those Newsbooks have been published.

Latin America was prepared in the news room of The National Observer. Assisting in the news reporting were Mark Arnold and Richard Egan. Heidi Fiske assisted in the research. The illustrations and page layouts are by Kathryn Henkel. The cover design is by Edwin A. Roberts, Sr. Photographs are from the Associated Press, United Press International, and various inter-American agencies, unless otherwise credited.

All the

On the beach in Ecuador: Throughout Latin America, a time to get under way.

Latin Americas

The Diversity of the Area,

The Broad Range of Its Problems

And Its Place in United States Policy

THE PEOPLE of Latin America are not like the people of Spain and Portugal, the chief mother countries of the lands south of the Rio Grande. Although a Latin culture predominates, especially in the cities, the old Iberian heritage has been influenced by the huge Indian populations of Mexico, Central America, Colombia, Ecuador, Peru and Bolivia, and by the huge Negro populations of the Caribbean islands, the Guianas and Brazil. And, to a lesser degree, Latin America has absorbed the values of immigrants from Ireland, Germany, Italy, India and the Orient.

This rich racial mix is today causing problems similar to the ones the United States has been troubled with for years. It is fashionable among Latin Americans themselves to claim they have avoided racial tensions—chiefly through a gradual process of inter-marriage—and this is partly true. Most Latin Americans are a mixture of various ethnic strains and such people do not generally see race as a divisive factor. But there are extreme racial tensions in British Guiana between East Indians and Negroes, and even in Brazil, which clams to be free of racial prejudice, one is not likely to find a Negro naval officer nor a Negro diplomat.

This attitude of ethnic inequality, while of less social importance than it is in other parts of the world, is still potent enough to keep the Latin temperament sovereign in most Latin American republics. And it is the Latin temperament that has given Latin America its erratic history and has contributed mightily to its present troubles.

Switches in Policy

Uncle Sam has always responded to his erratic neighbors in a fitting way. United States policy toward Latin America has been erratic for a hundred years, making its most recent turn in the spring of 1964. When Lyndon B. Johnson succeeded John F. Kennedy as President, he agreed to continue the whole Kennedy program with practically no modifications—except in the area of Latin American policy. On March 18, 1964, Thomas C. Mann, assistant Secretary of State and President Johnson's top Latin American policy-maker, told a group of high-ranking U.S. diplomats that the U.S. would discontinue the Kennedy policy of separating the "good guys and the bad guys" in the Latin republics. That is, the U.S. would no longer try to punish strong men who came to power by overthrowing democratic regimes. The explanation was that the Johnson Administration believed it should not get involved in the internal political affairs of Latin American nations.

Thus, President Johnson is borrowing a page from the Eisenhower administration guidebook. President Eisenhower not only was quite willing to keep hands off Latin politics, but several times his administration decorated Latin dictators.

While such policy zig-zagging doesn't affect the U.S. commitment to help Latin America economically—a commitment that jelled in the Eisenhower years and which was expanded and named (the Alliance for Progress) by President Kennedy—it is the kind of reversal that bothers people like the Latin Americans and General Charles de Gaulle. De Gaulle's primary message to the rest of the Free World is that U.S. foreign policy, because of the nature of the U.S. political process, is subject to sudden change. Therefore, he contends, it is unwise for other nations, though friendly to the U.S., to become too dependent on Washington for anything, including trade and national defense.

And this is the message De Gaulle delivered in person to Mexico in March 1964, and has recently delivered to the people of South America. It is a notion with great appeal for countries that, sometimes rightly, have felt misused by the North American giant. Beyond that, getting the word straight from Paris vastly increases its weight. Paris, and not Madrid or Lisbon, has traditionally been the intellectual oracle for Latin Americans.

But France's resources are limited and its own other interests are many. Indeed, the United States would like nothing better than for France and the other European powers to play a bigger part in the economic development of the region.

Although De Gaulle has no trouble drawing huge, happy crowds when he visits Latin America, it is doubtful he has done much to diminish U.S. influence there. On the contrary, recent developments suggest that the ties between the U.S. and the Latin American republics have never been stronger.

An Old Hostility

The Organization of American States, acting at the behest of Venezuela, declared Castro's Cuba officially an outlaw country and voted to break diplomatic relations with it. Of the four OAS members who still maintained embassies in Havana, only Mexico refused to go along with the OAS decision. Chile, remarkably, cut its ties with Cuba during a presidential campaign in which a leading candidate was a Marxist and a Castro supporter. Bolivia made the break under U.S. pressure; without U.S. aid, the Bolivian economy would collapse. Uruguay broke relations but with extreme reluctance; the country has a strong liberal tradition that makes it instinctively opposed to measures such as the OAS action, and it is expected to try to get that action reversed.

Mexico is determined to preserve its diplomatic ties with Castro because "they are mutually beneficial," but also because Mexicans would rather be poked in the eye with a sharp stick than do anything that suggested knuckling under to Uncle Sam. For while Mexico has received $301,000,000 in U.S. aid since the Alliance for Progress officially got under way in 1961, the country still nurtures an old hostility toward the U.S.

By means considered more foul than fair, both by Mexicans and many Americans, the U.S. in the middle of the 19th century acquired from Mexico territory that included what are now the states of California, Texas, Arizona, New Mexico, Nevada, Utah and part of Colorado. Mexico lost 40 per cent of its territory to the U.S.—not a small reason for a long-time grudge. A few years ago, without notice to the Mexican government, Congress drastically changed the U.S. cotton subsidy law in a move that had a serious effect on the economy of cotton-exporting Mexico.

One Mexican diplomat summed up his country's feeling this way: "The problems the United States has in dealing with the Latin American countries have long roots. The United States was thoughtless and overbearing toward the Latin nations for a long time. Since Franklin Roosevelt's day, perhaps a little earlier, the United States has tried to behave more humanly. Now, with the Alliance for Progress, we Latins have no serious doubt the United States is really out to help us, especially since it would be so uncomfortable if all of Latin America fell into Communist hands.

Paris Match

Kennedy in Colombia: *Muy Macho.*

13

A Peace Corpsman in the Dominican Republic: The Alliance combines self-help with a northern neighbor's good right arm.

"But the people in Washington should be helping us not only through the Alliance programs, but by considering how the trade and agriculture laws Congress enacts can hurt countries that depend so much on trade and agriculture. Beyond that the people of the United States should realize that there are many Latin Americas and many kinds of Latin American people. We do not seek to be loved, but we demand that our problems be understood."

Most Latin Americans do not consider the Communist menace among their immediate problems. The United States, on the contrary, sees the social and economic troubles of Latin America as grist for Communist propaganda and as opportunities for Communist subversion. So far, Castro has been isolated on his island and Communist parties within other Latin American countries have been kept from power. But Castro remains as powerful as ever, Communist intrigues continue throughout the area, and the overwhelming majority of Latin Americans remain pinioned by practically every problem a society can have.

This Newsbook attempts to give the reader a sense of the ferment that is Latin America today. Change is everywhere. Cuba under Castro is still trying to find its way out of the economic labyrinth it worked itself into by needlessly antagonizing its best market and most helpful friend, the United States.

An Assortment of Strategies

Cuba in one sense no longer belongs to the Western Hemisphere and its dependence upon Soviet Russia has caused tremendous problems. Cuba must get its oil from Soviet ports half a world a way, and it must somehow manufacture spare parts for all the Yankee machinery confiscated by Castro. True, the island country offers opportunities for the "New Cubans," young Castro supporters who suddenly find themselves promoted to jobs they never could have won under the old regime. But for most Cubans life is desperate and miserable enough to keep impoverished refugees, who flee their homeland at the risk of their lives, trickling into Florida.

In the rest of Latin America an assortment of Communist movements using an assortment of strategies are working on the minds of the peasantry and the urban slum-dwellers. Some

of these Communists follow the militant Peking line that screams for armed revolutions; others scramble for power through the existing political system; still others are Castroites who take their ideas from Cuba's leader, who in turn takes his ideas both from Peking and Moscow and out of his own head. Although the Communists were slapped down in the presidential election in Chile, these Reds continue to stir up trouble and, despite the split in the world party organization, they all seek the same goal: The end of freedom in Latin America.

The American Response

To combat the enticements of communism and to help Latin America cash in on its hoard of natural resources, the United States is pouring millions into the area through the variegated agencies of the Alliance for Progress. President Kennedy did not invent the Alliance but he did give it a big push. More than that, he appealed to the Latin American people to make a greater effort at helping themselves. Kennedy was more popular south of the Rio Grande than any President since Franklin Roosevelt. He embodied, in the words of one observer of the Latin American scene, *"muy macho,* which translates literally as 'much male' and which is a Spanish idiom for a 'vavavoom' man."

But it took more than *muy macho* to figure out the channels through which foreign aid would be given and by which the Latin peoples could make their own contribution to their economic progress and social betterment. The burden of the Alliance, as it was set forth in the Charter of Punta del Este, clearly rests on Latin America. Latin American countries are supposed to put up 80 per cent of the money along with bringing about broad-scale reforms.

Criticism of the Alliance has not been wanting. Some countries have been slow to keep up their end of the bargain and private capital, both internal and external, has not been forthcoming in the amounts hoped for. But for all these drawbacks, there is tangible evidence of Alliance progress—in new roads, houses, schools, water systems, agricultural programs, and medical and sanitation facilities.

If the problems of Latin America are to be understood, as that Mexican diplomat demanded, it's necessary to examine the peculiar brand of politics that has made it so difficult for the

For much of Latin America, today is a copy of yesterday, and tomorrow is an idea yet to be considered.

countries to achieve stability. Politics has rarely meant a contest of party principles. It has meant a contest of personalities, with the antagonists and their supporters villifying the top man on each side. Issues are personalized and passion often replaces reason. Revolutions have been so common in the area because they have frequently been the only means for getting the incumbent gang out.

A similar instability has existed in the economies of Latin American countries. The feudal *hacienda*, which is a large, self-sufficient farm worked by peons, has kept agricultural production low and the people of the country hungry and poor. In several countries, inflation has kept the economies in a state of constant crisis, as has the dependency of all Latin American countries on a few export commodities—commodities whose prices tend to fluctuate sharply on the world market. Too, there has been the nature of the Latin American people that has led them to regard their plight as "hopeless but not serious," ready to live for today and let tomorrow take care of itself.

But more and more there is an awareness that tomorrow does not take care of itself, that a little planning is necessary. Thus, 10 countries have formed the Latin American Free Trade Association, hopefully to create a Common Market after the West European model and similar to the trade area now being constructed successfully by the five Central American republics. There are signs that corruption and inefficiency are being seriously combatted, and there is more reason to hope for the eventual prosperity of Latin America than there has ever been.

Castro's Cuba, communism in the rest of Latin America, the nature of the Alliance for Progress and its record, the anatomy of Latin politics and the special problems of Latin economies—all these areas are closely examined in the first part of this Newsbook. But most of these topics are of a general nature, applying to the area as a whole. Each country has its own problem and character and so the second part of the Newsbook is devoted to the specific situation in the individual republics and in the Guianas, with emphasis on the most significant events that are occurring now in each.

These 16 special reports discuss the ominous stirrings among the *campesinos* in Mexico, the rewards of economic unity in Central America, the lingering anti-Yankee bitterness in Panama over the Canal and the attempts of that country to develop its interior, the lingering influence of the *caudillo* image in Argentina, the troubles caused by the violence-prone miners of Bolivia, and the nature of the military regime in Brazil.

Similar reports detail the situation today in Colombia, Chile, Ecuador, Peru, Paraguay, Uruguay, Venezuela, the Guianas, the Dominican Republic and Haiti.

This book is a news story about how it is now with the peoples, problems, dangers and ideas that describe the various Latin Americas. And which, in a time of profound change, give stamp to them all.

The story begins with Cuba.

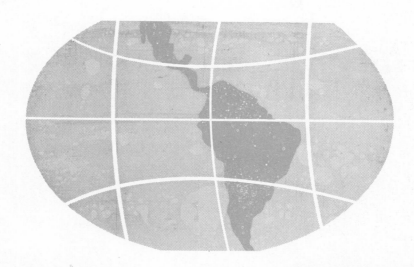

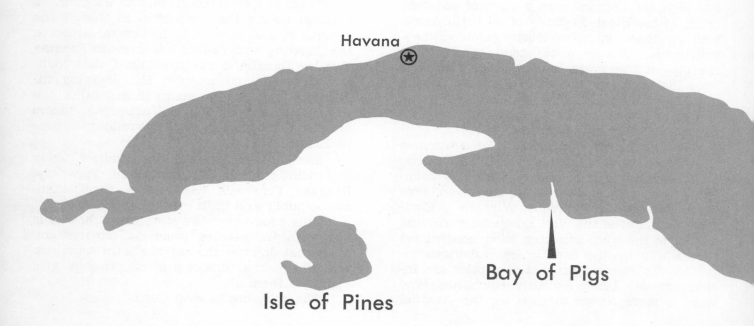

U. S.

Cuba

Havana ⊛

Bay of Pigs

Isle of Pines

Caribbean Sea

As It Is

Castro Accepts Soviet Aid, Chinese Polemics

But Remains His Own Favorite Marxian;

Boondoggles and Ingenuity

IT was once the Pearl of the Antilles. There were gaudy casinos and beautiful women. It was the home of Sloppy Joe's and music and gaiety, and it attracted tens of thousands of tourists for whom any kind of vice or madness could be arranged. It was ruled by a succession of dictators who filled their own pockets while preserving an unjust social order, but it was friendly to the United States and people did not continually risk their lives trying to escape. And it was one of the richest republics in Latin America.

Today, after five-and-a-half years of Fidel Castro, Cuba is, by almost any standard, an economic mess, an ideological mish-mash, and a misfit in the Western Hemisphere. It is also a ruthlessly run police state, and a Soviet satellite. So it appears to even the most dispassionate observer of the Cuban scene.

But that is not the way it appears to Paul Valdes, a wide-smiling, muscular mulatto, as he contentedly contemplates his lot from an easy chair in a small but comfortable first-floor apartment at 413 Clavel Street, not far from the old section of Havana. And how Cuba looks to Valdes may tell much more about the likely tenure of Castro and communism on that island than some of the more familiar indicators.

A visitor has no difficulty spotting evidence of decay and dissidence. He sees it in the stalled cars and wheezing buses, in the long string of rusting freight cars on a rail-

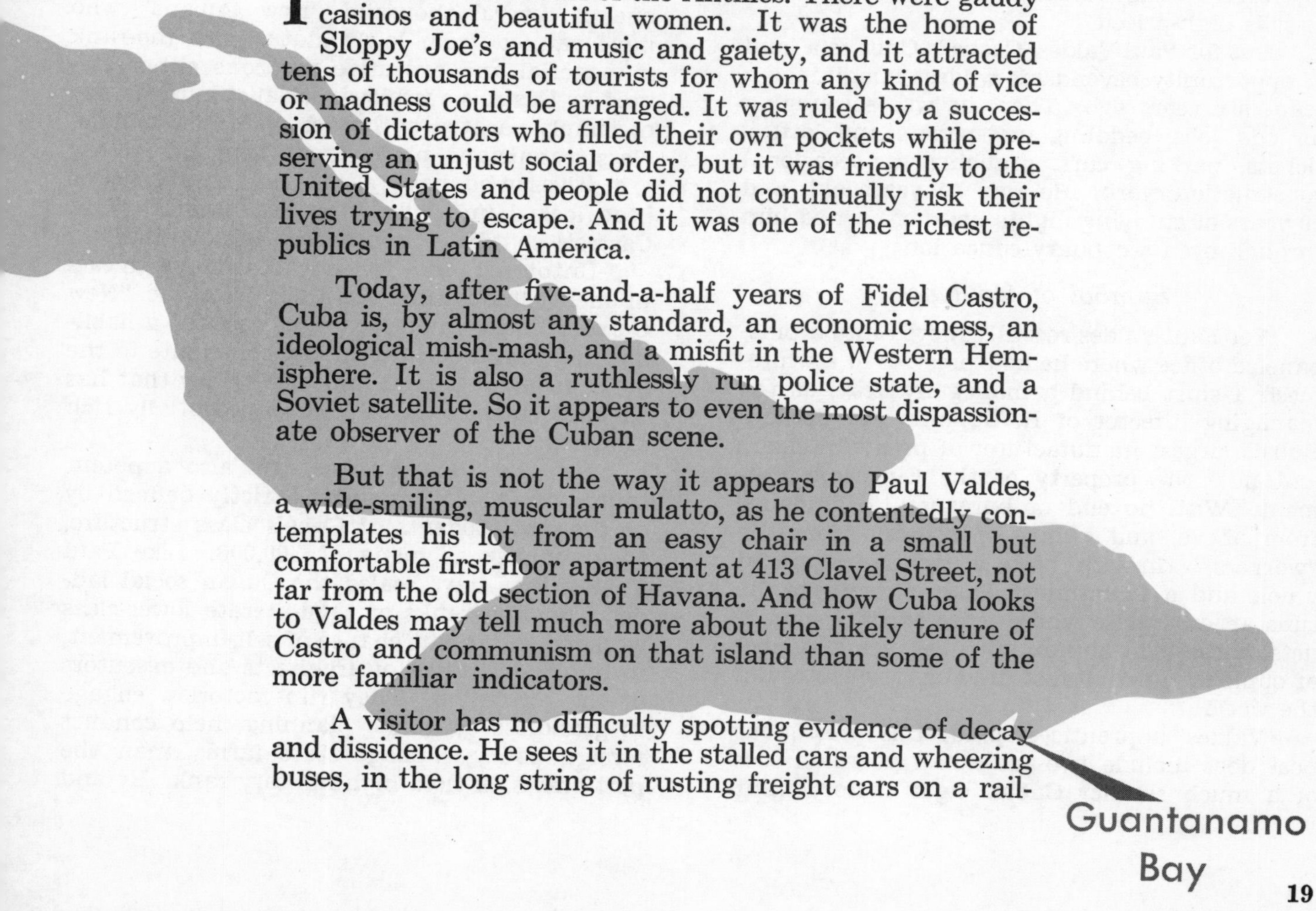

Guantanamo
Bay

road siding, in the industrial machinery idled for lack of spare parts, in the agricultural shambles and the rigid rationing of food and clothing, in the whispered complaints of citizens who accost an American reporter on the street.

Most of the clocks in government buildings have stopped; so have most of the air conditioning units in the once-plush Havana Hilton. Toothpaste is a rarity and so are taxicabs. The food even in fancy restaurants is as unappetizing as it is high-priced.

But for Paul Valdes, Castro's Cuba is a land of opportunity beyond his wildest imaginings a scant six years ago. Then, he was scrounging for odd jobs, peddling newspapers and lottery tickets, parking cars, grabbing at occasional construction work. He was 35 years old, and 20 years of studying nights had not carried him through even secondary education.

Symbol of Opulence

Yet Paul Valdes recently moved into a pine-paneled office where he now presides in a white-mesh T-shirt behind a mahogany desk, as the managing director of H. Uppman, for decades Cuba's largest manufacturer of premium cigars and now the property of the Cuban government. With no end of bureaucratic guidance from above, and plenty of counsel from the "workers," through both a tightly organized union and a Communist Party directorate, he runs an enterprise whose more expensive products, encased in aluminum tubes, are a symbol of opulence in capitalist drawing rooms around the world.

Valdes' apprenticeship for this prestigious post does include two-and-a-half years as boss of a much smaller Cuban cigar factory. But before that, his knowledge about cigars was strictly limited. As he puts it, "I smoked them." And all he knew about factory management was what he learned in a special one-year managerial course established by the Castro regime for deserving supporters of the revolution.

A Source of Castro Strength

Paul Valdes is in the forefront of a crucial element in contemporary Cuban society. He is one of several thousand "New Cubans" who have vaulted from lowly status into top-rank managerial and executive positions either created by Castro's overblown socialist bureaucracy or simply vacated by hordes of former middle-class technicians, professional men and factory executives who have either fled into exile or been locked up as "counter-revolutionaries" in Castro's political prison on the Isle of Pines.

Untutored and, by any reasonable measurement, unqualified for their jobs, the "New Cubans" must, in one sense, be counted a liability; in generous measure, they contribute to the gross mismanagement and inefficiency that has wreaked such havoc on Cuba's potentially rich economy.

But the "New Cubans" are also a potent source of Castro strength. Strictly defined by on-the-spot students of Cuba's class structure, they number as many of 300,000. Like Paul Valdes, they have scaled the Cuban social ladder from the ranks of semi-literate lower-class workers, with scant chance of self-improvement, to the heady status of architects and executors of the revolution. They run factories, engage in grandiose economic planning, help conduct foreign policy, manage state farms, man the post offices, or hold high military rank. By and

large they are a contented, dedicated and—above all—grateful lot.

And in addition to them are many thousands of others who spring from less humble origins, or perhaps have not risen to quite such dizzying heights, but have nonetheless profited, one way or another, from Castro's coming to power.

Good Times for Gloria

Gloria Marsan, for example, is the daughter of peasant parents still farming a private plot in Oriente Province on Cuba's eastern tip. At age 19, she abandoned a secretarial course paid for from her father's savings to become a courier, carrying messages, medicine and ammunition to Fidel Castro's guerrilla forces high in the rugged Sierra Maestra mountains until Batista police closed in and forced her to flee to the United States in 1958. Today she is back in Cuba, working six hours a day in public relations for a soap and shortening factory which once was the property of Proctor & Gamble.

Three days a week Gloria sports army fatigues and packs a pistol during her part-time training as an army nurse. A fervent *Fidelista,* she has not yet fully embraced communism, though she has abandoned her Catholic faith.

To the ranks of Paul and Gloria must also be added a host of other Cubans whose addiction or indebtedness to Castro make them a bulwark to his regime and a sizable obstacle to any policy Uncle Sam might devise for removing the bearded leader from the Cuban scene.

Thousands of students are pouring through Cuba's universities and technical schools, absorbing en route a heavy indoctrination in Marxism-Leninism and the glories of Fidel. Not only is their education paid for by the government, but those who need it get free lodging and a spending allowance. Already they number over 100,000 and comprise perhaps the revolution's loudest advocates. The average student is estimated to have two living parents and one grandparent. Thus there are probably three more Cuban citizens with some sense of gratitude to Fidel for furnishing their offspring an opportunity they themselves never had.

In addition to those who now hold jobs once held by exiles, some 80,000 Cuban families now inhabit houses or apartments abandoned by refugees who fled Castro's rule. This means yet another expansion of the number of Cubans with an acute vested interest in opposing any upheaval which might bring the exiles swarming back.

Pampered PURS

Finally, there is the army, better-fed, better-housed and better-clothed than the average citizen, and numbering 150,000 strong. There is the militia, a body of 300,000 part-time "policemen" for the revolution, authorized to pack guns, sport uniforms and enjoy special status and privilege.

There is also a growing political elite pampered by special privilege. Known as the PURS, it is an amalgamation of the old Cuban Communist Party, Castro's 26th of July Movement, and a second revolutionary grouping which went under the name of the Revolutionary Student Directorate. PURS membership is being strictly limited to the most devoted and trustworthy party workers, with no more than 50,000 recruits currently contemplated.

Nobody even pretends to know how many

Fidelistas all this adds up to. One Westerner, only guessing, figures that perhaps 35 per cent —and conceivably as much as half—of Cuba's 7,053,000 population look favorably upon the revolution to a greater or lesser degree; perhaps one third is passive, either by indifference or intimidation; and maybe one quarter is opposed. Another veteran onlooker puts it differently: "About half of the population," he declares, "spends a good part of its time keeping an eye on the other half."

More Moderate Loyalty

Even if one could safely conclude that the Castro government has backing from half the populace, it's quite true that the support of several hundred thousand Cubans who have received an education or a new house or free medical care can hardly be equated with the backing of the armed forces, or the loyalty of the secret police.

On this score, one can only accept the consensus of most authorities that there is precious little evidence of disaffection where it would count the most—among top military men—and not much evidence of meaningful dissension anywhere else.

There is, naturally, no guarantee of long tenure for Fidel. If he and his amateur Marxist economists make many more miscalculations comparable, say, to their original and abortive crash program to industrialize Cuba, the economy could conceivably collapse, bringing an end to all the socialist beneficence and sparking wider and deeper opposition to the regime. Some experts, including many American officials, have high hopes this will eventually happen. Certainly, for instance, the United States'

economic squeeze on the little island is compounding the damage the Castroites are doing to their own country. But it's probably unrealistic to count on a complete economic collapse.

For one thing, the Cuban economy is just naturally rich and difficult to destroy. For another, as Wall Street Journal correspondent Philip Geyelin reported after a recent trip through Cuba, Castro and his Communist cohorts have not only a flair but almost, it seems, a preference for improvising their way around the most awesome obstacles.

The "Socialist Vanguard Factory" offers a sample of this improvisation. From the outside it looks like a dingy steel mill not unlike the sort of family-owned foundry that once flourished in many an American small town. But its inner workings have no industrial counterpart.

Vanguard's owner is the Cuban government. Czechoslovakian technicians helped build it. East German experts advise on operations. One top member of management learned his trade in the hire of a United States construction firm in Haiti and Mexico; two of his underlings learned theirs in Kiev, in the Soviet Union.

Yankee Bits and Pieces

Spouting flames in one corner of the main factory building is an 11,000-volt electro-furnace, home-made from odd bits and pieces including some bearing such labels as General Electric and Allis-Chalmers. Nearby are a Czech pattern-making machine, a Canadian sand-rammer, an East German sand core, and a "Wheelabrator Tumblast" from the American Foundry Equipment Company, Mishawaka, Indiana.

This industrial hodge-podge is itself a measure of the disruption caused by Cuba's crash conversion to communism. But a much more impressive measure can be found in Vanguard's products. Scattered in untidy piles around the factory floor is a wide assortment, numbering in the hundreds, of replacement parts for the rest of Cuban industry.

Files, Dies and Molds

That the Castro government should have felt compelled, three years ago, to build a factory just for this purpose is explained by the fact that when Fidel embraced Marx, Lenin and the Soviet Union in the early days of his regime, Cuban industrial plant and equipment was more than 90 per cent made-in-America. Aid from the Red bloc, including almost two dozen complete factories for manufacturing locks, files, dies and molds, bicycles, and other light goods, has since shaved that figure to about 70 per cent. But this still leaves the bulk of Cuba's vital sugar mills and nickel-mining facilities, its railroads, much of its cotton textile industry and oil refineries, cigar and bottling plants, a tire company, a canning works, and a host of other factories dependent on machinery and equipment of Yankee manufacture.

Yet as far back as October 1960 the United States began clamping down on shipments of all but food and medicines to Cuba; and after the missile crisis in the fall of 1962, the shut-off of even indirect exports of American industrial goods to Cuba became nearly complete.

Hence the Cuban government's decision to build Vanguard in 1961, and a subsequent deal with Russia to construct another factory, wholly devoted to spare parts production, which went into operation a few months ago. And this only begins to measure the scale of the Cuban spare parts industry. As the Cubans themselves concede, factory after factory has been obliged to establish or expand facilities for repairing machinery and reproducing spare parts.

Yet a lack of replacement parts remains a significant industrial bottleneck. At the cigar plant run by Paul Valdes, for example, some 60 per cent of production, now totaling 98,000 cigars a day, is done by 17 machines made by International Cigar Machinery of New Jersey. Officials insist spare parts are being built on the premises; but they also admit that machinery breakdowns will keep the factory from filling its projected "norms" for 1964.

"The Alice Principle"

In some factories, officials say they are still living off a heavy inventory of replacement parts and suffering no disruption from parts shortages. But the over-all picture is perhaps best summarized by Vanguard's factory manager, 30-year-old Leovigildo Rodriguez, a sallow, affable and energetic man who picked up some of his manufacturing expertise in Miami while an exile from the pre-Castro regime of dictator Batista. "We have enough orders for spare parts to operate 24 hours a day," he declares. But a lack of skilled workers, he adds, has Vanguard functioning well below full capacity.

The boom in the Cuban spare parts industry appears to be solid evidence of what one authority calls "the Alice principle—the need for Cuba to run at a feverish rate simply to stay in the same place." A diversion of a significant amount of Cuban manpower and technological expertise to the costly process of what

amounts to hand-tooling replacement parts is a shining example of economic inefficiency. And other examples abound:

Though the much-publicized British buses are now moving into service on Havana's streets, much of Cuba's bus system is serviced by Czech equipment or other Iron Curtain products which experts consider unsuited for Cuba's tropical climate. Because the drivers are also ill-trained and the repairmen are inexperienced, Cuban buses have a life expectancy of little more than 18 months. Thus, the Russians have had to furnish a special "Cuban-Russian friendship" shop to handle repairs.

Cuba's oil refineries, seized from United States and British firms, are rated among the best managed of all of the country's nationalized industry. But the refineries are nonetheless completely dependent on Soviet petroleum, which must travel 15 days or more by sea, compared with a voyage of three days or so when Cuba was purchasing its oil in the Western Hemisphere. The result is a fivefold boost in transport costs, which automatically adds to the expense of producing a gallon of Cuban gasoline. This probably explains why the price of gasoline was recently doubled to its present level of 60 cents a gallon.

Job Security

Socialist doctrine contributes mightily to economic waste, as does the impulsive, or simply incompetent, policy-making of Castro and his band. A government decree insures workers, for all practical purposes, against being fired. The result, as one top government official puts it, is that "sometimes we have too many workers on the job."

Government outlays for social welfare are huge—and highly inflationary. Spending this fiscal year will total $2.4 billion, with Cuba's free education system alone accounting for $250,000,000 and free medical care totaling $114,000,000.

Shrunken Earnings

Meanwhile, some 77 per cent of government revenue, which is also pegged close to $2.4 billion, at least on paper, derives from the earnings of Cuban enterprises, now almost wholly in the hands of the state. And these earnings, in turn, are not only shrunk by the spare parts shortage, the overblown work force, a lack of competent technology, inexperienced management, and the high cost of Soviet-supplied raw materials, but by the profound philosophical convictions of many of Cuba's new disciples of Marx that "profits" should not become a preoccupation of factory managers.

"Anything that smacks of capitalism is immediately equated with corruption," sighs one high government official who obviously has yet to be fully converted to communism. "And yet," he adds ruefully, "I have yet to discover a better test for efficiency than money."

Such thinking, of course, is a long way from becoming official policy. Nor is there much evidence that the Castro regime can come up with an economic program that works. On the contrary, there's some evidence that the government may be on the verge of embarking on yet another experimental fling in the realm of economics that could prove as disastrous as an early, ill-fated, crash program to industrialize Cuba, or an equally unhappy attempt to offset the loss of food imports from the United States

by diverting badly needed sugar acreage to other farm commodities.

The latest Castro enthusiasm is for sugar, which is already Cuba's primary economic prop, accounting for 25 per cent of budget revenue and the big bulk of Cuba's earnings of foreign exchange. Fidel now wants to boost the country's 4,000,000-ton annual output to 10,000,000 tons. He is apparently not too concerned about his lack of facilities to process this much sugar nor the depressing effect such an output would have on world sugar prices (see special report on sugar that follows this chapter).

"A Monument to Ingenuity"

Nevertheless, if Castro is impulsive in making many wrong moves, he also is impulsive about correcting his mistakes, as is indicated by his rapid scrapping of the grandiose scheme of converting Cuba into an industrialized nation.

Also, if factories like Socialist Vanguard are a testimonial to economic weakness, they are also, in the words of one expert, "a monument to ingenuity." Soviet help, while hardly massive, is also easing some of Cuba's dependence on worn-out American machinery; in a pinch, the Russians would probably bail Cuba out of serious economic difficulties before allowing the Castro government to collapse.

For while Cuba is an expensive headache for Moscow, and while Castro's erratic behavior is almost beyond the ken of the Soviet hierarchy, Cuba does represent a solid Communist foothold in the Western Hemisphere. The Kremlin would suffer a severe loss of face if the island's adventure in state socialism went down the drain, even though Cuba may be tied closer ideologically to Peking than to Moscow.

Ernesto "Che" Guevara, the oft-proclaimed intellectual leader of Castro's peculiar brand of communism, wrote a handbook entitled *La Guerra des Guerrillas* (The War of the Guerrillas) in which he stated that, for the conditions existing in Latin America, a Communist revolution can form in the countryside and pick up steam as it approaches the cities, instead of the other way around. This thesis runs directly counter to standard Marxism-Leninism as espoused by most Latin American Communist Parties. Like Red China's Mao, Guevara advocates guerrilla warfare, and he has no .use for latent revolutionaries who do not actively seek to turn their society upside down. This implicit attack on Communists who are partial to the Moscow line, which holds that the aim is a dictatorship of the working class, has been continued in speeches by Guevara and Castro ever since.

Dangerous Intrigues

But wherever Castro buys his ideology, he has found it necessary to accept all the Russian material help he can get. He has managed, while often ranting and raving, to play off the Soviets, the Chinese, the Cuban Communist Party, his own 26th of July Movement, and the United States against each other with resounding effect. His intrigues with the Russians almost led to nuclear war in October 1962 when President Kennedy revealed the presence of long-range ballistic missiles in Cuba. Khrushchev, under extreme pressure from Uncle Sam, withdrew the missiles. It is an open question whether Castro ever considered that, should a war between Russia and the United States come

about, Cuba would literally be blown out of the sea.

There is no general agreement on whether Fidel was a Communist while he was still holed up in the hills of eastern Cuba. Certainly it was the more moderate 26th of July Movement that carried Castro to success against Batista. But once in power he turned against many of his old comrades and took up with the Communists, possibly to win the Russian economic assistance he desperately needed if he were to retain power in the face of Uncle Sam's trade embargo, an embargo imposed after extraordinary provocation.

An Unorthodox Communist

Castro is as unorthodox a Communist as he is a human being. What Communist government leader, for instance, would be likely to confide, as Fidel did to a diplomat in Havana, that he has not yet managed to make his way through *Das Kapital,* though he has read several times "The Invisible Government," a purported expose, published in the United States, of the Central Intelligence Agency? Where but in Cuba would one expect to see a group of Communist government officials at a diplomatic reception suddenly raise their glasses gaily in a mock toast to Senator Barry Goldwater? Only casual Fidel, among the world's Red leaders, could receive the envoy of a major country, not in any fixed and formal prime minister's office, but by driving his guest around town in an old Oldsmobile or taking him to any one of a number of secret hideouts.

Discipline, from all accounts, is slack, whether in matters of party dogma, maintenance of machinery, or smoking within the confines of the big oil refineries in Havana. *"No Fumar,"* warns a giant sign beside the road, but a passing truck driver nonchalantly puffs away. He can hardly be blamed: The same sign hung over the head of his "maximum leader" in a Santiago auditorium, but Fidel chain-smoked his way through a 3½-hour session with visiting newsmen all the same.

Newsmen from the States, by the way, call Castro "Max," a sort of familiar diminutive of "maximum leader."

Like Max himself, organization is helter-skelter in government bureaucracies, the turnover rate among top officials is high, and in economic planning, particularly, there's almost a compulsion to experiment. Now, after several sizable boondoggles, the government is off on its scheme to corner the world market for sugar. Whether the idea is feasible or not, there's doubt that Castro has the patience to see it through.

"Castro is a backlash man," says one diplomat of Fidel's tendency to react impatiently against whatever he thinks is the source of his troubles. He is also a conscientious, if not a profound, student. So are his aides.

Instant Inquiries

Che Guevara, for example, is studying differential calculus two hours a week; Fidel himself reads tirelessly, and has been known to call up an agricultural functionary at 2 a.m. and demand an instantaneous appraisal of a new theory on how to increase milk production.

"Fidel is an incorrigible theorist," declares one diplomat in Havana. "That's okay when you are 20. But when you are the prime minister it can be dangerous."

By almost everybody's reckoning, Castro

is restive under Russian dictum, uncomfortable about his economic dependence on the Soviets. Partly this reflects his distaste for direction from any source, but partly it's because he is thought to find his Red bloc tutors a stolid, uncongenial, demanding lot.

Difficult to Instruct

The Russians, for their part, describe the Cubans as unresponsive, irresponsible, and difficult to instruct.

"Pure socialism was simply not meant for this kind of people in this kind of climate," opines one European diplomat in Havana.

From all this it is tempting to conclude that maybe Cuba hasn't gone Communist—that it only likes to think it has. And if Cuba's conversion to communism is really no deeper than that, it might be reasonable to conclude further that it cannot be very durable.

It's a happy thought but one which needs quickly to be squared with reality. Whatever Cuba's compatibility with communism, Castro's public commitment to the cause is complete. Case-hardened Reds control key sectors of the government. The Cuban Communist Party is interlocked with that of the Communist bloc.

The consensus among most authorities in Havana is that even if Fidel wanted to—and there's no evidence that he does—he could not now renounce his Communist connections, at least not in any way meaningful enough to satisfy the requirements of current United States policy, and survive politically. The most that can be read so far into his recent concilia-

tory line toward the United States is that he would like to lighten his economic dependence on the Soviet Union, break out of his diplomatic isolation in the hemisphere, and allay the threat of American invasion or undercover efforts to topple him, while still strutting the stage as champion of socialist revolution around the world, and still actively working for that cause.

"Fidel has to make trouble—it's the only way for him to survive politically," says one Western diplomat who sees scant hope of "neutralizing" Cuba under Castro. Most experts also consider Cuba's communization irreversible under the present regime.

A Tito Status?

But all students of Castro's Cuba are not agreed on this. Some envisage a kind of Titoist status for Castro, which would leave him Communist, but not an active partisan of international communism's spread. A few think he could move even further, into a Nasser-style neutralism. Even assuming they are right, no such shift is possible without United States encouragement. And United States policy, at least for now, is quite firmly aimed the other way, toward making it just as difficult as possible for the Reds to make out of Cuba an argument for Communist takeovers elsewhere in the hemisphere.

But elsewhere in Latin America, local Communist organizations are conspiring to win what Fidel Castro has long since won—power. So they have even more basic concerns than cigars, spare parts and the price of sugar.

For a Cuban dissenter, a prayer before dying.

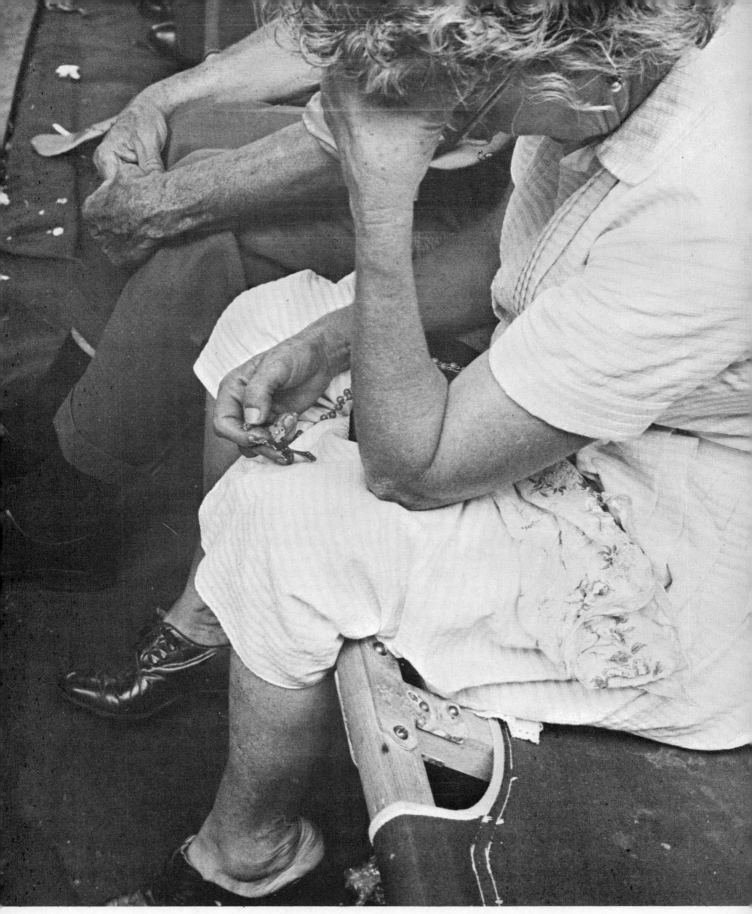

For a Cuban refugee, a prayer of thanksgiving.

SUGAR

As Fidel Learned the Hard Way, The Stalk Wants Careful Cutting

IN APRIL 1964 the relatively small purchase of 20,000 tons of sugar on the international market in London caused a flurry among sugar traders. The buyer was Cuba, the world's biggest sugar exporter. Veteran sugar traders in London couldn't remember Cuba's buying before in the world market.

But since Fidel Castro brought communism to Cuba the island's sugar fortunes have soured. The ruinous October 1963 Hurricane Flora and drought have crippled recent Cuban sugar crops. But, more importantly, just plain mismanagement and miscalculation by the Cuban regime have compounded the natural disasters. Cuba's sugar production in 1963 melted to about 60 per cent of the pre-Castro level and sugar is now being rationed on the island.

Cuba is overwhelmingly dependent on the vicissitudes of its sugar production, deriving approximately 80 per cent of its foreign currency earnings from that crop. Sugar plays an important part, too, in the economies of several other Latin nations and the ups and downs of the sugar industry can greatly affect Latin economies.

Of the 20 Latin American countries, only Honduras, Bolivia, Chile, and Uruguay export no sugar. Brazil and Mexico, as well as Cuba, are among the world's 10 leading sugar producers. The Dominican Republic, like Cuba, is over-dependent on a one-crop sugar economy. In Latin America, sugar accounts for eight per cent of the total export trade.

Sugar cane stalk was one of the earliest European visitors to the New World. In 1493 Columbus carried a few pieces of stalk on his return trip, giving them to Indians in the Caribbean islands. The cane, which grows best on a rich, moist soil under sunny skies in a tropical climate, thrived in the New World.

Cane sugar, a giant perennial grass whose prominently joined stalks each bear two ranks of sword-shaped, gracefully arching leaves, needs uniform, high temperatures and frequent showers during the growing season. Good drainage is essential for the carbohydrate, which is formed by the interaction of sunlight, air, and water in the leaves of the plant.

Latin American sugar is predominantly cane, although some beet sugar is grown. In the United States the melon-sized sugar beet, which develops best in 63-73 degree temperature, is more widely planted than cane.

In growing cane sugar, the soil is usually plowed deep. Stalk cuttings one to two feet long are laid end to end in rows four to six feet apart and covered with soil two to four inches deep. Each cutting includes a joint with a bud, from which the new cane plant sprouts. Subsequent cultivation is primarily for weed control.

Pests and plant diseases nowadays cause little harm to the cane. Pest control has been achieved through the use of insects that elimi-

Freshly cut sugar cane on the way to the mill.

The machette must be wielded with finesse.

nate the stalk-damaging species but do not themselves harm the plant. The development of new varieties of cane has largely controlled disease.

The harvest season is the key time for the sugar crop. The sucrose, or sugar, content of the plant reaches a peak, then falls off permanently after a few days. The cane must be cut speedily and expertly to assure a bountiful crop. To prevent harming the plant, the cane must be cut a short distance above the ground. The tops of the cane and the leaves are removed before the cane is transported to the mills.

At the mills, the juice is extracted from the cane and then concentrated until the sucrose crystallizes. In Latin America this sugar for export is shipped raw and refined in the importing countries.

The United States is the world's leading sugar importer and its aversion to Castro's communism has forced a restructuring of tradi-

tional Latin American trade patterns in sugar. Before Castro, the United States doled out "national quotas" to sugar-selling nations. Cuba supplied from 8 to 10 per cent of the United States' foreign needs. But in July 1960 President Eisenhower shut off further imports of Cuban sugar and Cuba's quota was divvied up among other, more friendly nations and domestic growers. It was naturally a boon to the other Latin American sugar-producing nations.

Faced with the loss of the growing U.S. sugar market, Cuba was forced to turn with outstretched hand to its new-found benefactor, Russia. Ironically, Russia is the world's leading producer of sugar and East European satellites Poland and Czechoslovakia also are big sugar growers. Nevertheless, Russia promised Cuba a long-term market for its sugar. At a guaranteed price of six cents a pound, Russia is gradually increasing its sugar intake from Cuba from 1,600,000 tons in 1964 to 5,000,000 tons in 1968.

Cuban sugar production under Castro, however, has fallen off sharply since 1961. Although production in pre-Castro years averaged approximately 6,000,000 tons, Castro's cuttings have averaged about 1,000,000 tons less.

After the 1961 crop, Castro began tampering with his sugar-buttressed economy. His goal: Diversification of the economy away from its one-crop status. Cuba began diverting skilled sugar workers away from the fields at harvest time to join an expanding militia. When national emergencies were declared and the militia called out, the sugar cutters were not spared. By early 1963 at least 350,000 sugar workers had been conscripted for full time military service. Other peasants called on to work in the fields became disgruntled over the low wages ($2.50 daily compared with $5.00-$6.00 before Castro).

From Russia, With Love

Other bungling added to Castro's sugar woes. An order to Russia for grinders to sharpen machetes, for example, was over-long in being fulfilled. When a shipment did arrive from Russia it contained thermometers, not grinders. With such consistent fumbling, sugar production skidded to 3,800,000 tons in 1963 and isn't expected to surpass that figure in 1964. Castro now is hoping Soviet-manufactured cane cutting machines operated by trained Russians will help offset the labor shortage in coming years. Undaunted by past failures, he has resorted again to heavy reliance on sugar as Cuba's chief cash crop and has set a goal of 10,000,000 tons annually by 1970.

But production is only part of the sugar story. Like coffee, sugar is highly vulnerable to price fluctuations. In January 1962 sugar was selling at 2.5 cents a pound. By May 1963 sugar prices in the United States had climbed to a 43-year high of 12.6 cents a pound because of low production in Cuba and Europe, where the weather was poor.

Continued high world prices could, of course, help offset Cuba's slumping production. But Castro's mishandling of the sugar industry has driven production costs to approximately three cents a pound, a cent more than in the United States. And that penny a pound, in an average Cuban harvest under Castro, could amount to as much as $100,000,000.

The tops and leaves of the cane are removed before the cane reaches the mill. There, the juice is extracted and concentrated until it crystallizes.

Communism

In the Continent and a Half

Moscow, Peking, Havana Reds Strike Different Keys

But There's No Discord About the Grand Finale;

Variations on the Theme of the 'Aquatic Ballet'

GUSTAVO DIAZ ORDAZ, the president-elect of Mexico, was discussing the strength of communism a short while ago and noted there were, in his view, three kinds of leftists: The genuine Marxists, those who talk like them, and those who are paid to be.

The distinction is useful in viewing the present Communist threat in Latin America. There are, in fact, many kinds of Communists at work in the Western Hemisphere today. Some take their orders from Moscow, others from Peking, still others from Havana. Their strategies vary; their tactics differ; their strength and their successes in various areas are wildly uneven. If there is one thing they have in common, it is simply a determined quest for power.

An American seeking to trace the Red line through Central and South America finds ragged edges. The tide seems to rise here, and recede out of sight there. It breaks through, momentarily, in Panama and rolls back in Chile. It surges in Venezuela, and slips from view in Guatemala. The threat seems to grow in British Guiana, and diminish in Brazil.

This is, in essence, the nature of communism today in Latin America. It is neither simple to define, nor easy to analyze. And yet it is necessary to understand better, for United States policy in Latin America is hinged heavily today on the immediate or potential chances of Communist advance.

In most countries, the Communist Party is outlawed; the party has legal status only in Mexico, Bolivia, Chile, Colombia, Uruguay, and, of course, Cuba. So it is difficult to get anything like a precise rundown on Communist strength. It is known, however, that in countries where the party is legal its growth has been less than spectacular. In most countries, party membership in recent years has actually lagged behind the population growth.

Wriggled Into Niches

Considering the nature of the reigning—that is the pro-Soviet—Communist parties in Latin America, this is not surprising. These parties date back in many cases to the 1920s. Many of the leaders now in power rose to prominence 30 or even 40 years ago. They have learned to operate with the governments in power, have wriggled themselves into niches from which they are not anxious to be dislodged for kicking up a revolution. They advocate collaboration, infiltration, propagandizing—anything but violence. They are old men heading old parties with ideas more comfortable to the old than to the young, zealous population of Latin America. Their membership, cut into by the numerous other far-left parties, dwindles.

Communist influence, however, is broader than the party's size. Though few in numbers, hard-core Communists in various disguises have reached positions of power, if not respectability, in universities, trade unions, and government. They are masters, in short, of the art of infiltration in Latin America.

It is a common mistake, though, to assume that the restlessness and agitation for reform so widespread in the area is all Communist-inspired or directed. Economic and political crises, to be sure, often are exploited by Communists because they fish most successfully in troubled waters. Yet their presence and power frequently are magnified for the political benefit of those in power.

A long-time student of Central American affairs puts it this way:

"Communism is important principally as a bogeyman, as an excuse for military intervention. There is an all-too-frequent tendency to lump together as Communists all forces working for needed social change. The chief danger in Latin America is not that the Communists will seize power but that they will cause a reaction that leads to dictatorship."

As evidence, supporters of this view point to military coups in recent months that have occurred in such countries as Guatemala, Brazil, and Ecuador. The pretext was the threat of chaos and the danger, real or feigned, of Communist take-over.

Still, the demonstrated capacity of the Reds to employ deviousness and violence in pursuit of power cannot be underestimated. And the presence of a Communist regime in Cuba since 1959 has aided their cause immeasurably.

Shortly after Castro came to power, Cuban Reds made their first overt attempts at aggrandizement. In April, 1959, a handful of Castroites set sail in shrimp boats for Panama. An uprising was planned there, to be led by Tito Arias, a Panamanian whose marriage to British dancer Margot Fonteyn earned the affair the title of the "Aquatic Ballet." The uprising fizzled and the Cubans were quickly rounded up by Panamanian police.

Still hopeful, Castro sent another flotilla to the Dominican Republic two months later. The outcome was the same.

Changed Tactics

Though both of these invasions were amateurish and futile, they did underscore Castro's ambition to spread his gospel. The tactics changed in succeeding years but evidence suggests there has been no diminution in Castro's determination to spread his revolution to other parts of Latin America.

The latest, most clear-cut evidence of the change in tactics to subversion and terrorism came in Venezuela in November 1963. During an outbreak of terrorism against the government of Romulo Betancourt, a staunch foe of communism, authorities discovered a three-ton cache of Cuban weapons in Falcón State. A subsequent investigation by the Organization of American States nailed down the fact that the arms had come from Cuba. That revelation prompted the OAS in mid-1964 to recommend the severing of diplomatic ties between its members and Cuba. In a matter of weeks, Chile, Bolivia, and Uruguay broke off diplomatic relations with Havana, leaving Mexico the only Latin nation maintaining relations with the

Castro regime. All other OAS members had already closed their Havana embassies before the general sanction.

The break-off of diplomatic relations fit neatly into the United States-supported policy of isolating, or "quarantining," the Castro government. The effect, at least as far as the Latin lands are concerned, goes beyond mere diplomatic formality. Castroites had used their embassies abroad as broadcast points for money,

propaganda, and instructions to local Communists. They also had been busy bringing Latin students and party people to Cuba for training and indoctrination.

Notable among the frequent visitors to Havana were such Latin leftists as Vicente Lombardo Toledano, head of the Popular Socialist Party (PPS) in Mexico and once Moscow's principal agent in Latin America; Francisco Julião, leader of the Red-dominated peasant leagues in

La Prensa, Lima

A Communist agitator gives villagers in the Peruvian Andes the hard sell.

northeastern Brazil; Guatemala's ex-President Jacobo Arbenz Guzman; and Chile's recently-defeated presidential candidate, Salvador Allende. If the break-off of diplomatic relations does nothing more than complicate Castro's communications system with other Latins, it will have had beneficial effect.

Cuba has a direct air link with only one other country in the Western Hemisphere—Mexico, where intelligence agents note all passengers flying to or from Castro's island. On September 21, 1964, Cuba opened an air route to the Bahamas. This service was suspended when the Bahamas, a British possession, refused to permit Cuban airliners to discharge passengers on its territory.

Other factors have tarnished Castro's initial appeal in Latin America. Firing squad executions of political enemies, shortly after Castro came to power, nauseated most Latin observers. When Castro was photographed at the United Nations hugging Soviet Premier Khrushchev, any doubts about the bearded leader's political inclinations were dissipated. And in October 1962, during the Cuban missile crisis, it became obvious that Cuba's course was being dictated in Moscow, not Havana. If anything disenchanted independent Latin Americans still sympathetic to Castro, it was this spectacle of the emergence of Cuba as a Soviet satellite.

Perhaps because of the brief bitterness that developed between Castro and Khrushchev after the missile confrontation, Cuba took an ambivalent position in another crisis within the Communist world—the fight between Communist China and Soviet Russia for leadership of the global Communist movement. Castro, initially

at least, seemed to favor the more militant attitudes espoused by Peking, as did some other Communist leaders in Latin America. In any case, the Soviet-Sino split has had, and continues to have, a profound divisive effect within Communist ranks throughout Latin America.

Today, for example, significant Chinese Communist factions are vocal and active in such countries as Bolivia, Brazil, Mexico, Paraguay, and Ecuador, competing with the pro-Russians. In one country—Peru—the pro-Chinese group actually controls the Communist Party. Pro-Soviet Communists are considered to be in control in 11 Latin lands—Argentina, Chile, Colombia, Costa Rica, the Dominican Republic, El Salvador, Guatemala, Honduras, Nicaragua, Panama, and Uruguay.

Working Against Itself

This dissidence within the Communist camp clearly has that camp working against itself in Latin America. During the 1964 presidential election in Chile, for example, the head of the Communist Party there, Luis Corvalan, was preaching the 'peaceful co-existence" line from Moscow while the pro-Chinese faction was howling for the violent overthrow of the Chilean government. In Brazil, Castro has refused to cooperate with the larger, traditional, Soviet-oriented Communist party and has sided instead with the pro-Chinese faction.

Thus, in general terms, the Communist threat today in Latin America might be summed up this way: Dangers do exist; though sometimes overstated, they are none the less real, particularly in such volatile places as British Guiana, Guatemala, and Venezuela. Where there is acute economic or political stress anywhere in the area, the Reds come running. Cuba's presence, as a Communist base in the hemisphere, enhances the chances for serious Communist advances in Latin America. But the increased awareness by Latin American authorities of Cuba's motives and operations, and the ideological dissidence within the Communist apparatus in Latin America tend to reduce the effectiveness of Communist strategy and tactics.

In specific countries, this is the current picture:

Argentina. In March and April 1964, the discovery of miniscule guerrilla encampments in

Part of the arms cache landed on a Venezuelan beach by Castro Cubans was
displayed to Hemispheric ambassadors.
The evidence led all members of the
Organization of American States except
Mexico to break diplomatic relations
with Havana. Castro's philosophy of
armed revolution is in line with the
predelections of the Red Chinese, who
are also at work in Latin America.

northern Argentina excited considerable attention in the Latin press. In those two months, three camps were found: One in Salta, the state on Argentina's northern border with Bolivia, one on the border of Salta and Jujuy states, and one in Córdoba. Six people were found at the camp in Córdoba, all members of the Argentine Communist youth organization which has warmer feelings towards Castro and Peking than the Communist Party of Argentina (PCA), which supports Russia in the Sino-Soviet rift.

continues as to the origins of the three depots.

The Communist Party of Argentina is probably not behind any of the encampments. Consistently a supporter of the USSR in the Sino-Soviet rift, the PCA is not likely to foment guerrilla activity in the north. But dissident members of the Communist youth organization, recently expelled from the PCA because of their zealous support of Havana and Peking, might instigate such action.

With approximately 45,000 members, the

In Chile, the people decided it was possible to veer to the left without going over the cliff. There, the Christian Democrats have harnessed the impatience of younger citizens by offering them drastic reform within a democratic framework.

In Salta, seven men were found at one of the camps. They had books by Mao and Che Guevara with them, arms, uniforms—the accoutrements of a guerrilla camp. These seven, who have never been traced back to any Argentine political group, called themselves "nationalists." One, who was killed, claimed to be a Cuban, vaguely supporting the conjecture that the arms came from Cuba. The third camp revealed only arms, no inhabitants, when discovered. Speculation ran rife at the time and investigation

PCA is the largest Communist party in Latin America, although its political effectiveness is strictly limited. It has fought for control on communism's main battleground in Latin America—within the labor movement—and has consistently lost out to the *Peronistas*. Of 2,300,000 union members in Argentina, estimates of *Peronista* membership run as high as 1,800,000, and most key leaders are *Peronistas*.

The outlook for the party, especially since it was declared illegal in 1963, is bleak, but the housing shortage and inflation which plague the city worker could channel explosive forces in communism's direction.

British Guiana. Communism could acquire power legally in this small British colony on the eastern coast of South America. Premier Cheddi Jagan is an avowed Marxist who incites and thrives on racial clashes between the colony's East Indians and Negroes. Although the East Indian supporters of Jagan are by no means all Communists, they have given their allegiance to the premier. Both the Negroes and East Indians want independence. A free British Guiana under Jagan's rule, however, would guarantee no lasting Communist regime. Racial enmity is so deep that the Negroes and East Indians would undoubtedly continue fighting. Whether Jagan could install a Communist regime under such conditions and in the face of U.S. opposition remains uncertain.

Brazil. The Communist Party was about to regain legal status when President João Goulart was ousted in April 1964. Goulart, although no Communist, had openly flirted with the Reds, presumably hoping to use their support in setting up his own authoritarian rule. But whether the overthrow of Goulart helped or hurt the Communists is debatable.

Most Latin experts believe the Goulart government was heavily infiltrated with Communists and would soon have handed over power to the Reds. Now, these experts say, Communist strength has been decimated and the efforts of the new government to effect reforms under a democratic system will lessen further the Communist threat to reach power by legal means.

Another View

Nevertheless, there are some liberal analysts who doubt that the Goulart government, while hostile to the United States and honeycombed with extreme leftists, intended to venture into communism. Democratic sentiment among the population was so strong and the pro-Communist forces so inept, they argue, that a Communist take-over was far-fetched. However, the new government's restrictions on civil liberties have been so harsh, they believe, that there may be a backlash effect. Brazil's economic and social problems remain unsolved and if restrictions continue, the Communists may flourish again amid popular discontent.

Peru. President Fernando Belaúnde Terry has accomplished the near-impossible in Latin American politics: Last year he let the Communists sit in the rumble seat of his election bandwagon; this year he's giving them the boot. Belaúnde didn't court the Reds—he just accepted their votes. But after consolidating his strength, he took firm measures against Communist agitation in unions; he also began a land reform program and jailed Castroite guerrilla leader Hugo Blanco. Thus the Communists in Peru have been rendered ineffectual.

Even Peruvian university students, traditionally more Communist-oriented than anyone else, are swinging away from the Reds. For the first time in several years, an APRA-backed student was elected in June 1964 as president of the student body at Lima's University of San Marcos, training center for politicians and proving ground for political trends.

Price of a Split Vote

The Peking and Moscow factions lost by splitting their vote. The Peking Communist faction in Peru holds a unique position in Latin America—it controls *the* Communist party of the country. But not by majority rule: From all appearances, the pro-China militants are in the minority.

Uruguay. The Communists in Uruguay make no attempt to infiltrate the government or overthrow it but are directing a frontal attack through propaganda. Uruguay cheerfully allows agencies of many Communist countries to operate unimpeded. The Uruguayan Communist Party, which broke once with Russia, is now strongly pro-Moscow. Russia has helped the country's economy through purchases of wool and grains.

Communist China, which has a trade mission but no embassy in Montevideo, is angling for trade arrangements with Uruguay. The Chinese put out much propaganda from Uruguay, often called the Latin American "mailbox of the international Communist movement," but have gained few converts among the Uruguayan people. Communists, however, do control the largest trade union federation here and run the student organization at the University of Montevideo.

Venezuela. The failure of the Communists to reach power through violence in 1963 has not

Where Communist promises sound sweet.

dissuaded them from trying.

Subversion efforts by the Armed Forces of National Liberation (FALN), the militant arm of far leftist groups, have taken two main forms: Support of several small military uprisings and sabotage of businesses, particularly those under American control. A favorite FALN target has been outlets of Sears, Roebuck & Company. FALN terrorists also frequently hit oil pipelines.

Headline-seeking stunts of the FALN have been smoothly executed. At various times in the past two years, the FALN has: Stolen five French paintings worth approximately $650,000 from an exhibition; hijacked the freighter Anzoategui 380 miles offshore, and kidnapped a visiting Spanish soccer star and an American army officer, both of whom were released unharmed.

Mexico. The left in Mexico is badly shredded. The Mexican Communist Party has the stigma of internationalism that weakens its efforts to proselytize in the country. When asked about the dangers of communism, one Mexican authority contemptuously remarked, "We've already had our revolution."

In the 1964 national elections, the Communists organized two parties: The People's Electoral Front, an organization of militant Communists that failed to gain 75,000 valid signatures on an election petition to run a presidential candidate, and the National Liberation Movement (NLM). The NLM urges the overthrow of the government by force, supports demonstrations, and engages in open criticism of the government. Former President Lázaro Cárdenas, the nominal NLM leader, strongly sympathizes with Fidel Castro. Cárdenas, however, infuriated the left when he came out in support of Diaz Ordaz for president.

The Popular Socialist Party (PPS) is the

Freedom is a child skipping home from school.

most influential of the Marxist parties. But it never openly criticizes a Mexican president and in 1964 supported the candidacy of Diaz Ordaz in hope of winning favors from the government.

Costa Rica. During the 1940s the Communists found two sympathetic presidents who welcomed their influence in the government— Calderón Guardia (1940-44) and Teodoro Picado (1944-48). As a result the Communists played a large role in the passage of a new labor code and the establishment of social security and income tax systems. They were helped by the Roman Catholic Church, whose leader, Archbishop Victor Sanabria, mistakenly believed the Communists had changed their revolutionary objectives when they changed the party's name to the Vanguardia Popular.

Costa Rica's 1948 civil war led to the formation of a junta, which declared the Communist Party illegal, although restrictions were later relaxed. In 1953, however, Jose Figueres Ferrer, an old foe of the Communists and the leader of the 1948 junta, was elected president. Figueres instituted a broad social reform program that stole the thunder of the Reds and their influence has waned since. Estimates of Communist strength now run from 50 to 300.

Guatemala. The Communist Party had little influence in Guatemala until the 1944 revolution against dictator General Jorge Ubico, who had cracked down hard on the Reds. The revolution, led by young military men and ex-students, was not Communist-oriented. Juan José Arévalo was elected president and introduced numerous social reforms, including a social security system and a labor code. But Communists did take over control of labor organizations.

Arévalo saw no danger in the Communists' activities, which continued to spread through

ESTÁ NA HORA DO

MONOPÓLIO INTEGRAL

TUDO DE PETRÓLEO PARA A PETROBRÁS

The Reds are quick to capitalize on nationalistic ardor.

the 1940s. His successor in 1951, Jacobo Arbenz Guzman, was elected with Communist support. If Arévalo considered the Communists no threat, Arbenz seemed to regard them as a blessing. The Communists were his close political allies and he made no move to stop them when they merged all their labor unions into one organization in 1952. Arbenz' chief goal was to carry out a sweeping agrarian revolution. He staffed the agrarian reform commission with Communists, who promptly capitalized on their positions to organize the peasants. By 1953 the Communists controlled the national radio, several influential newspapers, and the police.

The Army Wields the Power

In July 1954 an insurrection led by Colonel Carlos Castillo Armas, with support from the U.S. Central Intelligence Agency, overthrew Arbenz. Castillo Armas before his assassination in 1957, moved to modify the Arbenz reforms. His elected successor, Gen. Miguel Ydigoras Fuentes, continued the slackened pace of reform. The Ydigoras government, although anti-Communist, was beset with corruption and inflation.

When ex-President Arévalo slipped back into the country in 1963 the army staged a coup, fearful that Arévalo would win the presidency in coming elections. Communist guerrilla bands, totaling about 100 men, roam some areas of the country and Communists still are influential at the university in Guatemala City. But in Guatemala the army, strongly anti-Communist, wields the power.

Nicaragua. The Communists, as well as all other opposition groups, were kept down during the 23-year reign of dictator Anastasio Somoza, who was assassinated in 1956. The Communists, however, have made inroads in labor unions and student organizations. They played a role in violence that erupted in Managua during the February 1963 election of Rene Schick, hand-picked candidate of Somoza's sons. Small groups of Communist rebels still haunt the countryside. Although vigorously suppressed by the Somozas, the Communist movement is still alive and could prove troublesome.

Honduras. Communists were highly active among banana workers in the 1950s and tried to capitalize on a north coast banana strike in May 1954 but were deposed from the central strike committee by non-Communist labor leaders. The growth of the Liberal Party, which elected progressive President Ramón Villeda Morales (1957-63), further diminished the Communists' influence. In the October 1963 army coup that deposed President Morales, the Communists joined in anti-military rioting. But the Honduran labor organizations, among the most powerful in Central America, are staunchly anti-Communist.

El Salvador. The Communist Party in El Salvador was practically exterminated in 1932 when dictator General Maximiliano Hernandez Martinez got wind of plans for a Communist-directed military insurrection. Most of the Communist leaders were captured and shot. The party has been dealt with harshly in recent years, too. In 1952 a government roundup jailed the top Communist leaders. In 1962 Communist leaders again were arrested and exiled. The party, however, has strong student support and El Salvador, with its many landless peasants and tightly knit oligarchy, remains fertile ground for Communist activity.

Where Reds May Be Gaining

Panama. Anti-American feeling is stronger in Panama than anywhere else in Central America yet the Communists have never been a potent force in Panamanian politics. Their influence is strongest at the university and among the banana workers of the north and west. Government harassment, internal party feuds, and the growth of responsible labor organizations have enfeebled the Communists. Although the Reds can stir up anti-American feeling, they have seldom been able to turn it to their own ends. Since the January 1964 riots in the Canal Zone, Communist propaganda has been more stridently anti-Yankee and there is some feeling that the Reds may be making gains.

All in all, communism in Latin America has experienced mixed fortunes. The Reds are finding the area somewhat less vulnerable than they had supposed, although their conspiracies remain a constant danger. And it was largely because of that danger that the Alliance for Progress was urgently assembled.

The Alliance:

The signing of the Charter of the Alliance for Progress, Punta del Este, Uruguay, August 17, 1961.

What It Is and Why

An Act of Faith in the Latin Peoples Evolved Out of Hope, Charity and Fear

ALIANZA para el Progreso is a Spanish phrase that means a thousand things. To most Americans it means Uncle Sam's foreign aid efforts in Latin America, but this is only a small part of the Alliance for Progress.

In theory the Alliance is essentially a self-help program under which the Latin American republics are working to correct the causes of their monumental social and economic problems. In fact the Alliance is a multi-pronged instrument of foreign policy with which the United States is trying to help create the conditions in Latin America that are conducive to democratic government and free enterprise.

The poverty and hopelessness of millions of Latin Americans are the preferred compost of communism. Like toadstools springing from a rotting log, Communist cells pop up among the wretched peasants who are always hungry and among the bitter urban workers who live atop garbage piles and see their small earnings devoured by inflation. To such people the promises of communism are sweet.

The Alliance for Progress was designed to give Latin Americans an alternative by giving them hope. Despite widespread criticism of the Alliance's record so far—criticism often deserved but sometimes blind to the towering obstacles the Alliance faces—there have been considerable physical accomplishments that, when compared with the area's near-stagnation over many decades, are remarkable.

Since 1961, Uncle Sam, in pledging $2 billion a year to the Alliance, has helped Latin America acquire 222,600 new homes, 23,400 new classrooms, 6,800,000 school books, 207,000 agricultural loans, 1,056 new water systems, and 554 new mobile health units and hospitals. Moreover, daily meals have been provided for more than 20,000,000 people.

These are admittedly small numbers in an area much larger than the United States and having millions more inhabitants. Nor do they lend true perspective to the Alliance and the scope of its activities. To appreciate what the Alliance is, what it is doing and what it is failing to do, it is first necessary to understand how the Alliance came about, what its various components are, and the respective roles played by the United States and the Latin American republics in fostering a social and economic renaissance south of the Rio Grande.

On, By, And To But Not For

The Alliance for Progress, first of all, is not an organizational unit. It is not an office or a door or a building inscribed with that name, nor is it even a control center for coordinating the many agencies and projects that fit beneath its broad umbrella. True, there are tattered Alliance posters taped to the doors and walls of the Pan American Union, the U.S. State Department, the Agency for International Development and other institutions; and it is possible to point to persons who work *on* the Alliance or whose work is caused *by* the Alliance or who are representatives *to* the Alliance. But there is no such thing as working *for* the Alliance.

Furthermore, the Alliance for Progress is not a set of rules and regulations to which participating countries have pledged themselves. The Charter of Punta del Este makes recommendations to the various governments, but the representatives of those governments who signed the Charter did not bind themselves by it. The Alliance, therefore, is not an establishment but rather bits and pieces of various programs. It represents not a contract but an advisory memo.

Contrary to popular belief in the United States, the late President Kennedy did not establish something altogether new when he announced the Alliance for Progress on March 13, 1961. The Alliance is generally considered to have two specific forerunners: Operation Pan America and the Act of Bogotá.

Operation Pan America was proposed August 9, 1958, by the then president of Brazil, Juscelino Kubitschek, in a message to the other governments in the hemisphere. This message called for "a reorientation of hemispheric policy," and it listed eight basic objectives.

The objectives were: Strengthening hemispheric unity; correction of underdevelopment; employment of inter-American agencies for an accelerated attack on that underdevelopment; technical assistance to countries that needed it; market stabilization for basic commodities; expansion of international financing institutions; stimulation of private initiative; and overhaul of the fiscal and economic policies of individual countries in the interest of faster development.

The main idea of the statement was that economic and social progress were necessary if democratic political systems were to be sustained.

Operation Pan America was greeted with enthusiasm throughout the hemisphere, and endorsed later in 1958 by the 21 American republics. (In later agreements the number of signers is always 20, not 21. Cuba is the dropout.)

On September 22, 1958, the republics established a Special Committee to Study the Formulation of New Measures for Economic Cooperation. "The Committee of 21," as it came to be called, was to look for these new measures in the light of the proposals contained in the statement outlining Operation Pan America.

Inter-American Committee

At this same meeting, the ministers set up a second committee, one to work toward "establishment of an inter-American development institution in which all the American countries would participate." This was the most important inter-American action taken between the announcement of Operation Pan America and the second important precursor of the Alliance for Progress, the Act of Bogotá, which was signed late in 1960.

An inter-American bank had long been desired by the nations of Latin America—and long rejected by the United States. Now, with full support from Uncle Sam, work went ahead

Slow progress in Alto Beni, Bolivia.

The Andes, too, stand in the way.

on it. On January 8, 1959, the Specialized Committee for Negotiating and Drafting the Instrument of Organization of an Inter-American Financial Institution met for the first time (Inter-American committees often have longer names than the children of Spanish aristocrats), and on April 8, 1959, the participating nations agreed to establish the Inter-American Development Bank (IDB).

The purpose of the bank is "to contribute to the acceleration of the process of economic development of the member countries, individually and collectively." Its functions: To promote public and private investment and to use its own capital in projects aiding economic development; to help member countries use their own resources better; and to provide technical assistance.

Act of Bogotá

In September 1960, the Committee of 21 convened in Bogotá, Colombia, and at this most important of its meetings set down on paper the Act of Bogotá, the second ideological impetus to the Alliance for Progress.

The Act recommends "measures for social improvement and economic development within the framework of Operation Pan America." It also doffs its hat to the U.S. offer to support a special fund for social development to be administered by the IDB.

This Social Progress Trust Fund (SPTF) received its original allocation of funds in the late spring of 1961, when President Kennedy allotted it $394,000,000 of the $500,000,000 appropriated by Congress at that time for aid to Latin America. On June 19, 1961, the IDB agreed to administer the Fund. The Social Progress Trust Fund is one of the two major instruments (the other being the Agency for International Development) through which Uncle Sam provides economic help to Latin America directly.

The conviction expressed in the Act, "that within the framework of Operation Pan America the economic development of Latin America requires prompt action of exceptional breadth in the field of international cooperation and domestic effort," gives in a nutshell the principles of the Alliance for Progress which was to follow shortly.

Operation Pan America was initiated by Latin Americans. The Act of Bogotá was arrived at through the agreement of all the American republics. The next move came from the United States when President Kennedy announced the Alliance for Progress on March 13, 1961.

In his speech, Kennedy stressed the unity of the Americas, not just through geographical welding, but also through their common revolutionary heritage. Now, he said, the American republics must work together to prove that economic and social progress flourish best under democracy. To this end he dedicated the Alliance for Progress.

The Alliance as he saw it should be a "bold and determined" 10-year plan. He emphasized that the Latin American nations must help themselves, and that *all* levels of society must share in growth. He then listed the steps the United States was prepared to take. That day he had asked Congress for $500,000,000 for the Alliance (this sum had already been authorized by Congress in September 1960 under President Eisenhower, and was finally appropriated in May 1961).

Completing the Revolution

The United States would consider, "case-by-case," commodity programs; the Food for Peace plan would be stepped up; Uncle Sam would help any Latin American nation whose security was threatened from without; and Latin American teachers would be invited north to teach the United States about their countries. Kennedy also recommended support of economic integration and expanded training of economists.

"With steps such as these," he declared, "we propose to complete the revolution of the Americas."

In his speech Kennedy asked for an inter-America meeting to consider his proposal for such an Alliance. This meeting took place at Punta del Este, Uruguay, from August 5 through August 17, 1961. The so-called Charter of Punta del Este, establishing the Alliance as an inter-American agreement, was signed by all the American republics except Cuba.

The Charter of Punta del Este, and the Declaration to the Peoples of America which accompanied it, set forth a very generalized agreement, more *between* the United States and

Latin America than *among* the American nations, to work together toward a better economic, social, personal and political future in Latin America.

For its part, the United States agreed to help the Latin nations through Government grants, generous loans and technical assistance. On their side, the Latin American nations are supposed to adopt programs to improve the lot of all the people in all countries in the area, not just in their own countries and not just certain groups.

The Declaration and the Charter outline a program which would sweep every room in the Latin American house clean—a tall, tall order. The Declaration lists 12 all-encompassing goals: Strengthening of democracy through self-determination; acceleration of economic and social development; housing programs; agrarian reforms; better labor conditions; elimination of illiteracy; health and sanitation improvements; tax reform; streamlined monetary and fiscal policies; stimulation of private enterprise; control of price fluctuations for basic commodities, and economic integration of Latin America.

Emphasis on Self-Help

The Charter goes into the requirements for achieving the goals listed. Prime among these requirements are extensive, long-range national development programs—programs, a) in accordance with democratic principles, b) based on the idea of self-help, and c) allowing women the same status as men.

Local institutions would be bolstered so that local resources will make heavy contributions to the programs. Social reforms would be pursued to ensure a more reasonable distribution of wealth. These are the things which the countries were advised to undertake themselves; only one provision of this section mentions external aid. The emphasis is clearly on self-help measures.

The Punta Charter also deals with the steps capital-exporting countries in general should take to help Latin America, and what the United States in particular promises to do:

"The United States will assist those participating countries whose development programs establish self-help measures and economic and social policies and programs consistent with the goals and principles of this charter."

This contingency principle underlies Uncle Sam's participation in the Alliance throughout. It avoids the old error of enriching corrupt or inept leaders; occasionally it hamstrings some projects until various reforms are completed in the recipient country.

The Charter goes on to outline the Alliance structure to be set up. It mentions specifically the organizations which should work together, and in some cases even states *how* they should work together. Importantly, it calls for the creation of a panel of nine experts chosen "exclusively on the basis of their experience, technical ability, and competence in the various aspects of economic and social development."

From this panel, committees of no more than three men each decide on the soundness and "Alliance-ness" of national development programs. Countries are not obliged to submit their programs to this committee for approval, and may look for funds where they may find them, but the recommendations of the committee "will be of great importance" in the allotment of external funds for the program.

Nine Wise Men

The "nine wise men," as they are called fondly by their friends and facetiously by their detractors, have had their work cut out for them. Not surprisingly, considering the complications and scope of the plans submitted, some programs have waited as long as two years to get approval.

The Punta Charter is also concerned with the economic integration of Latin America (when the word "integration" stands alone in a discussion of Latin America, it can be safely assumed to mean "economic integration," much as "integration" in the United States immediately suggests "racial integration").

It urges the more developed countries to take a generous attitude toward any policies affecting the sale of Latin American commodities. It notes that "the active participation of the private sector is essential to economic integration and development."

Right here is one of the bow knots in the Alliance for Progress line. Although private participation is considered essential if not primary to the success of the Alliance, the agreement is among the governments of the countries involved, not its private citizens.

Food for Peace—and for work.

The final section of the Charter is devoted to basic export commodities, the major source of economic wealth—and worry—in Latin America. It recommends the elimination of export subsidies, import restrictions and a variety of other trade-doctoring devices that have traditionally bedeviled the area. But, oddly, the Charter fails to recommend the economic diversification which most experts believe is a prerequisite to stability in countries which rely on but one product for most of their foreign revenue.

A reading of the Charter engenders several feelings about it. One notices first of all that the language is exceedingly optimistic and the proposals are perhaps unrealistically all-encompassing. In the heady language of the Charter the seeds of disappointment were sown.

The Alliance for Progress has another, older ideological root which deserves mention if only because it has provoked some invidious comparisons: The Marshall Plan.

The vision of a bootstraps operation as speedily successful as the Marshall Plan was in Europe may have generated the exaggerated optimism which characterized President Kennedy's Alliance speech and the Punta Charter itself. The Marshall Plan, of course, operated under very different conditions from the Alliance for Progress: Much more money was poured into devastated Europe after World War II than has been allotted to the Alliance; the U.S. controlled the expenditure of the money it granted; the program operated in an area whose citizens were familiar with and trained to carry out a high level of political, social and economic organization.

If Kennedy's idea for the Alliance for Progress didn't originate with him, what was the reason for the publicity and enthusiasm that greeted it? What was different about the proposal?

First of all, this plan came from the U.S.,

and the U.S. would have to be, in any inter-American progress operation, the financial leader. Secondly, the Alliance, although it represented nothing qualitatively different from earlier proposals, did represent a quantitative expansion of U.S. aid commitments to Latin America. And probably most important of a ll, Uncle Sam seemed to be taking a more beneficent attitude toward countries that had long regarded the U.S. as something of a selfish ogre.

In the three years since the Charter of Punta del Este was signed, what has been the fate of this enthusiastically conceived Alliance for Progress?

Disappointing to All

It has disappointed almost everyone. Progress has been not nearly so rapid as envisioned in the Charter. And no wonder. One of the stated goals, for instance, was "elimination of adult illiteracy." How could such an educational level be achieved in 10 years in an area where the average literacy rate in 1961 was 50 per cent for those 15 years old and over (as compared with 97.3 per cent in the U.S.), and where the population in almost all countries bounds ahead of the school building effort?

Another complaint claims that the Alliance *per se* isn't accomplishing anything, that the successes attributed to it would have been achieved if the Alliance had never been called into being.

This charge has some merit. The Alliance has no central office through which all projects "under the Alliance" are filtered; thus, there's no way to tell what has actually been done through the Alliance and what has been done simply in line with the principles of the Alliance —principles which were in the air considerably before President Kennedy gave the phrase to the world. What's more, Uncle Sam's donations to Latin America have increased in size but have not changed in nature since Punta del Este.

The United States gives economic aid directly to Latin America through four channels: The Agency for International Development (AID), the Social Progress Trust Fund (SPTF), Food for Peace, and the Export-Import Bank (EXIM). All of these agencies existed prior to the Alliance except SPTF, and the proposal for it had been made even before the Act of Bogotá.

AID's aid and Food for Peace were expanded sharply as a result of the Alliance but EXIM's help has decreased rapidly since 1961.

In addition, Uncle Sam contributes substantially to the Inter-American Development Bank (also founded prior to the Alliance), and to other international organizations which, through loans, grants and technical assistance, help Latin America. Again, U.S. aid through these channels is affected more by the principles than by the fact of the Alliance for Progress.

A major failing of the Alliance to date has been that the internal reforms and long range national development programs in Latin America have been preached, but not practiced, with gusto. Those in power balk at instigating agrarian reform to leave them with less land, tax reform to leave them with less money, and educational and social reform to leave them with less status and power. Meanwhile, long range plans require time, money, and expert advice—all of which are in short supply, especially in the countries which need the plans the most. And even when such plans have been completed, they often must wait one to two years for Alliance approval.

Knotted Purse Strings

Another headache has been the apathy of the private sector. The Charter reckoned that 80 per cent of the economic stimulation of the Alliance would come from private investors, but this surge of investment hasn't been forthcoming. Political uncertainty and inflation in many area countries keep the purse strings knotted.

Finally, the Alliance failed to develop a true multilateral character. The Punta Charter had envisioned a genuine alliance wherein all member nations participated in all important decisions. Because U.S. help is still locked within pre-Alliance agencies, it has slid into the old routes and ruts: Bilateral agreements to give or lend money, rather than multilateral decisions on where capital should be put to work. Perhaps the idea of multilateralness was bizarre in the first place and impractical since only Uncle Sam would provide any big external aid. But it did suggest a degree of international cooperation among Latin Amercian countries that seemed desirable.

To achieve a measure of multilateralness, in other words to "Latinize" the Alliance a little more, a seven-member Inter-American Committee for the Alliance for Progress was established. The body is made up of six rotating representatives from Latin American countries and one permanent member from the U.S. There is also an eighth non-active member who serves as chairman. The Committee's job is to keep watch over all aspects of the Alliance and make recommendations to increase the effectiveness of Alliance projects.

But, like so many international bodies with imposingly listed responsibilities, the Inter-American Committee doesn't really have much power. It cannot, for instance, issue binding vetoes or approvals of programs and so its influence on the course of the Alliance is not likely to be profound.

The New Man Is Mann

When President Johnson shifted Teodoro Moscoso from his position as coordinator for the Alliance to that of U.S. representative to the Inter-American Committee early in 1964, it might have been regarded as a promotion since the Committee was supposed to be the new guiding force in Alliance policy. But Moscoso's sudden resignation a few months later suggested, among other things, that the Inter-American Committee was not exercising much influence in hemispheric affairs.

Moving to top place among President Johnson's Latin American advisers was old Mexico hand Thomas Mann. Mann quickly made headlines by reportedly "leaking" the information that President Johnson would take a more pragmatic approach to Latin America than did President Kennedy. Mann allegedly suggested that Latin dictators would not be denied U.S. aid just because they were dictators. This news, in a somewhat exaggerated form, brought a loud protest from the liberal press. The President replied with a dose of Johnsonian balm that stressed Uncle Sam's support of democratic governments—without closing the door on possible negotiations with Latin dictators.

Uncle Sam appears to be moving away from the heady idealistic notions that surrounded the Alliance for Progress at its birth. But the commitment to help Latin Americans help themselves remains unchanged. Methods, meanwhile, are being tested and refined in the field, as a close-up look at the Alliance in action will show.

Paul Conklin

They knew him.

The Alliance:

What It's Doing and How

The Size of the Challenge Dwarfs the Try

But Things Look Better in Tegucigalpa

NOT in the rankest Harlem flat, not in the most dilapidated mountain cabin, not in the length and breadth of the 50 states is there a hint of the kind of poverty that pervades Latin America. It is not just a poverty of purse. It is total poverty.

It is a poverty of housing, of food, of water, of sanitary and medical facilities, of roads, of schools, of public transportation, of administrative talent, of respect for and understanding of civil authority, and of individual incentive. In short, the situation might indeed be hopeless if it were safe to let it be. But Uncle Sam has decided such universal poverty is untenable and so, the Alliance for Progress, whose structure was discussed in the foregoing chapter, was created to see the job through.

In the few countries which have experienced important economic development in recent years, such as Mexico, the Alliance involvement tends to be more sophisticated than in such places as Northeast Brazil, the "bulge" in the South American continent where the human misery is so total it is all but undistracted by hope.

Alliance help to Mexico fits into four categories: Rural development, home finance, Food for Peace, and a new agricultural center to serve all of Latin America. Most interesting, in terms of Mexico, are the first and the last of these.

Mexico's rural development plan is chiefly a program of supervised agricultural credit for small and medium-sized farms. "We're trying," explains an Alliance official, "to focus the attention of the banking community on the agricultural sector, to see it as a source of commerce. Traditionally, Mexican banks have never lent to the countryside."

The program works this way: The U.S. provided a $20,000,000 loan to the Bank of Mexico (a government institution combining the functions of a national mint, treasury department, central bank, and home finance agency). The Bank of Mexico lends this money to private banks at 3 per cent interest and allows them to lend it to farmers for 6 per cent. In addition, the Bank of Mexico sends out specialists—there are 100 of them, mostly under 35 years of age and reportedly well trained—to investigate loan applications, advise the local banks on credit risks, and help the qualifying farmers increase their production.

The benefit to the private banks is that "they have a chance to make 3 per cent profit using someone else's money," says an Alliance man. So far, more than $7,000,000 has been lent to 2,000 farmers, with the average loan being $3,200.

Mangoes and Avocadoes

The benefit to the farmer is two-fold: He can get inexpensive credit and has between 2 and 10 years to pay, depending on the type of project he wants the money for.

"If he wants to plant mangoes or avocadoes, it takes five years before he begins to produce, so he'd probably get a 10-year loan; but if it's a loan to irrigate, it will give him immediate benefit so he'd take out a two-year loan," the Alliance man explains.

Alliance officials, who have some reason to be unenthusiastic about many things, are very optimistic about rural development. They expect the original $20,000,000 to be used up in a matter of months. Unfortunately, however, the small farmer who needs the money the most is a bad credit risk and can't qualify, or is too ignorant to know how to go about applying for it.

An example of private and public cooperation under the Alliance is the plan for an agricultural research center at Chapingo, which is presently the site of Mexico's national agricultural college. The plan would expand the college to include a new national extension service and agricultural research institution. The usefulness of such an establishment is clear.

"As of now," says an Alliance official, "a geneticist in a laboratory may develop a great new seed for corn but there's no technique for making this knowledge known and carrying it to the families planting corn every year."

Financing the expansion is a $2,000,000 loan from the U.S. Agency for International Development (AID), a loan for the same amount from the Inter-American Development Bank (IDB), $2,600,000 from the Mexican government, $300,000 from the UN Special Fund, and grants of $1,500,000 each from the Ford and Rockefeller foundations.

Taking the Credit

The college has an enrollment of 600 students and plans call for tripling that figure over the next five years. The faculty will go on a full-time basis, instead of part-time, and the whole curriculum will be sharply upgraded.

Mexico likes U.S. aid but gets sticky about telling Mexicans about it (see chapter on Mexico). Mexican politicians would rather take the credit themselves. And do.

In contrast to such up-to-date schemes as an agricultural research center are the bread-and-butter projects in countries such as hot, humid Honduras, just south of Mexico.

Honduras is a country where the average family income is $200 a year, where illiteracy is 65 per cent, where mountainous terrain and thick tropical forests have left vast areas uninhabited. Good roads are few and railways are non-existent in the south, where most of the population of 2,000,000 lives. Communication is so difficult, in fact, that until the past few years, the central government in Tegucigalpa, the capital, lacked effective control of all the provinces.

Says a Western diplomat in Tegucigalpa: "We have in Honduras all the problems of the classic underdeveloped country, exaggerated."

Newell Williams, the cigar-puffing local director of the Agency for International Development, supports this view and quickly sketches the size of the Alliance's job in Honduras.

A Chilean garbage picker and family at home.

"We had tried to do everything at one time, when we started out, like spraying buckshot. It was just about as effective as buckshot, too. We've learned our lesson. My objective is to increase productivity with loans, not grants."

American aid to Honduras now runs to $10,-000,000 in loans, $1,000,000 in grants. A large chunk of the latter is for training government administrators and tightening up on tax collection procedures. In 1964, says Williams, tax receipts were up 17 per cent, chiefly because of more efficient collection methods. "With our $1,000,000, we're trying to wag their whole donkey of $500,000,000—the gross national product."

One important step toward increasing Honduras' productivity has been the erection of its first hydroelectric plant, which began operating in April 1964. The Cañaveral Hydroelectric Project, with a 160,000-watt capacity, was financed with the help of a $2,800,000 U.S. AID loan.

The facility hopefully will entice industry to Honduras, particularly in the fast-growing area around the northern city of San Pedro Sula. But industrial expansion has been slowed by the lack of long-term, low-interest credit—although Uncle Sam recently signed a $5,000,000 loan agreement with a private development bank in San Pedro Sula.

AGENCY FOR INTERNATIONAL DEVELOPMENT LOANS AND LOAN AUTHORIZATIONS TO LATIN AMERICA

Fiscal Year 1963 (In Millions)

Country	Technical Assistance	Development Loans	Supporting Assistance	Total	Cumulative Fiscal Year 1948-63
Argentina	$3.3	$76.4	$20.0	$99.7	$154.5
Bolivia	7.5	18.3	9.9	35.7	224.6
Brazil	23.8	37.4	25.5	86.7	224.5
British Guiana (*a*)	1.3	. . .	. . .	1.3	4.0
Chile	6.3	35.0	. . .	41.3	259.1
Colombia	6.2	87.2	0.2	93.5	171.8
Costa Rica	2.4	10.6	. . .	13.0	35.5
Cuba (*a*)	*No aid since fiscal year 1961*				2.8
Dominican Republic	3.6	2.1	23.9	29.7	57.8
Ecuador	4.9	6.3	7.0	18.2	77.0
El Salvador	3.0	16.6	. . .	19.6	32.4
Guatemala	2.6	0.7	. . .	3.3	98.3
Haiti	. . .	. . .	4.9	4.9	57.0
Honduras	3.2	1.6	2.4	7.3	36.9
Mexico	0.3	. . .	. . .	0.3	28.8
Nicaragua	2.5	1.0	. . .	3.5	25.2
Panama	2.3	6.0	0.4	8.8	49.2
Paraguay	3.0	. . .	. . .	3.0	35.9
Peru	3.0	. . .	. . .	3.0	80.9
Surinam (*a*)	0.3	. . .	. . .	0.3	3.1
Uruguay	1.9	6.0	. . .	7.9	18.8
Venezuela	3.0	30.0	0.1	33.1	60.5

(*a*) *Not members of Alliance for Progress*

"Most commercial loans here," explains foreign aider Williams, "must be repaid in 36 months, with interest rates of about one per cent a month. In reality you almost have to throw in the Cathedral (in Tegucigalpa) and one or two other buildings for collateral to get a loan here."

Forty-five per cent of Honduras is forest, yet lack of roads and capital has left much of it unexploited. "The one long-term resource that can be exploited here is pine trees," Williams notes. "But how do you get to it? And how do you get it out? Obviously, by putting a road in. I'm working on a loan for that now."

In most of Central America—indeed in most of Latin America—progress is hampered by the lack of infrastructure—roads, water and sewage systems, power systems and port facilities. Of the $30,400,000 in U.S. AID loans to Honduras since 1957, half of that amount has gone for infrastructure projects.

Visits from the Doctor

But not all AID programs are on so grand a scale. The Honduras government and the U.S. share the $350,000 a year it costs to operate eight mobile health teams which travel from village to village dispensing medicine, conducting physical examinations, and innoculating the inhabitants against diphtheria, typhoid, and polio. Each team is composed of a doctor and a driver, who is also a "latrine expert." Bounding over the rugged countryside in jeeps, the teams cover a total of 35 towns, with between 50 and 100 people treated at each stop. The patients are asked to contribute the equivalent of 25 cents; the contributions go into a local fund for building community health clinics. All 35 towns have built such clinics.

Not all U.S. help is channeled through AID boss Williams' pine-paneled office in downtown Tegucigalpa. Two other aid devices are the military civic action program and the Peace Corps.

The civic action program, in Honduras as elsewhere, is an attempt to turn the Latin military, traditionally identified in most area countries with reaction and oppression, into an enlightened social force.

Explains a U.S. adviser: "We're trying to make the military a force for social reform, to have the people think of the soldier as the man with the hoe and the putty knife, not the man with the gun aimed at them."

The U.S.-supported School of the Americas at Fort Gulick in the Panama Canal Zone turns out 1,300 Latin American military men a year, trained in military techniques—including counter-insurgency—but also proficient in valuable specialties. The soldiers are taught to be radio operators, civil engineers, auto and airplane mechanics, bulldozer drivers, and medical technicians. After their schooling, they are sent home to build access roads, develop water supplies, and construct bridges.

Seventy-five per cent of all Latin recruits, according to one estimate, are illiterate upon entering military service. For this reason, a full 30 per cent of their time in training is given to elementary education.

"The hope is," declares a U.S. military adviser in the Canal Zone, "that they'll go home and teach others some of what they've learned."

Sometimes they don't learn so well.

In Honduras a military junta booted out the U.S.-backed democratic government of President Ramón Villeda Morales in October 1963, only a few days before the scheduled national elections. Ironically, several of the leaders of the revolt had undergone training in the States or at the School of the Americas.

Erasing the Past

A U.S. military adviser in Tegucigalpa shakes his head grimly and declares: "We are trying to undo and erase 5 to 10 centuries of thinking in these countries. It's not the kind of thing that can be accomplished overnight."

Nevertheless, Yankee military men say they are encouraged by the response of younger officers in the Latin American armed forces, and it is on the younger ones, imbued with more modern social concepts, that they pin their hopes for the area's future.

Under a program to eradicate pine beetle disease, a disease that attacks the roots of pine trees, the United Nations is supplying food to program workers in La Vente, 60 miles south of Tegucigalpa. But the UN provided no means for getting the food to the workers. So the Honduras army trucks it into the woods once a month and picks up the tab for gas and oil. During one recent month the army delivered 40 tons of food to the forest workers.

Other programs show the scope of the army's activities.

Under the Alliance for Progress school program, it had been planned to build 400 classrooms in rural areas. Now the Honduras army is working alongside local laborers in these self-help projects, and, without increasing cost either to Honduras or Uncle Sam, the total number of classrooms built will be 500.

There are four to six soldiers at every site, making cinder blocks, installing plumbing lines and hammering beams. Trained carpenters in other army units are making desks and chairs. The U.S. is giving the projects a push by supplying electric power saws.

Specialists in Action

The civil action program also provides Special Action Forces—specially trained Yankees and in some cases Latins—to work on specific problems. In Colombia, for example, where the government wanted help organizing and training a staff for a new military-civilian hospital, a U.S. Special Action team was sent out. It included the chief surgeon at Fitzsimmons Army Hospital in Colorado, a woman dietician (an Army captain) from Texas, and a blood specialist from the research center at Walter Reed General Hospital in Washington They were paid for their four-month tour in Colombia out of military assistance funds.

According to one U.S. military man, some "75 per cent of every U.S. military assistance dollar goes for non-weapons uses, mainly for teaching people new skills, usually with some civilian application."

Peace Corps activities in Honduras are directed by Edwin P. Astle, a crew-cut veteran of technical assistance programs in Paraguay, Haiti and British Honduras.

"Our object here," Astle explains in his cluttered office on Avenida Cervantes in Tegucigalpa, "is to try to get communities to help themselves, to realize their own potential for solving their problems."

Much of the Peace Corps effort in Honduras, as elsewhere, has been directed at self-help projects. A Corpsman is sent to a town or village requesting him. He talks to leaders of the communities to learn what needs to be done; usually, everything needs to be done.

"It may be a health clinic, a local school,

latrines, a recreation area, driving a well, or a beautification program for the village green," Astle declares.

One of the most ambitious programs in which the Peace Corps is participating is a radio-literacy course, which is supported by Honduras businessmen, the Honduras government, and the Catholic Church. Communities or individuals buy, usually on the instalment plan with small monthly payments, a fixed-frequency radio monitor. For two hours a day, a special station in Tegucigalpa broadcasts basic lessons in reading and writing.

Peace Corps volunteers travel from village to village appointing literate persons as teachers, a job offering no pay but considerable prestige, and also distributing school materials—books, notebooks, blackboards and pencils. Some 600 radio sets have been distributed and each one is listened to by 10 or 12 students.

In later stages of the project, lessons will involve instruction in more efficient farming methods, sanitation, and home economics. The idea seems sound enough, but it involves very hard work and interest in it is flagging. Peasants who miss a couple of days' lessons because of sickness or extra work in the field find themselves behind with little incentive to return. Weather interference with broadcasts and breakdown of radio sets have also hurt the program, as has the difficulty in keeping unpaid instructors.

Numbed by the Sun

Compounding Alliance problems in Honduras as well as in other Central American countries and in the equatorial lowlands of South America is a hot, humid climate that stultifies the human body and, often, the mind.

Says one AID official: "The ceaseless heat and the frequent rains that somehow do not lessen the humidity are one of our most difficult obstacles. It is hard for our people to stimulate the peasants when we ourselves begin to get numbed by the sun. The climate is especially rough when you consider how much trouble it is just to find a drink of clean water."

Take, for instance, the reeking slums of Lima, where tens of thousands of families live in filthy huts erected atop piles of garbage. For the inhabitants of Lima's slums there are two ways of getting water. They can either draw it from the occasional gullies which dribble through their neighborhoods bearing a not altogether coincidental resemblance to open sewers, or they can proffer barrels or buckets to the water truck which makes periodic visits to help them out.

Under these conditions it is practically a hopeless matter to bathe.

Said one woman who was washing her young children in a shallow wooden tub: "In the old days we lived in the mountains and there never was enough food. But we had water there. Here in the city (her hand surveyed the tattered shacks) there is more food but there is never enough water. Children must be kept clean. For a bath in the mountains I think I would give all I have."

In addition to the filth and inconvenience such situations create, there is always the threat of disease. In Venezuela, which has earnestly attacked its shortage of water facilities in recent years, more than 184 deaths per 100,000 persons took place in 1952 because of water-borne maladies. A dozen years later, because of new and expanded water supplies, the death rate from such diseases has been cut in half.

Chimbote, Peru: Peace Corpsman Joe Grant of the Bronx shows a youngster how to punch one to right.

Paul Conklin

Rio de Janeiro: No place to go.

Some 70 per cent of Latin America's rural population in centers having less than 10,000 people lack potable water. This doesn't just mean they don't have a tap or a well handy; it means they don't even have a stream or river from which they can take water with safety.

This unavailability of water is a major reason why the children of Latin America are perpetually scabby and dirty. And the larger the community, the more crowded the slums, the greater the health threat.

Rio de Janeiro is framed by the *favelas*, the worst slums in Latin America except, perhaps, for Lima's. Some 300,000 people now live in the huts of Rio without water or sanitary facilities. A reporter from the States recently toured these huts, which stand in the shadow of the huge Christ the Redeemer statue on top of Corcovado Mountain. It was a Saturday morning and many of the children were in school, but still the area was overrun with people.

"The children go to school six mornings a week," said a young Brazilian businessman who was serving as guide. "They are happy to get away from the terrible conditions here."

The reporter was ushered into the shack of Sam Kelley, a part-Negro, part-Latin laborer who came to Brazil several years ago from Trinidad. He and his wife had nine children, four of whom died in their first year. The Kelleys and their surviving children live in one room with one bed. There is no water, no latrine and no privacy. The shack reeks to high heaven.

"Yes, I hear of the Alliance for Progress," says Sam Kelley. "I have always listened to big government words. Maybe my mother in heaven cries for me. Nobody else cares. I have a job cleaning buildings but what good is a job when money is no good. Things cost too much. It was bad in Trinidad but it was better. I come here because my father was Portuguese and I speak the language. I drive a taxi until it won't go no more. Will the Alliance for Progress give me a new taxi?"

A taxi, no. But three agencies operating under the Alliance are pouring $35,000,000 into a water system for the Rio slums. The project will increase the city's water resources by 44 per cent.

"I am not a Communist," says Sam Kelley

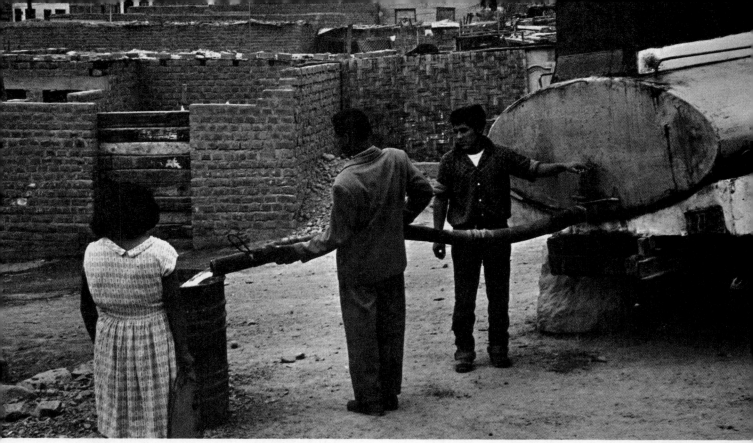

Lima: Once a week, running water.

slowly, "but many in the *favelas* are Communists. Yes, I know of the water that they say is coming. It should come quick because bad water makes my teeth hurt, and if my teeth keep hurting I will become a Communist."

But adequate water facilities, necessary as they are, must be part of a larger package, a package that stresses decent housing, according to Alliance officials.

Declares a U.S. banker in Brazil: "There is a serious motivational problem in Latin America. The slum people have been living far worse than animals in a zoo and they have become like animals themselves. Many of them have stopped caring. That sometimes makes it easier for them but it makes it harder for anybody to help them. I'm no do-gooder but if we could just get every one of those families into a nice little house I think you'd see them display different attitudes."

This view is widely shared by U.S. and Latin officialdom. In Chile, Uncle Sam has erected whole villages to house people dispossessed by the earthquakes of 1960. Rows of simple, cinder-block dwellings stand where shabby huts stood before, and the effect of the new homes on the people shines in their eyes.

Says U.S. AIDer Kay Ray in Santiago: "The people regain their self-respect, the children are far easier to discipline and all the other Alliance projects go better when the people have a livable home. It's the best way to give them hope and to make them try to improve themselves."

Homebuilding under the Alliance is far more than a giveaway program. In Chile, for instance, a man can buy a house with only a nominal down payment and a 20-year mortgage. He amortizes his debt not only with regular monthly payments, but also by keeping his children in school. For every year his children go to school—instead of dropping out to work in the fields—the mortgage on his house is reduced by a certain amount. Thus the Alliance provides an incentive to education, an incentive that does not spring naturally from the breast of a father who himself did not go to school.

In Peru, the Agency for International Development and the Peruvian government have

Santiago, Chile: Before and after Alliance aid.

teamed up to foster savings and loan institutions. Some $10,000,000—$6,000,000 from AID, $4,000,000 from the Peruvian government—has been pledged to Peru's Central Home Loan Bank, which is financing 80 housing cooperatives.

The important thing about savings and loan associations in spurring home building in Latin America is that they permit even very poor individuals to pay their own way in acquiring a house, thus providing that measure of self-help recommended at Punta del Este. The loans are usually granted on terms that would make the average U.S. banker bubble-eyed, but "easy" loans are the only loans possible in much of Latin America.

And the savings and loan association idea is spreading around the continent. Argentina has about 70 such associations, Chile has more than 20 and Peru has 15.

"Savings and loan associations teach people to budget, to save and to build on their own and accept some responsibility," says one Peruvain official. "They are a drop in the bucket compared to what is needed just in my own country, but after so many years of nothing just this beginning is very gratifying."

How to Build a House

Financial contributions, however, are not the only way in which Uncle Sam is helping Latins to have better living conditions.

Under various programs, technical advisers are sent to the area to plan and supervise construction. Peace Corps workers rally the residents of the villages in which they work to try to inspire them to build houses, finding materials either in the village or luring help from other groups in the country (the Peace Corps itself has no money for building materials).

Despite the progress that's being made—and the progress is impressive when a new housing unit is viewed against a background of squalid slums—the problems get no smaller. The need for housing swells as population growth cancels out gains. Building costs rise, especially in countries with inflation difficulties; those countries find foreign equipment increasingly expensive in terms of their own currencies. Sometimes, too, the necessary land is hard to wrest from its owners, or often title to building sites has not been clearly settled.

Not only is the population growing, it is growing disproportionately fast in the cities as a result of internal migration. Generally, the larger the city the more aggravated its housing shortage. Thus three countries with huge metropolises—Brazil, Argentina and Venezuela—lead the pack in housing needs. Brazil's problems in this area are by far the worst.

But another country whose cities are being pincered by slums is Colombia. Its capital and largest city, Bogotá, is especially blighted. For this reason, and because Colombia has taken the necessary steps to assure it Alliance approval, the largest single housing project under way in Latin America has taken root on the 770 acres of the old Bogotá airport.

On December 17, 1961, four months to the day after the signing of the Charter of Punta del Este, President Kennedy and Alberto Lleras Camargo, who was then Colombia's president, launched "Ciudad Techo."

Myriad Mishaps

The Institute of Territorial Credit, Colombia's equivalent of Uncle Sam's Federal Housing Administration, bought the bulk of the land needed for the development, built sewers, water systems and streets, supplied electrical facilities, and set aside parcels for community buildings. The original goal was 12,000 units, 40 per cent of them in multi-family buildings and the rest individual homes. Today the goal is 14,000 units and even that figure will likely be raised as additional land is purchased.

Myriad mishaps have plagued Ciudad Techo. The devaluation of the peso two years ago caused a slowdown. Loan money was harder to get and the government entered a period of austerity. Wrangles over land titles have only recently been settled, and inadequate transportation facilities serving the building site hampered the project.

Last year two events cast a shadow over the work. A tornado demolished some of the homes, and on November 22, 1963, John Kennedy was murdered. On that night the residents of Ciudad Techo solemnly paraded through their streets, and elected to rename their community "Ciudad Kennedy."

In harness with clean water and decent housing as pullers of the Alliance is nourishing food. Food in most of Latin America is not only scarce; it is often lacking in nutrients because of worn-out soil.

In Puno in the high mountains of Peru, the terrain is rugged and the air is thin. Some children have to walk three hours to reach school. Until recently few youngsters were inclined to make the trip, as a 40 per cent absentee rate showed. Today, absenteeism is almost unknown. The agent of this change is not a fiery-eyed truant officer, but food. Through the Food for Peace program, authorized by U.S. Public Law 480 governing the distribution of Uncle Sam's surplus crops, Peruvian schools are serving lunch to children whose main nourishment had been the narcotic *coca* leaf. The project is called *Operación Niños,* or Operation Children.

Operation Children is younger than most of the youngsters it serves. In its first year, 1963, the program fed 9,000,000 children, substantially raising their nutritional level and their educational level as well. There are few school dropouts when school means eating as well as studying. The U.S. is supplying $28,500,000 in food and equipment with the recipient countries chipping in $13,000,000 in addition to paying all operating costs.

Elsewhere in the Andes, in one of the Indian villages that ring two-mile-high Lake Titicaca, local men built a school. Their pay was not in *pesos bolivianos,* but in food.

Some 120 rural families migrated to develop new lands in a three-month Colombian project. As they made their way, Food for Peace meals sustained them and helped to pay them for work on roads leading to their destination.

In Ecuador, more than 1,000 workers built ovens, washing facilities, latrines and gardens. They received U.S. surplus farm products as compensation.

To many Latin Americans, particularly in the Andean countries, the most pressing need is for transportation. Without roads they can not get their products to market. Without roads fertile lands remain closed to development and peasants leave worked-out farms for the already teeming cities instead of for undeveloped land they could till.

In Moquegua, Peru, workers have only one

ALLIANCE FOR PROGRESS:

(Fiscal 1965 Figures Estimated)

Fiscal Years	New Houses			New Classrooms		
	1962 & 1963	1964	1965	1962 & 1963	1964	1965
Argentina	....	....	600	....	....	50
Bolivia	100	....	800	300	100	60
Brazil	3,000	2,500	4,500	1,000	8,000	7,000
Chile	22,500	10,000	10,000	1,200	1,800	1,000
Colombia	50,000	34,000	40,000	2,800	2,000	1,000
Costa Rica	4,000	1,000	1,500	50	30	300
Dominican Rep.	1,000	500	....	100	50	....
Ecuador	500	1,000	2,000	400	1,000	1,000
El Salvador	1,500	2,500	4,000	400	500	900
Guatemala	2,000	....	....	1,500	300	700
Haiti	....	....	....	100		
Honduras	....	200	500	300	200	200
Mexico	....	8,000	18,500	....	....	....
Nicaragua	2,000	2,000	2,000	100	300	300
Panama	2,500	1,000	500	400	300	300
Paraguay	....	....	....	10	100	100
Peru	5,000	4,500	9,000	....	....	....
Uruguay	....	....	....	....	....	....
Venezuela	23,000	38,000	10,000	....	....	....

way to reach their fields, which lie on the other side of a river. That is by climbing hand-over-hand across a rope stretching from a cliff above the river to the flatland on the opposite side. Along the Amazon, Indians carrying their bananas or chickens to market must undertake a tedious, hours-long journey in dugout canoes or on balsa rafts, braving alligators and piranhas and warding off insistent insects.

Improving the transportation system in the Andean lands is no easy task for the road-builder, even with modern techniques. The matted jungles of the Amazon must be penetrated; the lofty Andean mountains must be scaled. The separation of the Andes from the jungle lowlands to the east and the coastal strips to the west involves more than a difference in altitudes. It is also one of climate: Highland Indians, whose bodies are suited to thin air and cold weather, become highly susceptible to tropical diseases when they move downhill to areas of higher temperature and denser air. And it is one of culture and custom: Brought up in an isolated remnant of his herit-age, the Indian is unaccustomed to the Westernized society of his lowland countrymen.

Nevertheless, there are urgent reasons why the jungles and the mountains must be traversed. The populations of the Andean countries are squeezed into the few fertile areas of the coast or boxed up in the highlands while potentially rich lands to the east lie enmeshed in impenetrable jungle.

Three of the Andean countries—Ecuador, Peru, and Bolivia—are now working together on plans for a 3,720-mile road system through the jungles and mountains. The proposed Bolivariano Highway would begin in Colombia and run along the eastern slopes of the Andes through Ecuador, Peru, and Bolivia to the Brazil border. The Social Progress Trust Fund (SPTF) has provided the three countries with a $200,000 loan to pay half the cost of a survey of the proposed route.

In 10 to 15 years, most of the Bolivariano and marginal highways should be completed. Roads now under construction would become links in the long north-south chain.

PART OF THE RECORD

	Water Systems Built				Health Centers & Mobile Health Units			
	1962 & 1963	1964	1965	People Benefited	1962 & 1963	1964	1965	People Benefited
Argentina			(No external help requested)					
Bolivia	8	10	10	150,000	1	4	1	400,000
Brazil	15	178	280	15,000,000	170	110	110	3,000,000
Chile	38	24	5	350,000	41	20	4	2,500,000
Colombia	20	24	60	4,000,000	80	20	30	1,000,000
Costa Rica	....	9	10	250,000	6	5	...	300,000
Dominican Rep.	....	....	....	....	....	....	....	....
Ecuador	125	97	130	700,000	....	....	....	....
El Salvador	57	80	120	600,000	7	2	25	400,000
Guatemala	10	100	200	50,000	8	10	....	200,000
Haiti	....	....	....	....	....	....	....	....
Honduras	....	10	38	200,000	10	2	....	300,000
Mexico	5	4	3	450,000	....	....	....	....
Nicaragua	40	1	....	40,000	26	2	....	300,000
Panama	39	....	....	450,000	11	10	3	250,000
Paraguay	14	4	7	90,000	3	5	8	200,000
Peru	1	2	5	200,000	....	....	....	....
Uruguay	....	....	1	500,000	....	....	....	....
Venezuela	20	120	190	1,200,000	....	....	....	....

Because of differences in the present road systems, landscapes, and economic situations in the three countries, their transportation needs and land development possibilities vary.

Ecuador, northernmost of the three, has a large, fertile coastal area although most of its people live high in the Andes. Highways bear the brunt of Ecuador's transportation system, but of 9,375 miles of roads only about half are open to traffic throughout the entire year. Ecuador's fertile soil in the coastal west now produces the world's largest export crop of bananas. The country needs more and better roads to move this produce westward to the ports and eastward to the densely populated highlands and to facilitate migration from the mountains to the coast.

Unlike Ecuador's coast, the coastal area of Peru is a desert except for oases along the rivers that wend their way from the Andes to the sea. Peru has the same problem of over-population in its highlands (60 per cent of the people live on 12 per cent of the land) as Ecuador and could relieve this population pressure through migrations to large tracts of flatland in the east. Of Peru's 22,320 miles of road, only 20 per cent are paved.

The first paved road across the Andes in northern Peru now is under construction. It would provide a route for migration from the coastal deserts and the highlands to the eastern lowlands.

Landlocked Bolivia has neither the wealth of the Ecuadorian coast nor the woes of the Peruvian coast. Because the highlands produce little wealth except tin and the lowlands are largely undeveloped, the entire country remains poor. Migration to the eastern lowlands is considered essential if the country is to progress.

The road from Cochabamba to Santa Cruz demonstrates the value of establishing lifelines to eastern Bolivia. Before the road opened 10 years ago, Santa Cruz was a sleepy, quaint Spanish city. Today it is the booming center for the agricultural trade of the region.

Bolivians can travel over 12,500 miles of road. But only a fraction of these are paved and there is little regular maintenance.

But, while all areas south of the border need something, there are some that need everything.

Nations within nations are common in Latin America. Northeastern Brazil is such a place. If this nine-state region were considered as a

Sacks of flour distributed in La Paz, Bolivia, under the Food for Peace Program: The recipients are acquiring a stomach for change.

Carl Howard

This 47-ton "tree roller," used in Alliance road-building projects, bends back trees with the horizontal bar and then rolls over them, its blade-cylinders munching the wood to bits as it goes. The machine probably would not be suitable for backyard use—although some American suburbanites might appreciate its decisiveness.

separate entity, it would be the third largest country in South America and contain the second largest population. Its educational and income levels are dramatically lower than those of the rest of Brazil. The *sêcas,* Brazil's word for the droughts which have dried up attempts at progress in the Northeast since time immemorial, regularly hit the region.

The Northeast was the first section of Brazil to be settled, but it has only recently received attention for development purposes. United States aid to the region, as to all of Latin America, was erratic until the last few years. As Castro made his intentions clear, the U.S. began to consider all points where Cuba-like Communist take-overs might occur. An obvious spot was the poverty-stricken Brazilian Northeast. A serious Communist revolt had taken place there in 1958. In 1960, the militant Peasant Leagues headed by Francisco Julião received wide publicity. These groups agitated for land reform as a means to more even distribution of the small per capita wealth of this vast wasteland.

About the same time, SUDENE began to take shape. The Superintendency for the Development of the Northeast was to be a planning organization coordinating and instigating reforms in the Northeast; its first plan was formulated in May 1960.

As soon as President Kennedy took office, he pointed AID's finger at the northeastern bulge of the South American continent. On April 13, 1962, after consultations and visits between officials of the two governments, the U.S. and Brazil signed a pact which kicked off a two-year blitz program. Under the agreement, the U.S. was to provide $131,000,000 in dollars and *cruzeiros;* the Brazilian government was to ante up the equivalent of $145,00,000 over the following two years.

The money pouring into Northeast Brazil suddenly became a flood. Planners had to figure how to channel it effectively. Projects had to be worked out for improvement of this huge sweep of land. The SUDENE plan concentrated largely on road building and generating electric power.

Through SUDENE, the Brazilian government sought to do what Julião's forces sought through guerrilla activity: To restructure rural life and see to proper distribution of food. Neglected in this first plan were two areas which later would receive more attention: Development of industry and education.

71

Uncle Sam's large-scale entry into SU-DENE's financing changed the balance of projects. Much money has continued to flow into road building and maintenance—the bulk of U.S. aid in dollars, in fact. But in local currency, the largest proportion by far has gone for construction of elementary schools and teacher-training centers. U.S. aid in this field is designed to reserve Brazilian government funds for supplying and training teachers for the schools-to-be.

Saving the "Bulge"

Northeastern agriculture had received little help from AID resources, but in recent months money to develop this part of the area's economy has begun to flow. This change reflects specific political considerations. When Brazil President Castelo Branco came in, Celso Furtado, head of SUDENE, went out—forcibly. Furtado has a top reputation as a planner. His political leanings are to the left, but, most conclude, he is not a Communist. Several known Communists were on his agricultural staff, however, and they were also dismissed by the new regime. Experts believe agriculture in the Northeast must be developed if the Communist agitation there is to be neutralized.

The SUDENE faces the massive engineering tasks implicit in creating unified road and water systems for the primitive nine-state "bulge." It faces the equally large task of raising the standard of living of the dense population there, of educating them generally and training them for new employment specifically, and of reforming the social structure. In addition, the SU-DENE wrestles with knotty administrative problems.

Northeast Brazil is a powder keg. Practically the whole population is poverty-stricken and illiterate. The Communist agitators have long been at work in the area and if most of the people there have any political ideas at all, they are probably Communist ideas. In the words of an American long experienced in the Northeast, "If we can save Northeast Brazil from the Reds, we can save any place in Latin America."

But there is more to achieving an orderly society than nailing the Communists. Someone must fill the power vacuum. And here arises the singular shape of Latin politics.

A woman and a wall in Bolivia.

Hands Across the Border

THE two aid projects in Peru at first glance seem strikingly similar. One is a loan to help build a 48-mile road between the communities of La Morado and Tulumayo. The second is a grant to the Indian settlement of Congas for assistance in completing a 17-mile road reaching to the Pan American Highway along the Pacific Coast. Both projects involve road construction. Both will enable Peruvian peasants to carry their produce to large markets. Both are being financed by American dollars.

But there the similarity ends. The La Morado-Tulumayo road is an Alliance for Progress undertaking and the loan is for $1,900,000. The Congas project costs only $585, for the purchase of tools. It is being handled by a grass-roots, community-to-community program called "Partners of the Alliance."

Partners was founded by James Boren, an official of the Agency for International De-velopment (AID) who spent two years as deputy mission director in Peru. In those years, Mr. Boren watched helplessly as enterprising communities embarked on small-scale, local projects that subsequently foundered for the lack of small amounts of money. A school would be completed except for doors, windows, or a roof when the money ran out. Or, once a schoolhouse was finished, no money would be left for blackboards or desks.

When he returned to the United States, Mr. Boren swung into a personal campaign for a program to finance such small projects in Latin America. AID gave him a go-ahead in September 1963 and for almost five months Mr. Boren worked alone, establishing connections between individuals and groups in the United States who wanted to help and Latin communities that needed the help.

Thus was born Partners of the Alliance. By

mid-1964 Mr. Boren was working with a staff of four and had arranged projects linking groups in 11 states with Latin communities. An additional 12 states were considering joining the program.

Mr. Boren and his staff act as matchmakers. A professional organization, high school class, or town government might express interest in helping Latin Americans. A town in Guatemala or Ecuador might write to AID asking for chicken wire, insecticides, an incubator for a chicken hatchery, a projector to show movies on sanitation, or knitting machines for an industrial school. AID passes on the request to Mr. Boren and the Partners office tries to mate the American donor with the Latin American petitioner.

A request to Partners must be initiated by the Latin community, although Peace Corps volunteers or AID mission members often point the way. The community must show that the materials requested are vital to a self-help project.

Once a link has been established between a state and a Latin American country, Mr. Boren tries to arrange for the country and the state to remain paired in future Partners projects. Peru's regular liaison, for instance, is with Texas. The Texas AFL-CIO is providing Peruvians with picks and wheelbarrows. The PTA Student Forum Club of Navasota High School in Texas has sent Coleman-type laterns—at a cost of only $25 apiece—to illuminate night literacy classes for Peruvian Indians.

If a state organizes its own Partners clearinghouse for projects, AID drops out of the picture. Idaho has established such a set-up and sent four experts—a lawyer, builder, teacher, and public utilities man—to Ecuador to search for suitable projects. The four Americans drew up a master plan for the renovation of an Ecuadorean town that was damaged by a 1948 earthquake and unable to complete a rebuilding program.

While the Alliance for Progress is dealing in million-dollar projects, often a pressing need of a small Latin community involves a minute fraction of that sum: $25 donated by Colorado Springs to buy additional therapeutic equipment for a playground built by the fathers of three crippled children in San Gregorio, Chile, or $50 sixth grade students in San Rafael, California, earned washing cars that bought blackboards for a school near Arequipa, Peru. True, only small amounts are involved but they represent person-to-person help. That is to say, help to be remembered.

Latin Politics

*It Is a World of Passionate Partisans
In Which All Issues Are Personalized
And the Opponent Is the Devil's Twin*

THE MUSCLE-BOUND Venezuelan official stepped out of the swimming pool and, dripping and panting after a remarkable diving exhibition, lit a cigaret and collapsed into a bright yellow lounge chair. In a moment he was on his feet again, standing in front of a reporter from the States and threatening, in a friendly way, to toss the reporter into the pool.

"Before you do that," said the reporter, "why don't you finish what you were saying about Latin American politics and Albert Einstein."

The Venezuelan official, whom we will call Peréz because it might be awkward to use his real name in connection with this story, clapped both hands to his face and assumed an attitude of deep thought.

"Yes, I had almost forgotten. You asked about the turbulence of Latin politics compared with politics in the United States. Unfortunately, neither you nor anyone else from the States can understand politics in Latin America because you are too full of prejudice. You are like the people 600 years ago who could not conceive of the world being anything but flat, and you are like the people today who will not believe that time is the fourth dimension."

Peréz let his eyes roam for a few seconds over the swimming pool that was tucked into the Caracas hillside.

"What I meant was that it is impossible to understand Einstein's theories unless you put out of your mind what you had always thought of as common sense. When a rocketship flies through space at great speed, the passage of time aboard that rocketship slows down. Well, you say, how can time slow down? Time is time, eh? Well, time *does* slow down because it's related to velocity through space. To begin to understand this it's first necessary to forget common sense. This is what you must do if you want to learn the truth about Latin American politics. You have to throw out what you thought was common sense, because what is common sense in the States is not common sense in Latin America."

That Latin Impulse

With that, Peréz strolled over to the edge of the pool where a tall, good-looking blond was bending over to adjust the strap of her sandal. Peréz brought back his hand and gave her a swat that sent her sprawling into the pool. In the two seconds before the girl surfaced the reporter wondered whether Peréz would be able to flee the country before the girl had time to gather herself together and kill him. But when she bobbed to the surface, she simply laughed —they were apparently good friends—and hollered at Peréz in Spanish.

"That," said Peréz with a demonic smile, "was an impulse and in Latin America we obey our impulses. This explains all the revolutions and why constitutions are ignored. We do what we want to do because that is the way we want it. In the States you do not live that way. We don't judge you by our standards and we don't want you to judge us by yours. So the first thing you must do if we are to talk about this is to forget about how things are done in the United States. That is as irrelevant as common sense is in Einstein's theories.

"But what sense does it make," asked the reporter, "to perpetuate unstable government if the country continues to suffer because of it?"

"Here," answered Peréz, "we get into the area of values. Myself, I am a Betancourt man and I believe as he does that we must have more stability in Venezuela. And we are getting it as you know. Leoni succeeded Betancourt as president and there was no trouble. Power changed hands peacefully. But if the present constitution is some day thrown out by the people when they are tired of it, why shouldn't they be able to do it? That is only democratic.

"According to Yankee common sense, we love politics too much. We put our hearts into everything. That causes trouble the way love always causes trouble, but it is the Latin way and if you don't take the trouble to understand people like us you will go back to the States and write the same foolishness Yankee reporters always write. We are not good at running governments, that's true. But we know how to *live*. The poorest, stupidest Venezuelan knows how to *live*."

Wherever he went in South America, the reporter heard a similar refrain. Sometimes it was stated more defensively, but always there was the suggestion that Latins know how to unleash the human spirit and that this attitude of abandon is a noble, if not a holy, thing.

Tradition and Precedent

But there's much more to it than that. Latin America has been retarded politically (according to "Yankee common sense") because all political activity swirls about the persons and personalities of the leaders, because compromise is regarded as surrender, because extreme class-consciousnesses permeates all aspects of life, and because political parties lack a foundation of principles.

Beyond that, there is, with a few exceptions, no tradition of free elections and the orderly transfer of power, and it is tradition and precedent that gives a political system its momentum. Most of the people in Latin America cannot read or write, and most of those who can are poorly informed on problems and issues. The electorate, therefore, even when its gets a chance to participate in government, is incompetent for the job because it lacks the necessary education.

In many countries, too, the army and the Roman Catholic Church are, or have been, more powerful than the government, and therefore the government has often existed at the sufferance of these institutions. Dictator has followed dictator in Latin America because power is seen as a personal thing, and the leader symbolizes all power because he is the leader. The power is not in the laws or the system. It is in the hands of the president. And why not, many

Outdoor advertising, Caracas.

"I don't suppose you'd care to hear the rest of my inaugural address?"

months even though the *Apristas* have been crying for land reform for decades. And *Acción Popular,* the party of the country's democratic president, several times threw its support to the Communists in student elections just so the *Apristas* couldn't gain control of the student federations.

In Brazil, where the army remains in control after booting out João Goulart several months ago, General Castelo Branco has reluctantly decided to stay on as chief executive. The reason, heavily glossed over in official explanations, is that the Brazilian people can not be relied upon to keep damogogs out of power.

It is meaningless for American liberals to berate the army's continued rule in Brazil without frankly considering the alternatives. Castelo Branco is a moderate; there are no other likely moderate candidates for the presidency around. And this is the case not just because of the purges after the uprising in the spring of 1964; it is because the country's leading politicians, if they have wide popular support, are more anxious to engage in heady programs to please their constituents than they are to give the country

ask. The president is the boss, isn't he?

The only bona fide dictator still in business in South America is General Alfredo Stroessner of Paraguay, and even he is bowing slightly to changing times by permitting a small opposition party while going through the motions of democracy. Stroessner justifies his dictatorial role by claiming that without tough leadership his country would quickly drift into chaos. And he is right. With the few exceptions of Uruguay, Chile, and Costa Rica, continuing political stability has been beyond the powers of the other Latin countries.

Latin politics is never a confrontation of programs. It is rather a constant attempt to *desprestigiar* the other candidate. This means that all a political party's energies go into the job of making the opponent lose prestige or "face."

There is no limit to how far Latins carry this idea. The opposition must be discredited even if they share your beliefs and your tactics are paralyzing the life of the nation. In Peru, for example, the *Apristas* would not approve *Accion Popular's* land reform program for

From *The Wall Street Journal*

"I concede the election."

the period of austerity it urgently needs (see chapter on Brazil).

At the heart of the problem, along with the Latin personality and the widespread illiteracy, is the acute centralization of Latin American governments. There is no real self-government for villages, which are governed by an agent sent from the capital. In Bolivia, for instance, every municipal official is appointed by the president of the country.

Throughout Latin America, the tax collector, the school teacher and the policeman are almost always appointed by the central government. Most of the taxes collected go to the capital, and little of the money is used to benefit the villages. If the people of a village want their school painted, they will send a delegation to the capital where they may wait for days for an audience with the president. Finally, when the president has time to see the delegation, he will listen politely and then announce that the request is under consideration. Most likely, if the request is simple enough, the president will approve it. He will then tell a subordinate to see that the job gets done. Maybe the subordinate will follow through on it and maybe he won't. It will be months before the village finds out whether its school will get painted or not.

Neither Checks Nor Balances

The experience of the more progressive countries of the world shows that rule as close as possible to home is the most efficient. Even the Communists have learned this lesson the hard way. And at last some Latin American countries are beginning to get the idea (see chapter on Peru). But inculcating the notion of local responsibility into villagers with no understanding of the concept is difficult, especially in the Andean countries where most of the villagers are Indians and do not speak the official language of the country.

If the executive branch of the central governments in Latin America possess all-encompassing powers, it is partly because the other two branches have never had any important authority. Like the United States, Latin countries have legislative bodies and a judicial system. But the legislatures are largely debating societies with little power, and the courts, while usually fair in handling disputes between two citizens, would

never dare countermand the executive. Thus there is no system of checks and balances among government branches.

Very often Latin leaders begin their careers with the best intentions. They seek to be freely elected or, if they gain power by virtue of a coup (the French phrase *coup d'état*, which translates literally as "blow of state," is converted in Spanish to *golpe de estado;* it means a sudden, and often bloodless, takeover of all positions of authority by revolutionary elements) they will frequently set out to improve life in their countries. But so much corruption, inefficiency, nepotism and red tape choke the machinery of government that finally the president becomes frustrated by normal channels and turns into a dictator.

Dictators and Decrees

He is anxious to live up to the hopes the people have in him and so takes total control of the government to expedite matters. Men are usually not willing to give up any of their power so, once the dictator is entrenched, he remains a dictator until he is brought down by a revolution.

Even when a Latin president isn't a dictator he can, during much of each year, function like one. Latin legislatures are in recess for more than half the year and during this time the president can proclaim the *decreto*, or decree-law. This means that what the president says goes, and the supreme court that declared any such measure unconstitutional would find itself out of business.

Whenever the president wants to he can declare an *estado de sitio*, or state of siege. This amounts to a declaration of martial law which suspends the constitutional rights of the people. Peru's President Belaúnde declared a state of martial law recently when he feared that Communist agitators might foment a revolution in the wake of the Lima soccer riots that killed almost 300 persons.

Revolutions have occurred hundreds of times in Latin America, so often they are regarded as jokes by North Americans. Cartoonists for years have had a field day with the moustached Latin politician before the firing squad. The reason for so many violent uprisings is simple: In most countries in Latin America there has been no satisfactory means for the orderly transfer of power. Revolution is often the only way to get the party in power out.

But these uprisings (there have been 179 in Bolivia alone) rarely change anything except the people at the top of the power structure. The author of this Newsbook recalls many, many years ago the words of a Latin American student at a New Jersey boarding school. The Latin boy was immensely rich and the other boys marveled at his possessions, which included a full-size roller-coaster in his backyard and his own 26-foot cabin cruiser. The boy was 13 years old. A friend asked him if he were worried about reports of political trouble in his country. "No, I am not worried," he said. "My family is friendly with the people on both sides. If the side that is in power wins everything will stay the same. If the other side wins, everything will still stay the same."

A Tip for a Bureaucrat

In almost all Latin countries, graft is looked upon not as a crime but simply as the way to do business. In Mexico it is called the *mordida* (bite), in Argentina it is known as *coima,* and in Cuba it is called *chivo* (goat). It has become the way to do business mainly because government employes are paid extremely low salaries.

A Chilean newspaperman explained it this way: "Graft in this part of the world compares with the tips given to waiters and taxi drivers. They do not get paid enough to live on and everyone knows this. So everyone goes along with the system and gives them bribes. Is it any more sensible or honest to tip a waiter who is employed by someone else than to tip or bribe a lowly government official?"

An important obstacle to popular government in many, but by no means all, Latin countries has been the military. There has long been the inclination south of the border to possess armies and navies bigger and costlier than the countries need. Venezuela and Argentina are good examples. In those two countries the military has frequently controlled the government, or at least exercised a veto power over it.

To a North American it is puzzling to see a parade of tanks and cannons roll through the streets of Buenos Aires while jet fighters scream overhead. The chances of another country invading Argentina seem small. But the people of Argentina like parades and displays of mil-

itary power, even if they know in their hearts that the friendly Uruguayans have always minded their own business and that the Chileans are unlikely to come pouring over the Andes.

The Chilean army, for its part, has been notably apolitical, while the Brazilian army has generally acted as a watchdog, moving in only when a dictator has threatened the well-being of the country. Costa Rica doesn't even have a standing army, and Uruguay's army minds its own business much as Chile's does.

Because of the existence of the Organization of American States, under which the United States is committed to come to the aid of any member who is attacked, there is less need than ever for a Latin nation to have an army bigger than is necessary to preserve internal order. But colorful military uniforms are fun to strut about in, and parades wouldn't amount to much without braided hats and ceremonial swords. Tanks and war planes are also a tonic to a furiously flag-proud people.

Until the last decade or so, the Roman Catholic Church has, in many areas of Latin America, served as an obstacle to social progress. Ever since the first missionaries came across the Atlantic from Spain and Portugal, the Church has been identified with the Latin aristocracy; more importantly, the Church has identified itself with the aristocracy. Over the years the Church acquired huge land holdings, and it gave little thought to the social improvement of the people.

The Church As Reformer

Most of that is changed today. Where once a young, progressive priest who didn't keep his ideas to himself would be assigned to a remote village in the mountains, today the lead for social reform is being taken by the bishops. The Church, for instance, is behind many of the progressive—indeed, radical—measures that are going into effect in Chile, Peru, and elsewhere. Too, the Jesuits and the Maryknoll Fathers have long struggled to raise the standard of living of the *campesino* and the urban worker. But the effort of the main body of the Church to bring about social reforms is of rather recent origin.

The Church in Latin America is very much different from the Church in the United States. In Latin America, almost every village has its

A little oil here and there.

patron saint, and so does every large estate and most guilds and clubs. The biggest day in a child's life is not his birthday or even Christmas; it is the feast day of the saint after whom he is named. That day begins with Mass, followed by a great family gathering and parties and music and presents. At every important occasion, religious or otherwise, the help of patron saints is invoked and a member of the clergy is always in attendance. In Latin America the Church gives a special meaning to life, and it does it in a ubiquitous way that is unknown in the United States.

While the Church has helped to perpetuate an archaic social structure south of the border,

it has also been an insuperable obstacle to dictators who have sought to crush it. The biggest mistake Juan Perón made in Argentina was to declare war on the Church. In Brazil, at the time when demagog João Goulart was preparing to tear up the constitution and pave the way for a Communist takeover, the Church sponsored a huge demonstration by Catholic women in São Paulo protesting the scheme. The demonstration convinced the army it was time to depose Goulart; it also convinced the army that the people would be behind such a move.

The biggest failure of the Church in Latin America—and these are thoughts gleaned from talks with many of the clergy there along with material that has been appearing in recent years in Catholic intellectual publications in the U.S. —is that while it has always sought vigorously to save the souls of its charges, it has neglected to urge them to save their lives. This applies to the rich as well as the poor.

The Church regularly goes to the Latin rich to ask for alms because, obviously, the Church needs money to do its work. At the same time, it has urged the rich to give to the poor. Thus, it has stimulated the virtue of charity. But as a general rule the Church has not prodded its members to use their natural gifts to better advantage; it has not tried to convince the people of Latin America that there are temporal and spiritual benefits to be gained from hard work.

Because the Church is so extraordinarily influential among the Latin masses, its opportunities to change the unproductive attitudes of many Latin Americans have been very great. The Church as a whole has not taken advantage of these opportunities.

Young at Heart

After many generations of supporting the status quo, the Church is now changing rapidly as far as its political outlook is concerned. Some young priests, in fact, anxious to eliminate poverty, have come to support movements for social change so radical that they would substitute state socialism for what's generally believed to be the more prudent goal of popular capitalism. And some Catholic orders are busily establishing credit unions and farm cooperatives in the hope of improving the lives of the poor. All this concern for the temporal problems of the poor indicates that the Church, old and venerable as it is, still has a young heart and is ready to meet the future head on.

But there remains the danger that the Church, in its zest for modernizing its political and social outlook, will miss a vital target. In the July 1964 issue of *The Review of Politics*, a publication of the University of Notre Dame, Frederick B. Pike, associate professor of history at Notre Dame and an expert on Latin America, makes some perceptive points about the Church in Peru.

He writes: "Without doubt the economic problem of Peru is in part a moral problem, involving not just the hard-heartedness of the wealthy, but the laziness, irresponsibility, and lack of natural vigor of the lower classes."

Mr. Pike goes on to charge that "idealistic reformers who are most delighted by the more conspicuous aspect of the Church's new-found interest in social justice . . . concentrate their attention exclusively on . . . those who in attempting to modernize the Church stress only immediate lower class betterment, who fail to envision any difficult transition period, and who devote precious little attention to inspiring natural virtue and devotion to work among the lower classes."

Further on in his article Mr. Pike declares: "By preaching the solution to problems through adoption of new economic systems the clergy and the Catholic laity are causing the Church to shirk its primary responsibility, which is the internal reform of man."

The points that Mr. Pike makes are the same ones that are being discussed by leading churchmen in Latin America. They are basic to any discussion of the area's ills because the political instability of Latin America is traceable to the same characteristics of the people that keep them poor.

Whither Thou Goest

The question the Catholic Church is pondering in Latin America today is not whether it will or will not change. The question is what form that change will take and how the Church can best use its influence to help foster political democracy and economic freedom.

The Venezuelan official who slapped the girl into the swimming pool simply because she presented an inviting target believes his attitude is justified by his own peculiar notion of "spirituality" and the free flight of the soul. His disposition, however, to obey that impulse is harmful not just because it violates "Yankee common sense", but because it eschews the discipline that's basic to an orderly life. And no matter what any Latin poet may say or think, the human personality cannot blossom without political order, a respect for law, a respect for the rights and ideas of one's fellows.

An integral part of this orderly society is an energetic economy, and the problems in this area stem from the same curious behavior that has made Latin American politics so furious and so futile.

Magnum Photos

Don José Alfredo Martinez de Roz is representative of Latin America's few —and very few. He is a breeder of fine horses and a connoisseur of the good life. His house is just south of Mar del Plata, Argentina. You can't miss it.

Latin Economies

The Several Republics Advance

Against Inefficiency, Corruption, Myopia—

And It's Enough to Break an Iberian Heart

THE LIBRARY in Victor Andrade's home in La Paz, Bolivia, is simply but comfortably furnished. The books on the shelves look well-used, and it's clear at a glance that the former Bolivian ambassador to the United States has a taste for history. Near his desk stand the red and black spines of Churchill's six-volume *History of the Second World War,* along with many works on Spanish conquest in the New World. On the desk itself is an antique silver ash tray with two silver llamas mounted on its rim.

Andrade relaxes in a chair pulled around to the front of his desk. He is a handsome man whose coffee complexion and high cheekbones suggest a strain of Indian blood. He is wearing a blue and white sport shirt, open at the collar, and a brown, tweed sport jacket and brown slacks. He has already discussed Bolivian politics at length and now, as if suddenly stirred by the contrast between current events and life before the 1952 revolution, he lights a cigaret, blows smoke at the ceiling, and in measured tones begins to recall how it used to be.

"A few hundred miles from La Paz," he declares, "I own a farm in a valley that an Englishman once told me is the most beautiful place in the world. It is in the *yungas,* the subtropical region of Bolivia that separates the high mountains in the west from the hot lowlands in the east. We have hundreds of fruit trees and flowers in great number, and rising above the fruit and the flowers are the mountains that are topped with snow.

The farm has been in my family for maybe 200 years.

"Years ago, before the revolution in 1952, I visited the farm whenever my official duties would permit. When I arrived, the people who work there would be very happy.

"The men, women and children would come running to greet me. They would bow and call me 'lord' or 'master'. And they would bring me little gifts of fruit or things they had made themselves. Today, since the revolution, all that is changed. The same people who used to bow down before me now greet me with a handshake. They are clean and neatly dressed and they take great pride in their children's schooling and their own improved status. My farm is a different place now and, in that way at least, it is a better one."

One Real Revolution

Andrade's "farm" is in fact what remains of a *hacienda*. It is no longer the feudal kingdom-unto-itself that it was years ago; much of the land has been acquired by the government for redistribution among the *campesinos* or peasants. But Bolivia is the only country in South America where the *hacienda* has become a thing of the past. Bolivia, in fact, is the only country on the continent that has had a real social revolution. Other countries, such as Venezuela, Peru and Chile, are trying to reduce great land holdings through agrarian reform laws. But progress has been slow. In many areas of Latin America, the *hacienda* remains the keystone of society and an important reason why economic progress has come to the region so slowly.

True, the stagnation resulting from the *hacienda* system is not the whole story. Latin America has been impeded in places by an unfriendly climate, by wall after wall of towering mountains, by slavish dependence upon a single commodity, by amoral government officials at every level, by extreme economic and monetary policies that almost always boomerang, and by determinedly unproductive attitudes toward work and investment.

The old Latin American complaint that Yankee businessmen have unjustly exploited their countries, while erroneous in many instances, nevertheless is not entirely without basis. But even where such exploitation has not served the interests of the Latin nation involved, there is another side to the coin. Natural resources rarely have economic value if they never leave their natural state. Nor would Yankee exploitation have been possible in many cases if Latin American businessmen had had the faith and guts to gamble on the development of their own countries. Most of them preferred to run their big farms with antiquated methods, under-pay their employes and stash the profits in foreign banks.

These big farms, or *haciendas,* have historically been almost entirely self-sufficient; they produce everything that is wanted by the owners except for the luxuries that must be imported from abroad. Clothes are made on the plantation from fibers grown there. Food in variety is produced by the sharecroppers who usually work three days for the *hacienda* owner in return for the use of a parcel of land. These peons are almost always in debt to their feudal lords and they are not permitted to leave the *hacienda* until they have repaid all they owe.

Separate Countries

To such illiterate serfs, who generally were born on the land they work, there is little understanding of nationality. When Bolivia announced it was distributing land to its *campesinos,* hundreds of Indians from Peru applied for it—not realizing that Bolivia and Peru are separate countries.

The *hacienda* is not really a business by North American standards. It does not represent the owner's investment; he inherited it— land, animals and peons. If the place is sold, the peons in effect are sold with it. Because labor is so cheap and plentiful, the owner is not inclined to mechanize or modernize to increase the efficiency of his operation. Thus, the land gives but a little while teeming millions live on the brink of starvation.

Haciendas come in all sizes, from those of only a few hundred acres with one or two sharecropping families to estates spreading over a million acres and employing hundreds of peons. The larger *haciendas* amount to sovereign states, with their own laws and customs. A barter system prevails within them and almost no cash is ever exchanged. By their nature they propagate paupers, and by their existence they condemn their nations to economic servitude.

The burden of the *hacienda*.

It is because of the *hacienda* system that almost every country in Latin America is working toward agrarian reform, toward a more equitable and more efficient distribution of land. But it is not just a matter of breaking up vast estates. Some crops (such as sugar cane), for instance, can only be grown economically on large tracts. For this reason, Peru has exempted sugar and cotton lands from the provisions of its new agrarian reform law.

In Uruguay the great cattle ranches are getting bigger and bigger. When a ranch operator turns a profit, he tends to buy additional grazing land rather than improve the land and facilities he has. Increasing inefficiency is the result.

Land reform can also become a racket, as there is evidence it has in some areas of Venezuela. The Venezuelan government has bought thousands of acres from owners of *haciendas* for redistribution among the landless. But often times the government pays an exorbitant price

1963

RATES
OF
POPULATION
GROWTH

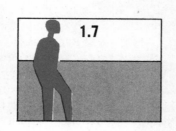

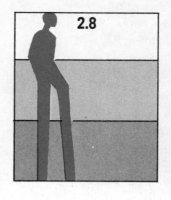

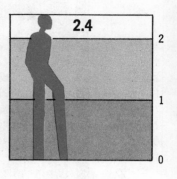

U.S.   LATIN AMERICA   INDIA

DENSITY
OF
POPULATION,
PERSONS PER
SQUARE MILE

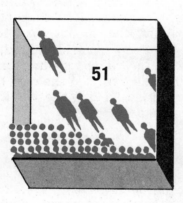

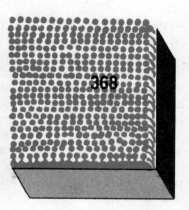

for poor land that its new owner has trouble working, that costs the government heavily, and that leaves the selling land baron with a fat profit.

Agriculture in Latin America cannot be stimulated without modern machinery and scientific land use. But to an illiterate *campesino,* a tractor can be a puzzling and often fearsome contraption. And as for scientific farming, Indians on the Bolivian Altiplano believe fastening white cloths to their oxen to chase away evil spirits is more useful than spreading manure.

The combination of centuries-old farming methods and the stagnating effects of the *hacienda* makes it profoundly difficult to get Latin America to the point where it can supply its own food needs. And although progress is being made in this direction thanks to legislation and foreign assistance, Latin America's explosive population growth (2.9 per cent annually) and the rising hopes of the masses breed frustrations that could lead to ever more serious political and economic breakdown.

Complicating the region's economic problems is the reliance of most nations on just one or two exports. It is from these exports that the countries earn money to buy the many imports they need, including in many cases, food. When the world price for one of these major export commodities falls sharply, the whole country suffers severely.

Latin Americans, therefore, view with some urgency their plans for diversifying their economies. But it is difficult for an underdeveloped agricultural country to build a well-rounded economy, partly because the domestic market is usually not big enough or vital enough to support, for instance, a steel industry or a machine tool plant. For this reason 10 Latin American republics have formed an organization that hopefully will evolve into a "common market," after the successful European model. By joining together, the 10 nations hope to achieve a level of economic activity none could hope to achieve by itself.

The Latin American Free Trade Association (LAFTA) is based on a philosophy exactly the opposite of the one that motivated the feudal *hacienda*. The *hacienda* is a stagnant, self-sufficient, inward-looking unit. LAFTA, with its emphasis on freer trade, is dynamic in concept because it is designed to provide more goods for more people. LAFTA subscribes to the notion of economic inter-dependence and is therefore outward-looking.

The problems facing LAFTA are greater than those that faced Western Europe at the birth of the European Economic Community. Although both groups had to overcome deep-rooted political suspicions among member nations, the European Common Market was from the outset composed of countries with advanced systems of public education and wide experience in industrial production.

Latin America, in contrast, is a largely agricultural area in which most people can neither read nor write, and in which social and economic progress must be preceded by the most basic reforms. It has only been in recent years that broad-scale programs have been adopted to break Latin America's circle of poverty.

Illiterate people, for instance, cannot prosper because they can qualify for only the most menial manual work. The average *campesino* is fortunate if he can scratch enough food from the soil to feed himself and his family; he is almost never able to produce the marketable surplus that would mean greater security for him and a more ample larder for his hungry country.

Similarly, the urban worker who can offer only the strength in his back is worth but a pittance in an area where manual laborers are abundant. Such a worker's productive capacity is small.

A Dollar a Day

A reporter recently spent a night and a day with a Chilean family whose head was both a *campesino* and an *obrero,* or worker. The Valdez clan lives in the hills a few miles from the old port city of Valparaiso. The family owns a cow and some ducks and geese, and grows vegetables on a small parcel of land. The father, Pablo, occasionally rides a bus to Valparaiso in the hope of finding part-time work around the docks or in the warehouses. If he earns a dollar for loading 100-pound sacks on a truck he feels he has had a good day. On returning home he works in his vegetable patch, perhaps cultivat-

ing the dry soil with a primitive tool or prying out unwanted rocks with his bare hands.

Mrs. Valdez makes most of her family's clothes in a corner of the crude, one-room shack that is their home. In July and August, the Chilean winter, the temperature falls to near freezing and sometimes it is too cold to sleep, even when the family, which includes three young children, huddles close under one great wool blanket.

Wine, which is made nearby by a neighbor and which is bartered for whatever vegetables the family can spare, is one of the very few pleasures Valdez can afford. Chilean wine is good and cheap, and Valdez drinks it out of a cloudy glass jug that probably has not been washed since it first was filled.

"I am not a drunkard," says Valdez, "but I like my wine very much. Aside from my wife and children, it is the only thing that can make me smile. That is the way it is when a man has no money."

Breaking the Circle

The chances are good that Pablo Valdez will never have much more of the world's goods than he has right now. But his children will probably have more. Chile, like most other Latin American countries, is taking steps to break the circle of poverty. There is no beginning to a circle and there is no single right place to combat the country's economic problems. But education, land reform, economic diversification, tax reform, and trade expansion represent the major avenues of attack.

If Walter, Valdez' 10-year-old son, can be taught to read and write, and then taught a trade, he will be ready to answer the call for skilled labor that is likely to follow the growth of LAFTA. The Latin American Free Trade Association, by dropping the tariff barriers among member nations, will increase the demand for finished products. To produce its share of what is wanted, Chile will build new factories and install machines to do the work men alone cannot do, or cannot do so well.

Chile will then look to young men like Walter Valdez to run the machines. If by that time he is literate and has taken vocational training, he will become a candidate for the kind of orderly middle-class society that nurtures political stability and economic progress.

But before Walter Valdez and millions like him in Latin America can make the most of their abilities, there must first be a need for those abilities. The economic diversification promised by LAFTA is one important means of providing diverse job opportunities.

Without LAFTA, the outlook for Latin America would be bleak. The area's population is now well over 200,000,000. By 1975 that figure will be increased by another 100,000,000, which means the region must provide at least 38,000,000 new jobs, of which agriculture can supply only 5,000,000. In view of this, it's little wonder the idea of a Latin American Common Market was enthusiastically received in many quarters. When and if LAFTA matures, it will unite more than 170,000,000 consumers with a gross national product of $60 billion and an import capacity of $5.7 billion.

Because the need for millions of new jobs was clear, and because Latin American export revenues in the 1950s were declining at a time when the cost of the area's imports was rising, nine countries decided to begin working toward free trade among them. The original participating countries were Argentina, Brazil, Chile, Colombia, Ecuador, Mexico, Paraguay, Peru and Uruguay. Venezuela joined the group later.

Borrowed Ideas

LAFTA borrowed ideas not only from the Western Europeans, but also from the economic integration movement in Central America, begun in the early 1950s by Guatemala, Honduras, El Salvador, Nicaragua and Costa Rica. The Central American movement is discussed further on in this Newsbook.

The basic idea of a common market, of course, is the eventual elimination of tariffs among member nations. In 1961 and 1962, LAFTA's first years of operation, tariff walls began to be lowered substantially—no small achievement among republics that have historically viewed each other with little trust or affection. Although the tariff reductions for 1963 were not as impressive as those made in 1961, many more manufactured products were added to the list.

LAFTA experts confidently predict that by 1972 the total exports among member nations will climb to 40 per cent of all Latin American exports. This would mean a diversion of about $1.8 billion worth of goods now coming from sources outside Latin America to sources inside LAFTA.

All this sounds fine and, as far as it goes, it is. But the 10 member countries are faced with problems beyond the basic ones of tariff reduction. They must, for instance, with little experience to guide them, set up continental sales networks, solve complicated credit problems, and combat the prejudice against Latin American goods that exists within Latin America. Bureaucratic red tape, which Latin Americans excel at sticking on to almost everything, is another source of trouble. Then, too, there is the difficult job of setting up adequate banking facilities to accommodate greatly enlarged trade within Latin America. Notoriously unstable currencies in many of the member nations present special problems, as does the lack of efficient inland transportation systems.

Climbing Trade

But even with these formidable obstacles, LAFTA's record so far indicates it is on the right track. Trade among members climbed 44.3 per cent between 1961 and 1963, the first three years of operation under the Treaty of Montevideo, which established the organization. Intra-LAFTA trade reached $526 million in 1963, up from $360 million in 1961.

LAFTA is a dramatic attempt at self-help, and self-help is a concept that formerly engendered little enthusiasm in Latin American countries. The organization, beyond what it is actually accomplishing, seems to be representative of a new sense of responsibility among area political and business leaders. Wealthy Latin Americans still seek safety by putting their money in Swiss banks, the New York stock market and Florida real estate—instead of investing it in their own countries. But the old fears about putting money to work locally appear to be abating; Latin America is beginning to accumulate capital.

The area's gross national products, for example, totaled about $74 billion for 1963. Capital investment by Latin Americans in Latin America that same year amounted to about $8.2 billion. This represents a capital formation rate of about 11 per cent, which is remarkably high for an area so underdeveloped.

A fish meal plant in Peru: By 1975, Latin America must provide at least 38,000,000 new jobs.

Such indications of self help are far more encouraging for Latin Americans than any amount of foreign aid, because the area's hopes can only be realized when its resources—people, materials and money—are put to work at home. Only then can a viable economy for the area be attained. But the willingness of growing numbers of private investors to put their money to work locally must be augmented by an equal willingness to pay their taxes.

No one in any land likes paying taxes, and in Latin America the people are no different, except that they seem to like it even less. Area governments are only beginning to learn, with the help of Yankee advisers, how to establish a reasonably just system of taxation.

It is necessary, first of all, to persuade the people that the tax laws will be fairly administered. This will take some persuading because countries south of the border are infested with corrupt tax collectors. Bribery has become so much a way of life in some countries that often a taxpayer must fork over almost as much in bribes as he would if he paid his taxes honestly.

Says one Brazilian official: "I think various studies have shown that if our tax laws were obeyed and all tax collectors honest, Brazilian taxpayers would actually have to pay less than they have been paying under the dishonest system."

The "dishonest system" has enabled a few Latin Americans to accumulate huge fortunes. Nobody in the region, for instance, has his income taxed at a rate higher than 37 per cent, and most wealthy people pay a good deal less than that, if they pay anything. In most Latin American countries, tax collections equal less than 15 per cent of the gross national product. The burden on the American taxpayer, whose funds are used to aid Latin America, is much greater. In the U.S., some 28 cents of every dollar earned is taken away in taxes of one kind or another.

One stumbling block on the road to tax reformation is that many national legislatures are made up of short-sighted men of wealth who have little taste for a change in the status quo. A rigorous enforcement of realistic tax laws would certainly hit them in the pocketbook, and hit them hard. Too, there is the basic inability of many Latin American governments to set up the administrative mechanism an

LATIN AMERICAN TRADE WITH THE U.S. 1963

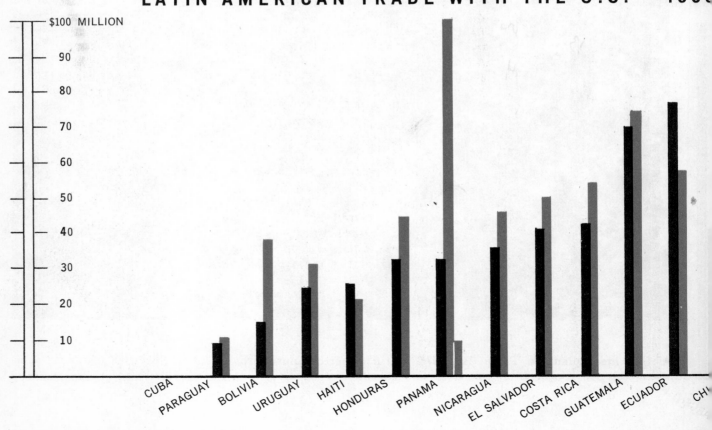

orderly system of taxation requires. A revamping of the tax laws, therefore, has been slow in coming.

Insufficient tax revenue, however, is only one of several causes of Latin America's most ruinous economic problem—the problem of inflation. Inflation in the United States has been a persistent trouble-maker since the Depression, reducing by more than half the value of the savings of the American people, and hurting particularly those who must live on fixed incomes. But inflation in the U.S. has not been chaotic. In many Latin American nations inflation has been extremely chaotic for generations (between 1850 and 1950, prices in Argentina, Bolivia, Brazil and Chile increased 2,000 per cent), and it's only been in the last two or three years that most area governments have realized that inflation is the cruelest enemy of economic growth.

In an inflationary situation interest rates soar. Money paid back on loans is worth much less in terms of purchasing power, so money that ordinarily might go into business loans is rerouted instead into such things as land speculation. People stop saving because money is

no longer a safe form in which to put one's assets. Domestic currency flees abroad, so that it may be repatriated later at a far higher value in domestic currency.

Most of all, the economy is severely braked by a feeling of uncertainty. People with money to invest tend to convert their funds into land or durable consumer goods and sit tight. Business activity slows, unemployment rises sharply, and the nation is threatened with economic collapse.

What have been the causes of inflation in Latin America?

Along with inadequate taxation, the causes are a combination of such things as a reduction in the value of exports (from which countries get the money to buy the goods they need from abroad and to finance economic development at home), a refusal to employ central banking controls designed to restrict inflation, deficit government spending as well as deficits of government-operated enterprises, costly social security programs, politically inspired spending of all kinds, and a desire to eliminate debts.

Behind much of the trouble has been the popularity of Keynesian economics in the area.

■ Exports to the U.S.   ■ Imports from the U.S.

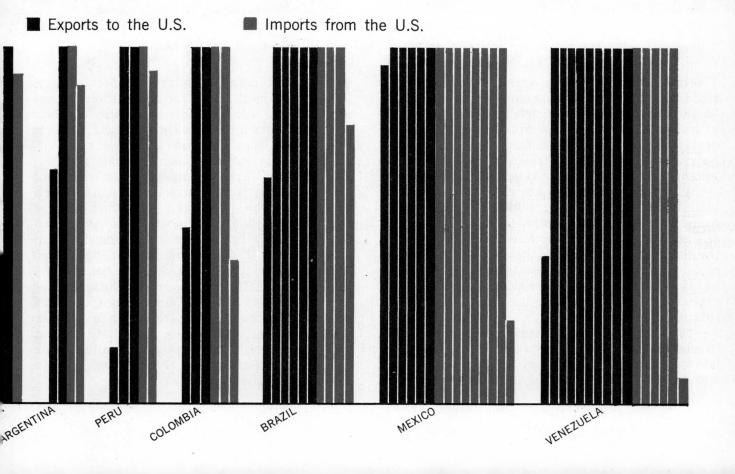

ARGENTINA   PERU   COLOMBIA   BRAZIL   MEXICO   VENEZUELA

Paul Conklin

The cloths are whiter than white, but a little manure would be better.

The ideas of Lord Keynes, including such concepts as the multiplying-income effects of public works and the uses of deficit financing, are at least questionable when applied to a highly developed economy. When they are applied to poor, undeveloped countries, the Keynesian principles are extremely dangerous.

But for years Latin American economists have clung to Keynesian notions despite the havoc caused by those notions. It is a matter of historical fact that poor nations do not have the economic stamina to withstand heavy doses of deficit financing. The results are always unhappy, and the poorer the nation that tries to get away with inflation, the worse are its ravages.

Since 1960 area governments have begun to change their ideas about how best to stimulate their economies, and they are turning more and more to such proven methods as the common market concept and sound fiscal policy. But Latin American politicians, although they may seek to adopt prudent policies for their countries, have a difficult time persuading their constituents that prudence is necessary.

Economic orthodoxy—and especially austerity measures—are so unpopular in much of Latin America that efforts to implement such policies have brought down governments. That kind of discipline rubs most Latin Americans the wrong way, partly because it seems to them a dreary way to run a country and partly because they believe Uncle Sam is behind the whole thing. Attitudes toward the United States vary in the area but they don't vary much. It's probably safe to say that Latin Americans either dislike the United States or they hate it, and even the minority who are not vocally hostile toward Uncle Sam regard their big neighbor to the north with suspicion.

This feeling would be understandable even if the United States were completely guiltless, which it isn't. That Americans can be so rich while Latins are so poor is a continual source of resentment. Also resented are the substantial profits American companies have made by working the natural resources of Latin America. Nor does the existence of thousands of reminders of Yankee influence throughout the area—from huge electric signs hawking Yankee wares in every major city to the presence of Yankee factories and mining operations—do anything but increase the sense of being dominated from the north.

"Humiliating" Help

Indeed, foreign aid from the States is not the least irritant to many Latins. A veteran U.S. diplomat in Latin America tells the story of the Bolivian official who admitted that while his country needed outside assistance, he couldn't help but resent the shipments of food and clothing from the United States. He described foreign aid as "humiliating."

The diplomat replied: "You say it is 'humiliating' for you to have to accept such basic needs as food from the United States. What you would prefer, I suppose, is for the United States to magically increase the incomes of all Bolivians. But this responsibility belongs not to Washington, but to Bolivia."

Nevertheless, it would be inaccurate to suggest that Latin Americans do not appreciate help from the States. Generally, it is the intellectuals who suffer from hurt pride in this regard. The masses, the poor, desperate people who live wretched lives in rural and urban slums, are not only appreciative of American aid, they are often incredulous. The Communists tell them such aid is merely a form of Yankee imperialism, but that does not strike a man with a full belly as much of an argument. (For a detailed report on United States aid to Latin America, see the chapters on the Alliance for Progress.)

There is another—perhaps the most basic— economic problem in Latin America that in one way or another affects all the others. It is the one economic problem that Latin Americans like least to discuss and which often brings from them bitter denunciations of Yankee "materialism" and "snobbishness". Nevertheless,

the main reason Latin America has stagnated for generations is that the Iberian character is poorly suited to efficient, orderly management of resources.

It is not that the descendants of the Spanish and Portuguese colonists are an "inferior" race, although many North Americans have fallen into the trap of thinking so. The Iberian character is a complicated mixture of high energy and spirituality, of hot pride and *personalismo*. and history shows that these qualities in combination are not ideally suited to economic progress or, for that matter, the gaining and retention of political freedom. And this is as true of the motherlands of Portugal and Spain as it is of the Latin American nations.

Sex, Soccer, and the Samba

Brazil, a former Portuguese colony, accounts for half the population of South America, and the country's inhabitants represent almost every racial strain in the world. But Portuguese culture predominates, and it is this culture that even many Brazilians agree causes the people to have an inordinate interest in "sex, soccer and the samba."

Explained one well-educated Brazilian businessman recently: "The Latin love of fun and games is an inescapable part of Latin America's troubles. It is an impatience of the blood. Hard work has never had much social standing here. But leisure is loved and honored. Soccer is so popular in Brazil and other countries in South America because it gives the opportunity to release the spirit, to release the passions. Work for most people does not do this."

The Brazilian, who was dining by the swimming pool of a beachfront hotel in Rio de Janeiro, paused as a beautiful girl in a bikini strolled by. He gestured with a fork in the girl's direction and added: "Most Latin men like women for the same reasons they like soccer and dancing. In everything that is enjoyed in this part of the world there is an element of abandonment. Deep in their hearts, Latin Americans, including myself, want to escape order because order reminds us of the confinement of the spirit within the body. We look for the chance to let the spirit soar. Such a temperament is not the best one for working on an assembly line. But I suspect it can be ennobling nonetheless."

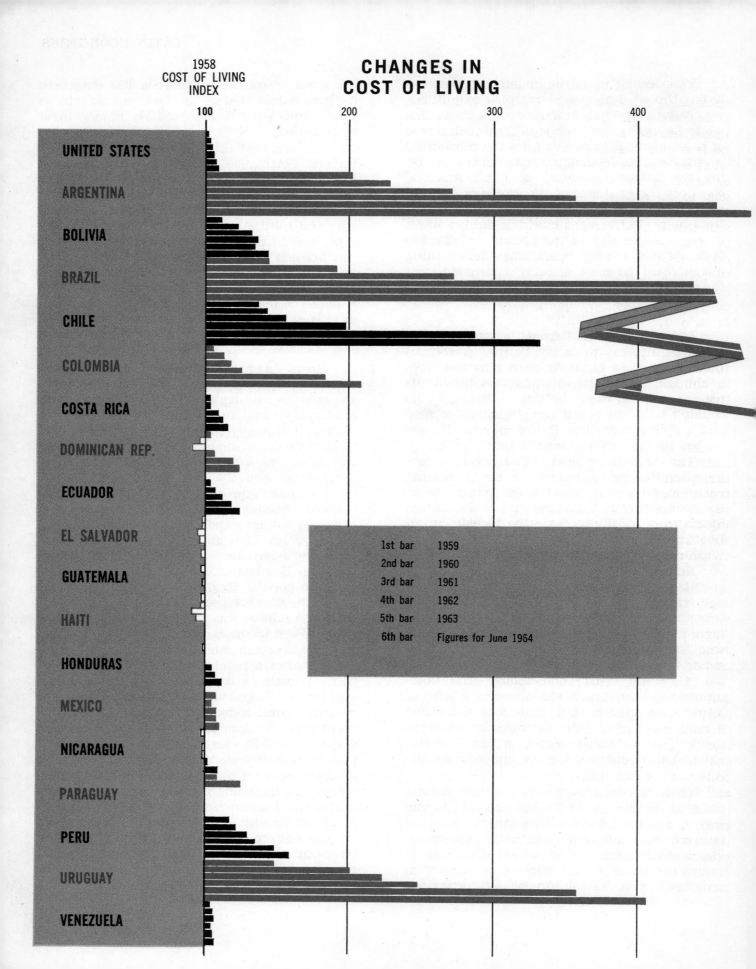

1958
COST OF LIVING
INDEX

CHANGES IN
COST OF LIVING

100   200   300   400

UNITED STATES

ARGENTINA

BOLIVIA

BRAZIL

CHILE

COLOMBIA

COSTA RICA

DOMINICAN REP.

ECUADOR

EL SALVADOR

GUATEMALA

HAITI

HONDURAS

MEXICO

NICARAGUA

PARAGUAY

PERU

URUGUAY

VENEZUELA

1st bar	1959
2nd bar	1960
3rd bar	1961
4th bar	1962
5th bar	1963
6th bar	Figures for June 1964

Woven into this Latin American version of spirituality is Latin pride, which is unlike the pride most other people feel within them. In Latin America a man is proud first of all that he is a man. He is proud not so much about what he *does* as what he *is,* and this *"is"* refers as much to the fact of his being a man as it does to his station in life. He sees himself and those around him in acutely personal terms, and this is one reason Latin American politics is often so unrestrained: Political debate becomes a matter of personal honor and friendly disagreement is made almost impossible.

Pride of such an intense kind can, ironically, drain a country of its economic vitality. It is a quality which, in some ways, hardly seems like pride at all because it excludes the most useful pride—pride in a job well done. If there is no pride in work, or workmanship, it is difficult to raise a country's standard of living.

"Shame Pay"

An isolated case points up how far Latin Americans can carry their notions about what is respectable and what isn't. In Rio de Janeiro, truck helpers on the piers get 25 per cent more pay for loading or unloading bathroom plumbing fixtures. This is known as "shame pay." Helping to transport plumbing fixtures is, in the mind of the Brazilian working man, somehow shameful.

In the Dominican Republic there has long been a popular feeling that harvesting sugar cane is beneath the dignity of a human being. Cane cutters, therefore, have been imported from Haiti to do the job. Haitians are Negroes and don't share the Dominicans' peculiar notion.

This notion of pride is a feature of the Latin character, but Latin America isn't all Latin. Along with a variety of other races, Indians account for a large part of the population, especially in the Andean countries. In Peru, for instance, 45 per cent of the people are descendants of the great Inca empire, and in neighboring Bolivia the population is 70 per cent Indian.

If the Latin is, by Yankee standards, too spirited, the Indian is too dispirited. The South American Indian is among the most melancholy creatures on earth. He goes through life in a trance-like state, partly because he chews a narcotic leaf to help him forget how awful

things are and partly because he still can't forget how awful things are.

Helping the Indians to cross the time gap between their present existence and modern society isn't easy, but Peace Corpsmen and others claim it can be done.

"Behind that blank expression—far behind it—is a human intellect," says a Peace Corpsman in a small Bolivian village. "We've had our best success with the children who are anxious to learn. The Indians can be taught and they sometimes surprise themselves at their own intelligence. The Indians have thought of themselves as being pretty pathetic for a long time—since the Spanish conquest—and they like the idea of learning and bettering themselves in the simplest ways. We are trying here to awaken dormant minds."

A Long, Discouraging List

Feudal farm systems, poor transportation, distrust of local investment, self-defeating tariff walls and internal fiscal and monetary regulations, ruinous inflation, dishonest government, inadequate tax laws and enforcement, reckless public spending, popular disparagement of hard work, misplaced pride combined with a sulking defeatism—these are the important obstacles to Latin America's economic progress.

It is a discouraging list, but there are at least two saving factors. Latin America is changing. More and more educated Latin Americans are beginning to understand both the scope of their difficulties and the causes of them. These emerging leaders are no longer satisfied to entertain some vague spirituality while damning Yankee materialism. They are becoming less and less convinced that economic efficiency diminishes the human spirit; indeed, they are finding out that the truth is quite the opposite.

The other saving factor is so far only a possibility, but it is an enchanting one. It is conceivable that the singular Latin spirit, when harnessed by economic orderliness, could generate the kind of production that will bring prosperity—and, far less importantly, an admiring nod from sober-sided Yankees.

There comes a point, of course, beyond which generalizations will not do. Each Latin American country has its peculiarities and special problems, and these are discussed in the following pages.

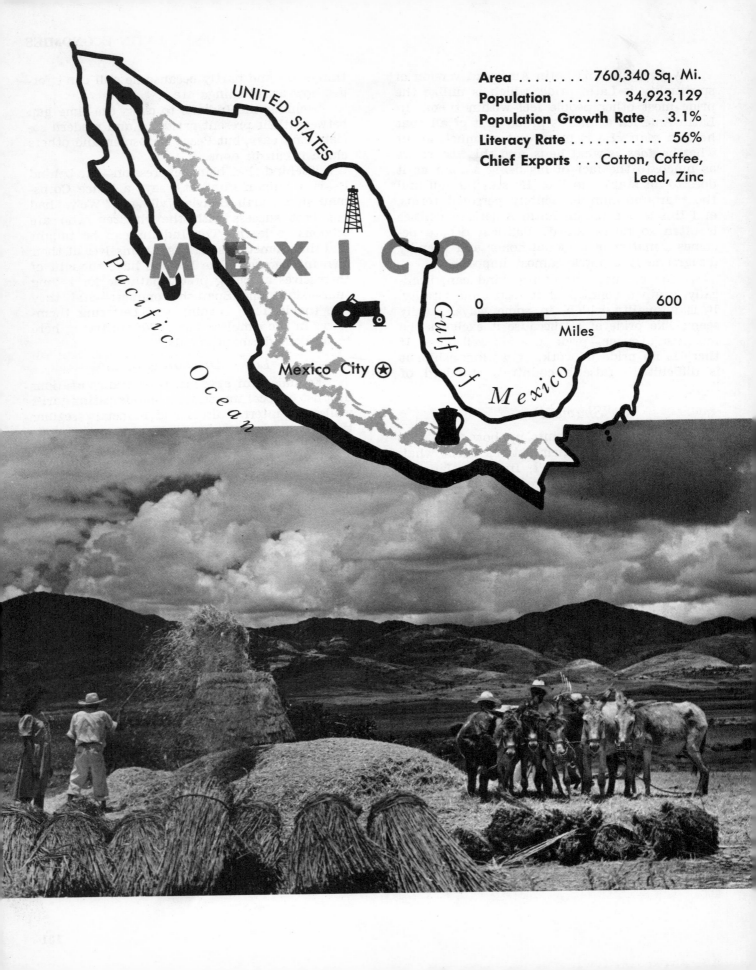

UNITED STATES

Area . . . . 760,340 Sq. Mi.
Population 34,923,129
Population Growth Rate . . 3.1%
Literacy Rate 56%
Chief Exports . . . Cotton, Coffee,
Lead, Zinc

MEXICO

Pacific Ocean

Gulf of Mexico

Mexico City ⊛

0   600
Miles

MEXICO

La Laguna and the Disenchanted

SANTA CLARA DEL COBRE, a tiny copper-producing and wheat-growing village 200 miles west of Mexico City, possesses the colorful grimness of all dirt-poor little Mexican towns. Some 2,000 people live there in mud adobe huts without water, sanitary facilities or the prospect of a better life.

In the village square are long-braided Tarascan Indian women who carry their babies papoose-style, serape-clad men with dirt-lined faces and wide-brimmed hats, and dark-eyed children without shoes. They applaud their governor who is making his annual trip to Santa Clara for the opening of the copper exposition. The governor praises their handiwork and the villagers forget for a moment that only the tourists can afford to buy what they make. The villagers barely have enough to keep themselves alive.

The people of Santa Clara are poor Mexico. Rich Mexico is somewhere else.

In Mexico City there are millionaires. There's Bruno Pagliai, an Italian immigrant married to actress Merle Oberon, who commands a $100-million steel and aluminum empire from the five phones in his spacious office. Sixty-year-old Carlos Trouyet, product of a Mexico City slum, rules Mexico's telephone company and almost two dozen other major enterprises. The two men personify the industrial revolution on which Mexico has pinned its hopes for prosperity.

But there is only one Mexico City, and there are 145,000 peasant towns and villages like Santa Clara del Cobre, and the contrast is a natural rallying point for disenchantment.

Mexico's newly-elected President, Gustavo

Diaz Ordaz, 52, who succeeds personable Adolfo Lopez Mateos, is acutely aware of the disparity. Says Diaz Ordaz: "Prosperity can not be healthy for one part of Mexico if it rests upon the poverty of the other part." Diaz Ordaz, a hollow-cheeked intellectual of pragmatic bent who served as President Lopez Mateos' minister of government, considers the problem of his country's 18,000,000 peasants, or *campesinos*, "the gravest on Mexico's political, social, and economic horizons."

It is indeed. For while the Mexican economy is experiencing an unprecedented boom, the lot of the *campesino*, in relation to that of the industrial laborer, is deteriorating. Exports have climbed 25 per cent since 1957; steel-producing capacity is four times the 1950 level; the rise in the gross national product topped six per cent last year, and Mexican economists talk proudly of a new middle class comprising one-third the population of 38,000,000, a growing market for the developing consumer-goods industry. Thirty-five years of government by the ruling Party of Revolutionary Institutions (PRI) has given Mexico political stability rare in Latin America, and U.S. firms have responded with $1 billion in investments over the past three years.

But while periodic increases in the minimum wage and a new profit-sharing law fatten paychecks for factory workers, millions of *campesinos* scrape their soil for enough produce to maintain their families at a bare subsistence level. Most peasants earn no more than $115 a year, one-third the national average. Twenty-four per cent do not customarily drink milk or eat meat, eggs, or fish. One-third of school-age children are not in school.

In the huge baroque-style office he occupies on Avenue Tacuba in Mexico City, Secretary of Agriculture Julian Rodríguez Adame rejects the suggestion that the *campesino* is the forgotten man of the Mexican revolution of 1910. He mentions the billions of dollars that have been spent since the 1920s on irrigation projects, road-building, electrification, and communications in the interior. He adds: "We pioneered in land reform before anyone else, and we're still at it. Our efforts have made us the model for other countries seeking to distribute land."

Mexico is the model of agrarian reform throughout the hemisphere, where the cry of the impoverished, like the cry of the Mexican revolutionaries of 1910, is for *Tierra y Libertad* — Land and Liberty. That revolution, and the bloody civil war that followed it, destroyed the old system of landed estates or *haciendas* that had reduced the peasants to peonage. Mexico has met the demand for land by distributing 130,000,000 acres to the *campesinos* since the 1930s. President Lopez Mateos is responsible for giving out 30,000,000 acres during his six-year term.

President Gustavo Diaz Ordaz.

But the distribution of land, while meeting the peasants' demands, has not fulfilled his needs. Now, after being told for 40 years that land was the answer to his problems, the Mexican *campesino* is being told that it is not. And he is being told by no less an authority than his new president, Diaz Ordaz. His stand is not calculated to win favor with the peasants.

An Exploding Population

One of the reasons for Diaz Ordaz' position is that Mexico is fast running out of good land to distribute. "More than three-quarters of the cultivable land is already in the hands of the peasants," he recently told a sullen crowd of *campesinos* in Cuernavaca, the capital of the state of Morelos. "There is hardly any allotable land remaining, and the number continues to grow of those who do not have land and are clamoring for it." In fact, there are close to 3,000,000 landless peasants in Mexico today—more than there were in 1937, because of the staggering population increase of 3.5 per cent a year.

But there's another reason too that the future chief executive is downgrading the promise of land as the cure for the plight of the peasantry. Explains an agricultural expert here: "It's become abundantly clear in the last 30 years that simply giving land to people who never had it before has not made it more productive, unless they know what to do with it. Where progress has come, it's been the result of modern technology and irrigation, not giving title to land they've been squatting on all along."

Thus, Diaz Ordaz is insisting: "Land reform that is not thorough and productive is not land reform at all." His farm program would shift the emphasis from distribution to increased outlays for irrigation, technical assistance, rural schools, and long-term low-interest agricultural credit to help small farmers finance new machinery, or purchases of poultry or livestock.

His message may be sound economics, but it doesn't satisfy the age-old quest for land. And agitators are stirring up the peasants to keep the land issue alive. They're aided by latent resentment of the graft and corruption that plague the government's farm bureaucracy.

In the rich valley around Ciudad Obregón, Mexico's bread basket, thousands of landless *campesinos* are demanding the breakup of large,

For the campesino, bad times.

productive estates, whose owners drive expensive cars and live in air-conditioned homes within view of their own mud huts. Federal troops routed 5,000 squatters who had invaded cattle ranches in depressed Durango state in 1963. Diaz Ordaz, as he was campaigning in Mexico's northern states, was besieged with angry complaints about violations of land reform laws. In Chihuahua City his presence touched off a riot.

Many of the sporadic disturbances are instigated by two left-wing organizations, the General Union of Workers and Farmers, whose leaders refer to each other as "Comrade," and the two-year-old *Campesino Central Independiente*, a group supported by fiery ex-President Lázaro Cárdenas and dedicated to whipping the landless peasantry into a potent political force.

The agitation is centered in the politically seething northern area of La Laguna, where efforts to irrigate too much land with limited resources have turned a once-flourishing cotton zone into a sterile dust bowl. The government's response to the plight of the *campesinos* there is instructive, for it offers one answer to the problems of rural poverty. The answer: Relocation.

Since early last year, 5,000 families, responding to government promises of rich, fertile land, have left La Laguna to colonize the deep, unexplored jungles of Mexico's southeast. If they are successful, the government plans to relocate 270,000 farmers in the states of Campeche and Yucatán, at a cost of $240,000,000. It is hoped that 30-year repayments from the profits of the new farms established there (each family will receive a 123-acre plot) will liquidate the government's investment. But the traditional distrust of the peasantry and the social dislocations such a move entails lead many to doubt that colonization can provide a long-range solution to the problems of the *campesino*.

So far the peasant uprisings have been localized incidents. How long they will remain so is an open question. Predicts one pessimistic observer: "Six years, eight years, maybe sooner. If nothing's done, with the population explosion, there'll be a real eruption unless things get better first."

But several factors militate against such an event. For one thing, the Mexican left wing is split into factions, all feuding among themselves. Secondly, the Mexicans have had their revolution, and their search for solutions to continuing problems is channeled through the ruling Party of Revolutionary Institutions, not outside it. PRI, which has not lost a major election since its founding in 1929, is so closely identified with the government, that to oppose it openly, or criticize its head, the president of Mexico, is regarded, even among the peasants, as unpatriotic, or worse.

Finally, PRI's influence extends down to the village level. Eighty-five per cent of the peasants belong to the Federation of Mexican Campesinos (CNC), an arm of PRI. Its elaborate system of controls is so pervasive that the government can, and does, move swiftly to choke off dissident movements.

But the same factors responsible for PRI's power will limit the hand of Diaz Ordaz in providing new solutions to the Campesino problems. It is true that he won over 90 per cent of the popular vote in the election. But he won not because he was Diaz Ordaz, but because he was the candidate of the PRI.

A Benevolent Dictatorship

The key to the success of the government party has been its ability to absorb and monopolize the main currents of Mexican political life: The demands of the wealthy, the demands of the weak, the energies of youth, the needs of the aged. The conflicting pressures that filter into PRI's gleaming $1,200,000 headquarters on Insurgentes Avenue in downtown Mexico City exercise more restraint on the President, its hand-picked candidate, than do the judiciary or bicameral legislature, both of which are little more than rubber stamps. "In many ways," says a political observer, "Mexico is ruled by a party dictatorship, but a benevolent one, generally."

Some critics of Mexico's agrarian reform program contend that what is needed is a "reform of the reform," a thorough-going revision of the ejido system, the country's basic form of land tenure. Eighty percent of Mexico's campesinos labor on ejidos, lands owned by the community and parceled out in small plots for private cultivation by campesino families. Critics argue that division of the land into small parcels (the average is about two acres) and the lack of full ownership rights (ejido land can not be sold or mortgaged) perpetuate the traditional pattern of subsistence agriculture.

But so drastic a course of action could not be envisioned by Diaz Ordaz. "A Mexican president," says a senior diplomat, "is like a man walking down a corridor. He can walk straight, or he can veer slightly to the left or to the right. But he can't go very far to either side or he'll slam into a wall."

Factories for the Farmers

Nor is the new president likely to attempt to break up the large estates. For one thing, it is the big commercial farms that produce most of Mexico's export crops of cotton, wheat, coffee, and sugar. For another, the estates that are the focus of peasant resentment are technically legal. Private landholdings of more than 247 acres of irrigated land are against the law, but it is legal for owners to pool their land for more efficient cultivation while listing their holdings separately.

Diaz Ordaz is expected to encourage industrialization of rural areas as one solution to the campensino problem. Indeed, industrial decentralization has already begun. Until recently, most of the nation's economic activity was centered in Mexico City, and the large population centers of Guadalajara and Monterrey. Now new plants dot the landscape of the Gulf Coast around Veracruz, and are transforming the mountainsides of Queretaro state, three hours drive north of Mexico City. In the state of Mexico, which borders the national capital, General Motors, Chrysler, Ford, and Willys have invested $110,000,000 in new plants and equipment. The industrial work force is expanding due to the growth of the feeder industries as a result of a new law requiring that Mexican parts account for 60 per cent of the value of each car built in Mexico.

Village fountain.

But some farm experts are convinced that industrialization is not the answer to rural poverty. Says Rodríguez Adame: "Farming, in general, is not a business, it is a way of life, with no possibility of changing occupations." The Agriculture Secretary's solution for the parched northern states is to follow the examples of two American states.

"Our mistake is to have tried to grow crops where it's too dry to grow crops. We should have begun sooner what you have done in Texas and Arizona: Switched to cattle raising." Rodríguez Adame adds that both the United States and Argentina get 55 per cent or more of rural income from cattle and its products. "We are on the way to that goal," he says, "because Mexico is eminently a cattle-raising country."

Diaz Ordaz, son of an obscure civil servant in the city of Puebla, is a firm believer in what Mexicans like to call their "continuing revolution." It is a philosophy holding that enlightened leadership, the energies set off by the revolution, and the resources of the land are sufficient to provide a better life for all Mexicans. "I belong," he boasts, "to the liberal and progressive historical current which since the revolution against the colonial system has been forming the national conscience against social injustice."

There's little doubt that the new president is committed to ending the misery of the *campesinos*. But the pressures against decisive action are great. They will come from the industrial sector, which demands continued priority, from grass-roots political bosses, money lenders and entrepreneurs who profit from the present system, and, most important, from his own party. He will, no doubt, face resistance, too, from the peasantry, ever distrustful of change. "If it comes too fast," says one observer, "it could bring about the very rural revolt they're trying to avoid."

The new president's dilemma is that while working for change, he must take care not to rock the boat.

MEXICO

BRITISH HONDURAS

Caribbean Sea

GUATEMALA

Guatemala
⊛

HONDURAS

Tegucigalpa
⊛

⊛ San Salvador

EL SALVADOR

NICARAGUA

Managua
⊛

0   300

Miles

Pacific Ocean

COSTA
San José
⊛

RICA

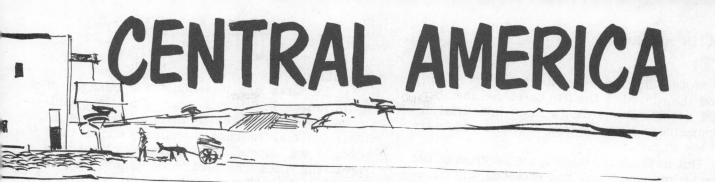

CENTRAL AMERICA

A Good Score for a Young Quintet

GEORGE CABOT LODGE, tall, lean, 37-year-old son of former Ambassador to Vietnam Henry Cabot Lodge, looked nervously about as he spread a one-page statement on the wooden rostrum of a restored museum in Antigua, Guatemala, picturesque one-time capital of Spain's Central America empire.

When he began to speak, the accent was pure Boston Brahmin, but the language was Spanish, and, when he finished, the audience of 44 businessmen from the five Central American republics and their wives rose to applaud his hesitant effort in an unfamiliar tongue. Lodge was one of five lecturers down from Harvard University to lead a six-week course in business administration in what may one day be a Central American institute of business administration. Now, at graduation exercises, he was telling the businessmen that they could be a model of enlightened leadership for all of Latin America.

A school of business administration? For the bucolic banana republics? The idea would have sounded preposterous five years ago. But now the five nations—Costa Rica, Nicaragua, Honduras, Guatemala, and El Salvador—have joined in forming a movement for regional development that American officials regard as perhaps the most significant development in Central America since the countries declared independence from Spain in 1821.

The five have already established a Common Market, eliminating tariff duties and other charges on 98 per cent of the locally produced goods they trade with each other. By June 1966 all goods produced within the area are to be tariff-free. The Central American Bank for Economic Development, capitalized at $20,000,000 ($4,000,000 from each member country), has financed expansion of more than two dozen industrial plants in the region. A Central American clearing house, working to establish a monetary union, last year cleared 75 per cent of regional transactions on the basis of a new Central American peso, valued on a par with the U.S. dollar. Market leaders are pursuing plans for an integrated network of roads, telecommunications, and electric power.

By 1970 Central America should be well on its way to welding into a single economic, and perhaps eventually political, unit a population of 11,000,000 people who live in an area a bit smaller than the state of Texas.

Explains Dr. Pedro Abelardo Delgado, gregarious, round-faced secretary general of the Common Market's supervisory organ, the permanent secretariat: "Five nations, averaging 2,000,000 people each, can't possibly find the resources to develop their economies if they work separately. So we combine."

That Dr. Delgado can speak casually about "combining" is surprising to anyone who has followed other efforts at economic integration. Nine South American countries plus Mexico are taking their first, hesitant steps toward developing a free trade area, but traditional rivalries and unstable currencies have kept most of their plans on the drawing boards. A continent away, the European Common Market has recovered from France's rejection of Britain's application for membership, only to become snagged on the issue of designing a joint policy on farm commodities. Russia's counterpart of Western Europe's Market, the Council for Mutual Economic Assistance, is floundering upon the refusal of the less developed members, most notably Rumania, to forgo industrial development and remain raw material producers for the bloc.

But in Central America, the progress of the integration movement has exceeded the hopes of its founders. Trade among the members, a mere $8,000,000 in 1950, has doubled since 1960. It now totals $66,000,000, or 12 per cent of the region's total trade volume. And last year, for the first time, the value of manufactured goods traded among the members outstripped the value of agricultural commodities—one sign of growing industrialization.

Several factors account for the success of the regional movement: Stable, convertible currencies, a traditional yearning for unity, and the relatively small volume of trade they exchange, which minimizes economic dislocations. Another factor, suggests an economist here, is that "nobody outside the movement took it seriously when it started. When 95 per cent of their goods were declared tariff-free at the outset, no one who could be hurt bothered to fight it. It seemed like too visionary a scheme to worry about."

Three Chief Crops

More important, the implications of continued dependence on a few basic agricultural products for export revenue became all too clear in the late 1950s, when world prices for coffee and bananas plummeted to disastrous lows. Interdependence, says Dr. Delgado, became "a matter of survival."

Lying on the narrow, mountain-spined isthmus that divides the Western hemisphere, these five nations have much in common. All except El Salvador, the smallest yet most developed of them, front on two oceans. Their topography varies from dense tropical forests to high, rugged mountains. None has extensive natural resources. All of their economies are dependent on one or more of the area's three chief crops, bananas, coffee, and cotton, which together supplied 80 per cent of the region's export earnings during the 1950s.

They share, too, a common poverty (average per capita income: $275 a year), a tradition of domination by foreign interests or by a landed aristocracy and a history of political instability.

Honduras has undergone 130 changes of government in the 143 years since independence. In three of the countries—Honduras, El Salvador, and Guatemala—military cliques have overthrown elected governments within the past four years. The election of Rene Schick as president in 1963 nominally put an end to the 30-year dictatorship of the Somoza family in Nicaragua, but the family maintains its power through the well-disciplined National Guard. Only in Costa Rica, where successive governments have implemented a social reform program pioneered 10 years ago by then-president Jose Figueres, has democracy taken a firm hold.

Pragmatic Leaders

Perhaps because of the instability of the governments with which they must deal, the integration movement's leaders are sternly pragmatic men. "We try to act as Central Americans, not representatives of our respective countries," says one of them. "That way, we're more insulated from pressures." Nowhere is that pragmatism better reflected than in the headquarters of the integration movement, a converted house opposite a small grocery store in a rundown section of Guatemala City.

Closets serve as filing cabinets; six secretaries are crammed into a former bedroom; one room, jokingly referred to as the library, is stacked to the ceiling with cartons of books and maps.

In contrast to the European Economic Community's headquarters in Brussels, which runs Europe's Common Market with a staff of 2,500 and an annual budget of $52,000,000, the Guatemala-based movement is a penny-ante affair. Operating expenses and salaries for 120 employes will total less than $400,000 this year. Comments Dr. Delgado, when asked why his headquarters is so cramped: "The only thing we need is a room where to work, and that we have."

Dr. Delgado's work started in 1960, when Guatemala, El Salvador, Honduras, and Nicaragua signed the General Treaty of Economic Integration, which is the market's constitution. It provides for tariff-free trade on all locally produced goods and the erection of a common external tariff by June 1966. Costa Rica joined the market in 1962. Panama is presently negotiating to become the sixth member, but many Panamanians fear that such a step would jeopardize her "special relationship" with the United States.

By 1970, according to present plans, the economic union will be complete. Among other things this will mean the elimination of passports and visas for travel by citizens of the region, unification of customs services, equali-

processing. Now, however, a sprawling cement factory employs hundreds of Costa Ricans. El Salvador is building bus frames. New textile plants have sprung up in Guatemala, and Nicaragua has a new refrigeration plant.

These projects, and others like them, have been promoted by the Central Americal Bank for Economic Integration (CABEI), a creature of the Common Market that claims to have created 7,000 new jobs and a $7,500,000-a-year

Planting time in Costa Rica: There are advantages in pulling together.

zation of industrial tax incentives, and conversion to a common monetary unit, replacing the *quetzal* (Guatemala), *lempira* (Honduras), *córdoba* (Nicaragua), and *colón* (one value in El Salvador, another in Costa Rica).

Each of the countries, to be sure, boasted its own industries before the start of the Common Market. But they were of a type common to developing countries: Clothing, chemicals, leather goods, metals, wood products, and food

payroll in the region since making its first loan in December 1961.

Agustín Gutiérrez, a 46-year-old banker from Costa Rica and one of CABEI's five directors (one from each country), explained the bank's purpose recently in the modern, glass-front building that CABEI occupies in the heart of Tegucigalpa, the Honduran capital.

"We make long-term capital available at low rates for economic expansion or establish-

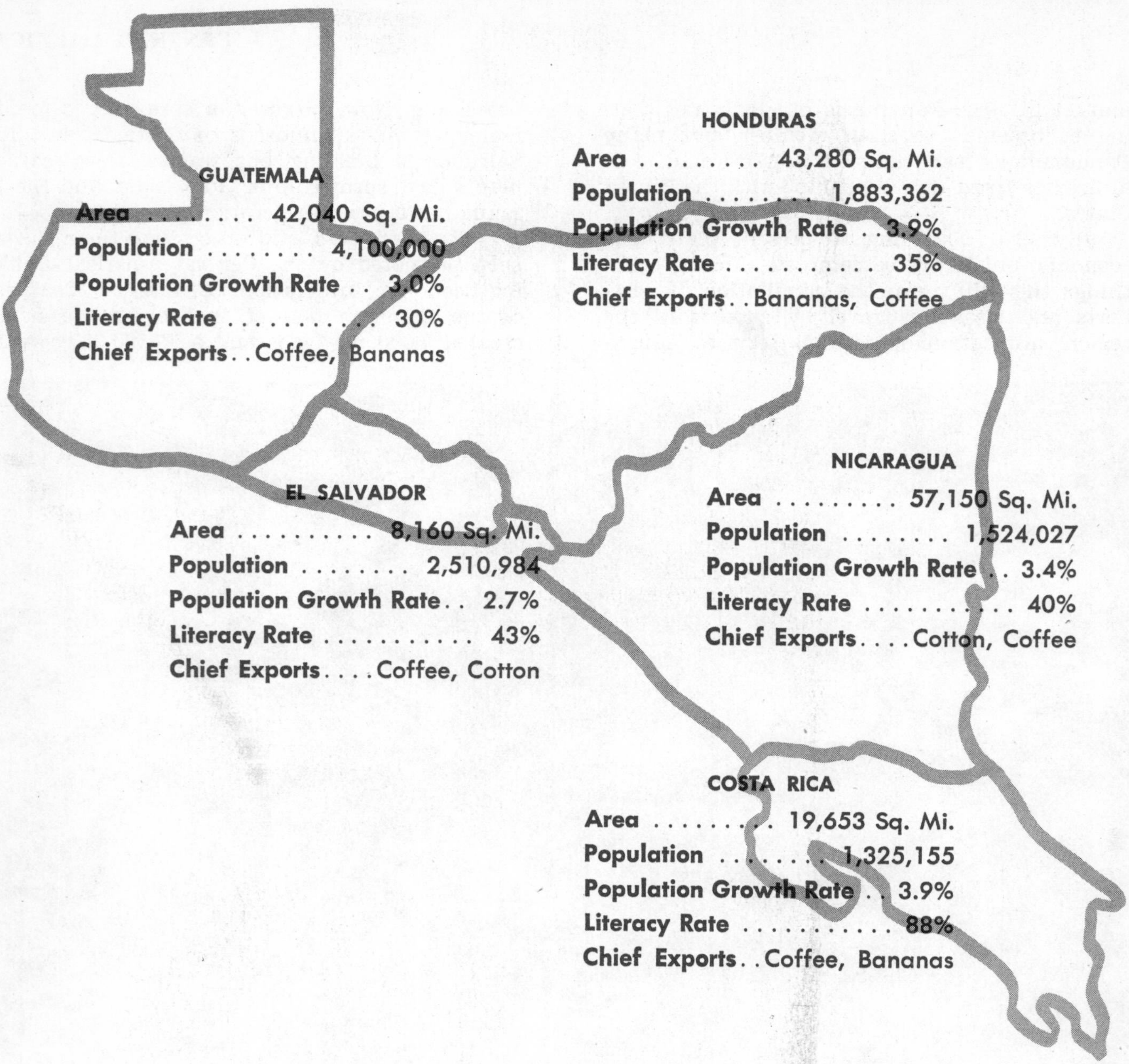

GUATEMALA

Area .... 42,040 Sq. Mi.
Population 4,100,000
Population Growth Rate .. 3.0%
Literacy Rate 30%
Chief Exports .. Coffee, Bananas

HONDURAS

Area .... 43,280 Sq. Mi.
Population 1,883,362
Population Growth Rate .. 3.9%
Literacy Rate 35%
Chief Exports .. Bananas, Coffee

EL SALVADOR

Area .... 8,160 Sq. Mi.
Population 2,510,984
Population Growth Rate .. 2.7%
Literacy Rate 43%
Chief Exports .... Coffee, Cotton

NICARAGUA

Area .... 57,150 Sq. Mi.
Population 1,524,027
Population Growth Rate .. 3.4%
Literacy Rate 40%
Chief Exports .... Cotton, Coffee

COSTA RICA

Area .... 19,653 Sq. Mi.
Population 1,325,155
Population Growth Rate .. 3.9%
Literacy Rate 88%
Chief Exports .. Coffee, Bananas

ing new industries of regional importance, that is, of benefit to more than one country. Generally, we finance 60 per cent of the total cost of a plant, including building, equipment, and working capital. What we look for are industries that will create new jobs, diminish the need for imports, and contribute to the gross national product."

The bank has already committed $17,000,-000 for industrial projects in member countries. It has granted special tax concessions to attract two new industries, GINSA, a tire and tube factory in Guatemala City, and a caustic soda and chlorinated insecticides firm being erected

in Nicaragua. In addition, it is conducting, with U.S. help, a property survey of each of the nations (a step toward reforming the archaic tax structures), and seeks to finance a modern communications system and complete a regional network of 1,000 miles of roads by 1969.

To emphasize the problem of communications in Central America, Gutiérrez points to the heavy, black telephone on his cluttered desk. "I can get through to New York within 20 minutes," he says, "but if I want to call Managua (Nicaragua), it may take all day. We have no direct telephone links between countries. All international calls go through Miami."

Paul Conklin

Maya Indian women mark Monday morning.

The need for highways is most acute in Honduras, a Mississippi-size country whose mountainous terrain is broken by a mere 250 miles of paved roads. Traditionally, farmers have found it more economical to transport their surpluses to neighboring countries than to send them greater distances within Honduras. But the pattern may be shifting. By 1970, U.S. assistance and funds from CABEI and the World Bank should have completed a modern highway linking Tegucigalpa with the northern industrial city of San Pedro Sula, with spurs leading to El Salvador, Guatemala, and Nicaragua. As a result, Tegucigalpa, the only Central American capital not served by a railroad, may not need one.

Despite the benefits of the Market to the region as a whole, the integration movement is not without internal conflicts. There is some fear in Honduras and Nicaragua that the more developed countries of El Salvador, Costa Rica, and Guatemala will drain off potential new industry, widening the economic disparities among them. Many small businessmen in all the countries are wary of the breakdown of trade barriers. Says an economist: "If I were a small businessman with a monopoly on my local market, I would be scared of foreign competition

Sunday morning in El Salvador: Can the Christian spirit apply to tariffs?

coming in and spoiling my show." Rivalry is developing, too, over the kinds of new industries to be promoted.

El Salvador and Guatemala are at loggerheads over the meaning of the integration treaty's stipulation that only goods "produced or manufactured" in member countries qualify for tariff-free movement in the region. For example: A brassiere firm in Guatemala is stitching together its product from materials imported from the United States. A Salvadorian company, which manufactures its own bras from local materials, contends the Guatemalan product is not "manufactured" in Guatemala.

Such disputes, resolved ultimately by the economics ministers of the five countries meeting as the Market's economic council, are an encouraging sign to leaders of the regional movement. "They show," says one, "that firms are beginning to think in terms of a regional market."

Dutch and Danish Milk

There is still the problem of eliminating tariffs on the two per cent of regional commodities still protected by duties. Under the 1960 treaty, all tariff walls among the five are to crumble by June of 1966, but no agreement has yet been reached on such products as wheat flour, dairy products, coffee, sugar, petroleum, and electrical appliances. The example of milk and dairy products is instructive.

Costa Rica has invested millions of dollars over the past 10 years in developing its dairy industry, and raised its tariffs high to protect it from foreign competition. Less-expensive Dutch and Danish dairy imports could level a damaging blow at the Costa Rican economy when national tariffs are eliminated, unless Costa Rica can convince her neighbors to build the common external wall, also to be erected in 1966, high enough to keep out the competition. But Costa Rica's neighbors who buy the European products might balk at a high tariff that would make their milk more expensive.

Market economists are resigned to continuing tariff protection for such commodities beyond the 1966 deadline. They reason that other Market countries may accept Costa Rica's argument for protection of her dairy industry if they, in turn, are also granted a few exemptions.

Though the primary benefits of the Market are economic, the movement extends to other fields as well. Regional planners are encouraging an integrated curriculum among the five understaffed national universities. "It's a tremendous waste of resources to have five separate departments of microbiology and five engineering schools without modern equipment," argues one planner. "If we could consolidate and, say, send all the microbiology students to Costa Rica and the engineers to Guatemala, they'd all get a better education."

Political Implications

Primary schools are feeling the effects of the movement. The first in a series of Spanish language readers, financed in part by the U.S. Agency for International Development, were distributed to 850,000 first and second grade school children in the republics last year. A Central American textbook research center in Guatemala is working with the five education ministers to design a new curriculum for all primary school children.

Regional development has become a focal point of activity among businessmen, intellectuals, and others who despair of erasing social injustice through the established power structures in their countries. Suggests one foreigner in Guatemala:

"New economic forces are coming into being that are not tied to the ruling oligarchies, who have worked against reform. As long as the land they owned has been the basis of the local economy, the oligarchs have called the tune. The new economic activity is a threat to their influence. The surprising thing is that there's been so little resistance."

Establishment of a Central American institute of business affairs in Guatemala is thus an event of social as well as economic importance. As George Cabot Lodge told the graduating class:

"We hold a priceless opportunity to improve a region, to assist in welding a Central America for the benefit not only of its business enterprises but of all its people, and beyond that to show new ways which may be useful to all Latin America in the achievement of true progress."

BANANAS

Economies Based on Them Tend to Bruise Easily

THE words "Banana Republic" usually conjure up the image of a downtrodden Central American country whose economic and political fortunes are controlled by the machinations of American banana interests, backed up by American military might. This image, even if there was some substance to it in bygone days, no longer holds true.

Bananas, to be sure, do play an important role in the economies of four Central American countries—Honduras, Panama, Costa Rica, and Guatemala. But only in Honduras are bananas the chief source of foreign exchange. The biggest exporter of bananas in the world is, in fact, not one of the Caribbean nations but Ecuador on the west coast of South America.

The American-owned United Fruit Company, whose name south of the border once was synonymous with "Yankee imperialism," has been attempting to freshen up its own image in the Latin countries and in the United States. United Fruit controls about 28 per cent of the total Latin American banana market. In recent years the company has been modernizing the industry with new boxing operations, branding of products, and developments of strains of bananas that are more resistant to wind and disease. The United Fruit banana worker now makes about $3.50 a day, triple the average pay scale for other banana workers in Latin America.

The United Fruit innovation period comes during a period of expanding consumer demand for bananas. Since 1950 per capita consumption of bananas in the United States, the world's biggest importer, has increased 10 per cent. Canadians and West Europeans are eating more bananas nowadays, too. More than 98 per cent of the bananas imported by West Germany come from Latin America.

Latin American banana exports to Western Europe, however, could drop sharply because the European Common Market has granted special trade preferences to several banana-growing African lands. The Common Market is considering the imposition of duties and quota controls on Latin American bananas. Latin banana-exporting countries nevertheless remain optimistic about preserving their West European markets because their bananas are superior to those grown in Africa.

The loss of the growing West European market would have a serious effect on the economy of the leading banana-growing Latin countries, particularly Ecuador where bananas account for more than half of the export earnings. Bananas had been a minor item in Ecuador's trade until the late 1940s when the Central American banana plantations were overrun by disease. Ecuador began growing banana trees on its coastal lowlands and within a few years was out-producing each of the Central American countries.

In Ecuador, bananas of the taller and more

A random harvest just won't do.

marketable Gros Michel variety can be grown easily in the fertile coastal areas where high winds, which can devastate an entire banana plantation, are rare. Inland rivers afford convenient transportation to Ecuadorian ports. Ecuador, too, has been fortunate so far in avoiding any prolonged attacks of banana plant diseases, which spread mysteriously and rapidly. Researchers have yet to discover a preventative for Panama disease, whose ravages cost the banana industry millions of dollars a year.

The banana is believed to have originated in the moist tropical regions of Southeast Asia. In 1516 a Spanish missionary, Father Tomás de Berlanga, brought banana roots from the Canary Islands off the west coast of Africa to the island of Hispaniola. Only since the turn of the century and the advent of more rapid maritime transportation has the banana gained extensive markets throughout the rest of the world.

Thirsty Plant

Bananas are grown in tropical zones and flourish best where temperatures range between 55 and 105 degrees. The banana plant requires large quantities of water and where rainfall is light during part of the year the plantations must be irrigated.

The banana is a non-woody plant similar to the canna lily or the orchid. The trunk of the banana plant consists of overlapping leaf sheaths. It is more than 85 per cent water. The top leaves are from 8 to 12 feet long and about 2 feet wide.

A banana plant reaches the harvesting stage about 14 months after the rootstock, or rhizome, is planted. The rhizomes, which weigh from 8 to 10 pounds, are inserted in foot-deep holes about 12 to 16 feet apart. Each rhizome must have at least one "eye," or sprout. Occasionally, sections with a number of eyes are planted.

When the eye sprouts three to four weeks after planting, it develops into a plant with a rootstock of its own. Only the strongest sprouts are allowed to grow; the others are pruned off. Each sprout bears one bunch of bananas. A bunch is made up of clusters called "hands," each containing from 12 to 20 bananas, or "fingers." A bunch may have from 6 to 14 hands.

After the growth of the plant a second shoot, known as the "daughter" plant, is allowed to grow. Three to six months later a third shoot, usually derived from the daughter plant and appropriately called the "granddaughter" plant, also is allowed to grow. By the time the fruit of the mother plant is harvested the next two generations are being tended to provide a continuing supply of bananas.

It is always harvested when hard and green because the ripe fruit falls prey to insects.

Importance of Timing

Fruit for shipment is first washed with a sodium bisulfate solution to remove spray residues applied to prevent disease and ward off insects. After drying, each stem is covered with a perforated polyethylene bag for protection during transit. During the entire growing, cutting, and harvesting procedure great care is taken to avoid bruising the fruit, which damages easily. United Fruit Company since 1960 has been packing the fruit in boxes at the plantation, thereby avoiding badly bruising the bananas during handling.

On the banana's journey from plantation to exporting point, timing is highly important. Shipping arrangements must be closely coordinated because the fruit ripens rapidly after harvesting. Ship breakdowns or port strikes in importing countries can result in the ruin of a banana shipment.

Speedy, refrigerated ships carry the bananas to the importing country. The temperature in the bins where the bananas are stowed usually is kept at around 50 degrees.

At their destination, the bananas are moved from the hold by conveyor belts and sold to a wholesaler if shipped independently. The wholesaler keeps the bananas in a "ripening room" until selling them to the retailer. Through temperature and moisture controls the wholesaler can time the ripening process to the exact day the fruit reaches the local grocery.

On board ship, bananas have airconditioned quarters.

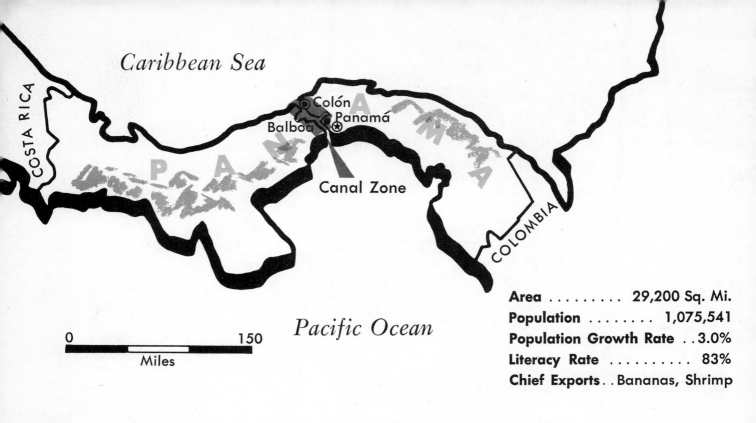

Caribbean Sea

COSTA RICA

Colón
Panamá
Balboa

PANAMA

Canal Zone

COLOMBIA

Pacific Ocean

0   150
Miles

Area . . . . 29,200 Sq. Mi.
Population 1,075,541
Population Growth Rate . .3.0%
Literacy Rate 83%
Chief Exports . . Bananas, Shrimp

PANAMA

An Open Wound Keeps the Fever High

MONTHS after the bloody rioting over flying the Panamanian flag alongside the Stars and Stripes in the U.S.-controlled Panama Canal Zone, reminders of the bitter conflict are everywhere in Panama City.

Take a drive along the Pacific coastline on picturesque Balboa Avenue here, and you can't help but notice a hand-painted message, in black, on the seawall: Panama The Hungary of America. Visit the gleaming Legislative Palace, just across President Kennedy Avenue from the Canal Zone, and guides will show you the places where the granite is pock-marked with American bullet holes, circled in red and yellow paint so they won't be forgotten. Ask Marco Aurelio Robles, the reform-minded ex-banker who is Panama's new president, what his country's primary need is, and he'll answer: "A new Panama Canal treaty."

Panama has other needs, of course, and many of them are more critical than its differences with the United States over the 10-mile-wide strip of American territory that splits this S-shaped isthmus. Chief among them is development of the agricultural and mineral resources of Panama's interior to lessen the economy's vulnerability to the vagaries of world commerce through the canal. Today, some of the most dedicated men in the Panamanian government are working to improve the lot and productivity of the *campesino*—illiterate, ill-fed, and ill-housed—before Communist agitators turn him completely against democracy.

But Marco Robles has good reason for considering the future of the canal his prime concern. It is the one issue on which his countrymen are united. Robles is handicapped as he begins his term by pressures from Panama's wealthy elite, who drafted him for the presidency. His effectiveness will be diminished, too, by a belief among a broad segment of Panamanian workers that the real victor in last May's election was fiery, Fascist-leaning Dr. Arnulfo Arias, a mystic and Harvard-trained surgeon who served two terms as president in the 1940s. To find the support needed to achieve his goals of economic and social reform, Robles may have to exploit the canal issue.

To be sure, relations between Panama and the United States have improved in the past few months. Outgoing President Roberto F. Chiari has restored the diplomatic ties he broke in the aftermath of the rioting that left 22 dead and more than 300 wounded. Negotiations between the two countries will eventually give Panama more control over canal operations and a considerable increase in the present $1,930,000 U.S. annuity to Panama. Another source of contention was swept away this summer when the Pentagon reduced the 25 per cent pay differential that favors the Panama Canal Company's 4,000 American employes over the U.S. Government-owned firm's 11,000 Panamanian workers.

But the presence of a foreign power on Panamanian territory in a subcontinent of growing nationalism can not help but remain an issue. It is the U.S. presence there itself, more than the conditions of it, that explains much of the resentment. "The January riots," says an American military man close to that crisis, "were a symbol of the average Panamanian's frustrations. If it hadn't been the flag issue that set it off, it would have been something else."

Still, except in moments of passion, most Panamanians are too realistic to seriously want the departure of the Canal Zone's 40,000 Americans (including military personnel and dependents). Panama's revenues from the zone totaled $92,000,000 last year, including the annuity, wages to Panamanian workers, and purchases by Zonians in the Republic. In addition, tourists, most of them Americans, pour an estimated $14,000,000 into the national economy annually. The Canal Zone provides low-rent housing to most of its employes, Panamanian and American. It provides services free or below cost ranging from health and sanitation to schools and police protection.

The Price of the Riots

All Panamanians understand these benefits, but that doesn't lessen their resentment. They see the contrast between the shaded lawns and comfortable homes of the Zone, and the squalid, rickety slum dwellings along the narrow, dirty streets on its borders. Many Zonians, second and third generation residents, are disdainful of the native population. Some freely boast they haven't been into the Republic in five or six years. To the Panamanians, they are colonials. Says a taxi driver in the capital: "Those people living in the strip, they look at us like enemies."

Just how heavily Panama depends on the United States became clear during the January crisis. Commerce, a healthy climate for foreign investment, and a few steps toward industrialization have given this nation one of the highest economic growth rates in Latin America. The construction industry was booming, and a new oil refinery was doing so well that petroleum replaced bananas as the nation's main export. (Panama still imports almost three times the value of its exports, however.) Favorable tax laws resulted in a considerable infusion of foreign capital, providing easy credit for business expansion.

All that changed with the riots. Within six weeks, one-fourth of all foreign capital was withdrawn from the country. Credit was curtailed. The government, which relies heavily on borrowings to finance recurring budget deficits, faced an inflationary spiral. Since the election of Robles, who was backed by President Chiari, business confidence has been restored, but it

will be several months, or longer, before the economy achieves its former level.

But Panama is not alone in having suffered setbacks as a result of the crisis. Partly as a result of anti-American propaganda that the government has taken no steps to discredit, most Panamanians consider the U.S. action against the Panamanian nationals who stormed the zone to have been vicious and unprovoked. Indeed, a high school textbook, which carries the approval of the Ministry of Education here, describes the events of January 9-12 as "the most despicable and cowardly aggression ever registered in the pages of American history."

The furor stems from a perplexing question of sovereignty. The 1903 treaty, signed only 15 days after a U.S.-backed insurrection won Panama's independence from Colombia, gives the United States not sovereignty, but "all the rights, power, and authority within the zone ... which the United States would possess and exercise if it were the sovereign ... to the entire exclusion of the exercise by the Republic of Panama of any such sovereign rights, power, or authority."

The Titular Sovereign

Theodore Roosevelt paid the fledgling republic $10,000,000 in cash for construction rights to a canal joining the Atlantic and Pacific Oceans, and an annuity of $250,000, which has been raised over the years to its present level of $1,930,000. In 1959, after six Panamanians were killed in riots over an attempt to plant the national flag in the zone, President Eisenhower acknowledged Panama as titular sovereign. President Kennedy went a step further in 1962 by ordering that both flags should fly together in civilian-controlled areas, "in an appropriate way."

The January riots were prompted by an order from Zone Gov. Robert J. Fleming, Jr., a U.S. Army Major General, that neither flag should fly outside the Zone's 18 schools. When American students at Balboa High School raised the Stars and Stripes in defiance of his order, 200 angry Panamanians attempted to hoist their standard at the two-story, yellow stucco school. They were turned back by Canal Zone police after an argument in which the Panamanian flag was torn. At nightfall, 3,000 Panamanians stormed the zone in protest. Snipers took up

When Yankee students raised Old Glory . . .

. . . Panamanians raised Old Nick.

positions in apartment houses across President Kennedy Avenue outside the zone, and behind the Legislative Palace. Other rioters roamed the streets of the capital, Colón, and other cities, looting stores and setting fire to American businesses.

In the wake of the riots, President Chiari charged the United States with an "unprovoked, armed attack," and demanded action by the United Nations Security Council. The National Bar Association of Panama requested an investigation by the International Commission of Jurists.

Few Panamanians are familiar with the report released in June by the investigating team that was appointed by the Commission of Jurists. It had been given scant publicity there. The report rejected the charges of American brutality, and pointed out that five American soldiers and one U.S. civilian had been wounded by Panamanian snipers before the troops were directed to switch from ineffective shotgun fire to .30 caliber rifles. It also criticized the Panamanian government for ignoring all pleas by U.S. authorities to dispatch the National Guard to help quell the rioters. Most Americans there

The Panama Canal

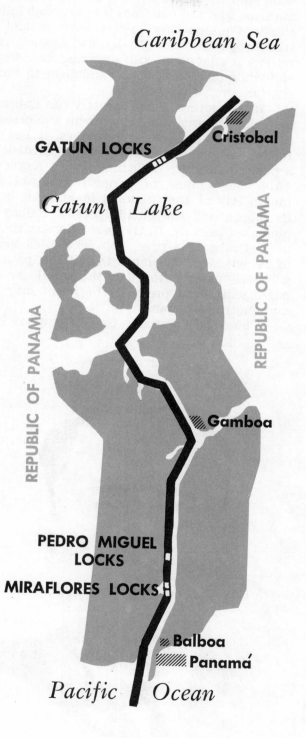

Caribbean Sea

GATUN LOCKS

Cristobal

Gatun Lake

REPUBLIC OF PANAMA

REPUBLIC OF PANAMA

Gamboa

PEDRO MIGUEL LOCKS

MIRAFLORES LOCKS

Balboa

Panamá

Pacific Ocean

believe President Chiari's government would have fallen if he had acted. Suggests one: "He thought it better to have the crowd take out its wrath on the Americans."

Despite the lingering bitterness over the events of January, some diplomats are hopeful the conflict may prove to be a blessing in disguise. "We've been trying for years to shake Panama loose of its canal mentality and begin developing other sectors of the economy," says an American spokesman. "Now that this has happened, they're beginning to try."

Whether they will succeed or not depends to a large extent on the leadership that Marco Robles can provide. Robles, a wavy-haired man of angular features who was noted for cracking down on Communist activity as Chiari's Minister of Justice, is possessed of neither great intellectual depth, nor charismatic appeal. He was picked as the government's candidate only after two other Liberal party hopefuls became deadlocked. His 11,000-vote victory out of 300,000 ballots cast was fairly impressive, but he was backed by a wobbly coalition of eight parties, and Arias, running without a formal organization on the strength of his own personality, received a third of the vote.

Nevertheless, Robles has the support of the all-important National Guard, and a vision of a new Panama that, in the long run, will benefit a majority of his countrymen.

Tapping the Interior

Robles told a reporter recently: "Our biggest need, after a new treaty with the United States, is the economic and social development of the interior. For this we will depend on the Alliance for Progress. We have a situation in which there is extreme wealth and extreme poverty side by side. This must no longer be. It is in the interior that our untapped potential lies, in rural development. After four years I hope to be able to look back and see the interior starting to contribute and share in the prosperity of the country."

An ambitious start toward rural development was made two years ago with passage of an agrarian reform law, which seeks to turn rural areas into a means of subsistence for the impoverished *campesinos,* and a food source for urban areas. The plan is to plow roads through wilderness for marketing produce, develop the

Arnulfo Arias.

livestock industry on unused grassland, build slaughterhouses, food processing plants, and make use of the nation's forests for lumber mills. The revenue produced would be plowed back in the rural sectors for schools, housing, health centers, and other social projects.

The law is administered by 45-year-old Porfilio Gómez, a mild-mannered agriculturalist with a master's degree from Cornell University. Gómez hopes to be able to distribute 50,000 acres of new land this year and, by giving titles to squatters, allow them to qualify for credit and technical assistance now denied them. However, the land reform program will also require relocating an estimated 15,000 families, now on private property. Though the law provides that no one can be evicted until provided with as good or better housing, Gómez is meeting stubborn resistance in some farm sectors.

Explains Gómez: "We are faced, here as elsewhere in Latin America, with an explosion of expectations, which we are trying to meet with our programs. But we are severely impeded by certain persons who are moving into these areas to tell the people we are actually trying to take away their land and help the rich imperialists."

These "certain persons" are primarily left-wing students, some of them Cuba-trained Communists, who fan out from the National University in Panama City (where they control the student government) to agitate against rural reform. "They will kill animals, cut fences, and commit other acts of vandalism to inhibit the farmers," says Gómez.

If the rioting of last January has impressed upon the Panamanian government the necessity of building up its other resources, it has also revived talk in the United States of constructing a new canal. Since the canal opened August 15, 1914, the volume of cargo passing between Limón Bay at the Cristóbal breakwater in the Caribbean and the Pacific port of Balboa has increased steadily. In the past 10 years the volume of cargo has risen from 36,095,349 tons to 62,247,094. By 1980 more than 60 ships a day will seek passage through the canal, as compared with 30 at present. The result may be a mammoth traffic jam.

Though the Panama Canal Company is en-

Marco Robles.

gaged in a constant modernization program, its ability to keep up with the volume of commerce is limited by the canal's construction. Ships must pass through a series of three locks. Entering from the Caribbean side, the first, Gatun Lock, raises the vessel 85 feet in a continuous flight of three steps. Each lock chamber is 110 feet wide and 1,000 feet long. The ship then steams through Gatun Lake, one of the largest artificial bodies of water in the world, to Gaillard Cut, and on to Pedro Miguel Locks, where it is lowered 31 feet to Miraflores Lake. At Miraflores Lock, the Pacific-bound ship is lowered in two steps to sea level.

The lock system is not only costly to maintain, but it prohibits transit to an ever increasing number of ships that exceed the locks' dimensions. In contrast, a sea-level canal—in Panama or elsewhere—constructed perhaps with the aid of nuclear explosives, could handle all cargo and would require less than 1,000 workers, as compared with 15,000 in the present canal.

Marco Robles has more immediate concerns, of course, than the vague possibility that one day a new canal may be constructed. The real power in this country rests with the 3,500-man National Guard of Colonel Bolívar Vallarino. Colonel Vallarino favored Robles for the presidency, and is said to view kindly the projected reforms. But the Colonel's allegiance is to the ruling elite, and the elite may become easily disenchanted with the new president if he shows as much ardor in carrying out his reforms as he did in pledging them.

Waiting in the wings is Arnulfo Arias, who twice before has been ousted from the presidency for introducing a Fascist-style constitution that discriminated against non-Panamanians. There is a mystique about Arias that makes him the idol of the poorer classes. Many of them firmly believe that within a year's time, Arias will "answer the call of the masses."

Whether he does or not depends on the course Marco Robles chooses to follow. Robles can pursue a course of moderate reform without much resistance. Or he can seek, at the risk of falling victim to his own supporters, to promulgate his vision of a new Panama.

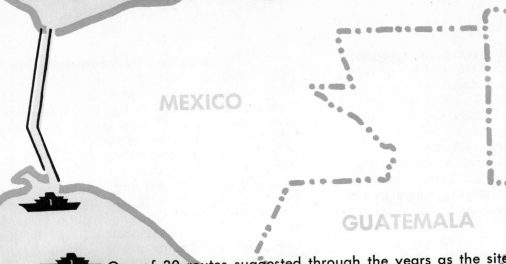

MEXICO

GUATEMALA

HONDURAS

EL SALVADOR

1 One of 30 routes suggested through the years as the site of a new canal connecting the Atlantic and Pacific Oceans, Route 1 would be highly expensive. It is long (170 miles) and would need locks. Another isthmian canal, or the widening of the present one in Panama, is needed because of expanding shipping traffic.

8 Route 8 along the Nicaragua-Costa Rica border is also long but would be constructed at sea level, which is less costly than a canal with locks. Nicaragua has dropped earlier opposition to the 139-mile route because of the proposed drainage of Lake Nicaragua, which would provide the country with hydro-electric power.

16 Route 16 in Panama is unquestionably the shortest and cheapest if nuclear explosions are used for excavation. But this 40-mile route is so near populated areas that blasting with nuclear devices would be unsafe. Building a new canal by non-nuclear means would be economically unfeasible.

17 The most likely site if a new canal is dug is Route 17, the 58-mile Sasardi-Morti Route through the jungles of lower Panama. Nuclear explosives could be used without danger in this thinly populated area. Building the new canal in Panama would avoid any political repercussions in that country, which is edgy about losing economy-propping revenues through diversion of traffic from the present canal.

25 Because of the many political difficulties with Panama through the years, the United States again is eyeing the 95-mile Route 25 in northwest Colombia. The Atrato and Truando Rivers nearly connect in this area, which would lower construction costs. But the danger of ship collisions arises because of heavy rainfall and fog in the area.

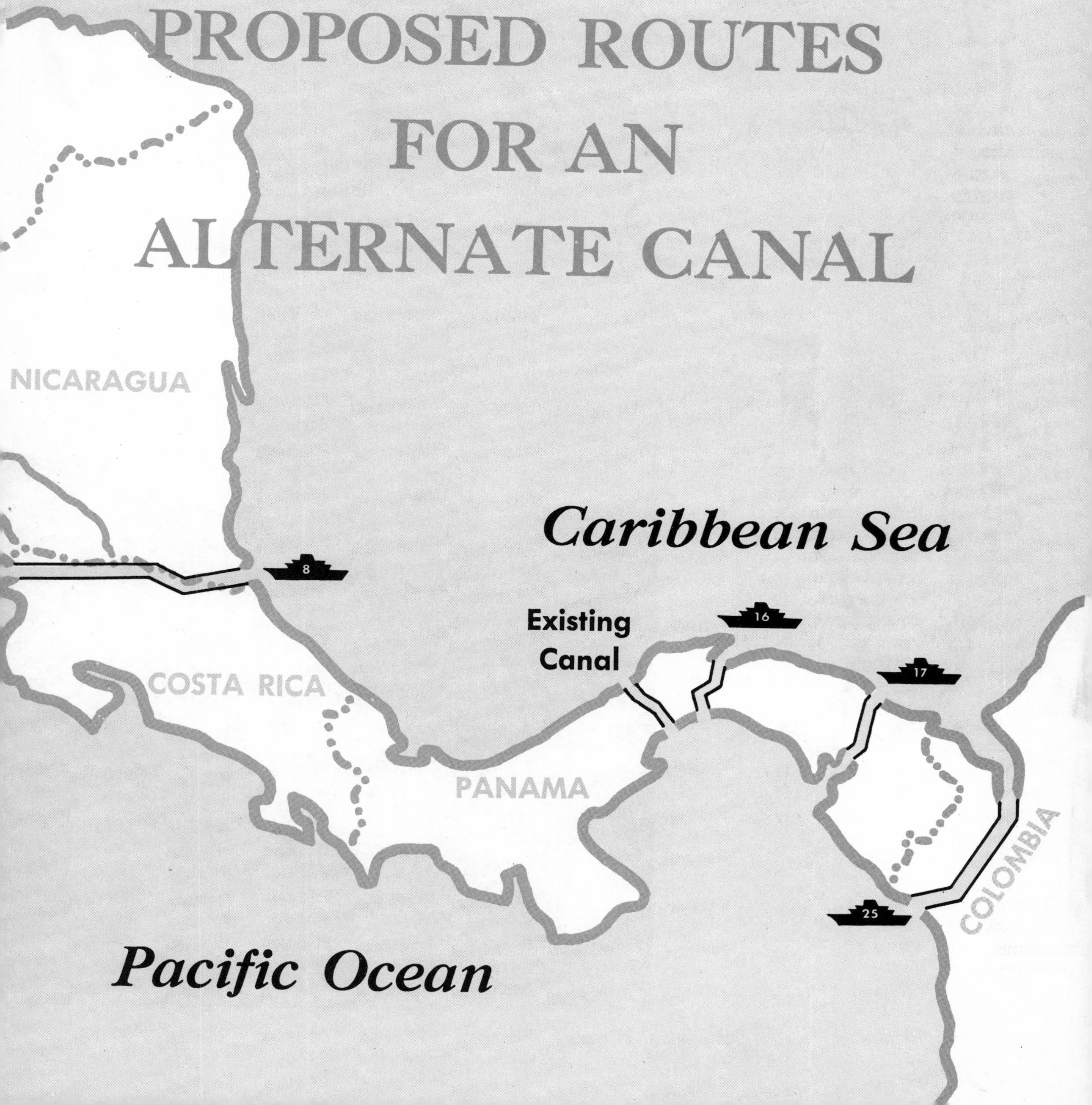
PROPOSED ROUTES
FOR AN
ALTERNATE CANAL
NICARAGUA
Caribbean Sea
8
Existing
Canal
16
17
COSTA RICA
PANAMA
COLOMBIA
25
Pacific Ocean

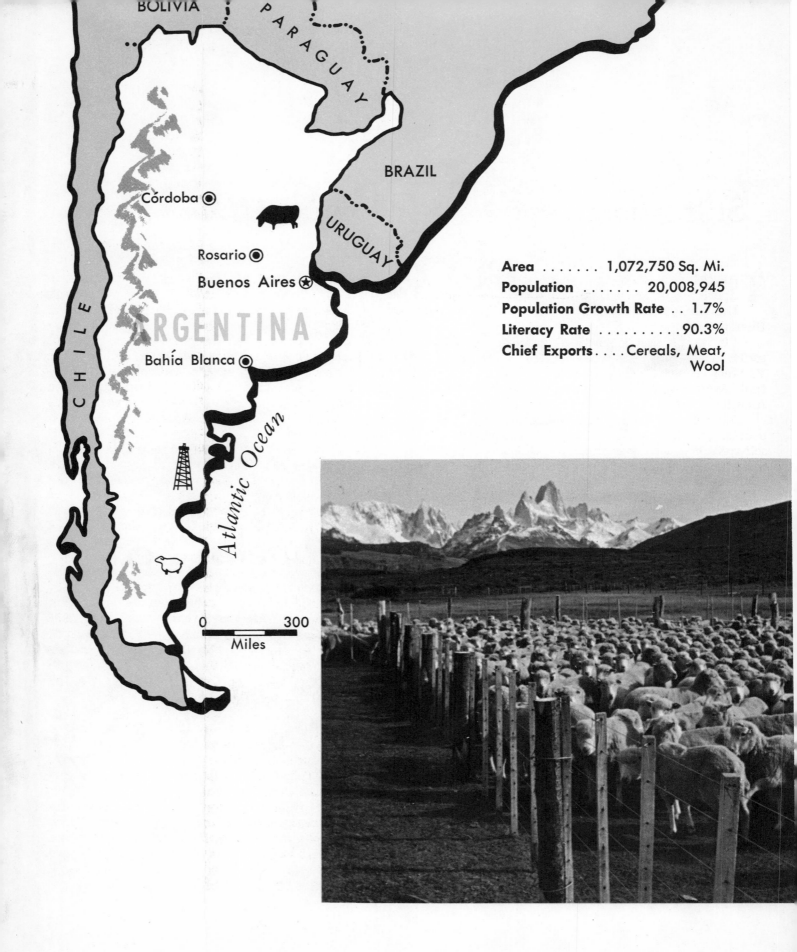

BOLIVIA

PARAGUAY

BRAZIL

URUGUAY

CHILE

Córdoba ◉

Rosario ◉

Buenos Aires ✪

ARGENTINA

Bahía Blanca ◉

Atlantic Ocean

0   300
Miles

Area . . . . 1,072,750 Sq. Mi.
Population 20,008,945
Population Growth Rate . . 1.7%
Literacy Rate 90.3%
Chief Exports . . . . Cereals, Meat, Wool

ARGENTINA

Still in the Long Shadow of *El Caudillo*

THE ARGENTINE businessman sipped his aperitif and slowly scanned the patrons of the fashionably old-fashioned restaurant in Buenos Aires.

"It is not entirely untrue," he said a little sadly. "Argentines in many ways are the Yankees of Latin America. But it is not true that Argentina is the United States of Latin America."

He went on to assert that Argentines, as a people, tend to be self-satisfied and haughty, self-righteous and materialistic—qualities that most Latin Americans believe Yankees possess in abundance.

"The rub is," he added, "that the U.S. has managed to achieve political continuity and this continuity has permitted the orderly accumulation of wealth and the national confidence that wealth brings. But Argentina has been unable to restrict its political debate within an orderly framework. Many other Latin Americans think of us as haughty but that is only because we are trying to cover up our basic insecurity. We know we are not a backward nation. We have just had our progress interrupted by meddling military men, outright demagogs, and greedy labor leaders."

The man who is now president of Argentina is neither a military man, a demagog nor a union chieftain. He is Arturo Umberto Illia, a kindly, soft-spoken physician who was elected in July 1963. The Argentine president, who promised in his campaign to restore "order, peace, and law," has turned out to be an unusual leader. In the sense that he has done relatively little since he took office, he is a model of restraint. But what measures he has taken hopefully to bolster the country's flagging economy have, in the opinion of most impartial observers, been radical enough to suit the likes of Perón himself.

Argentina is still suffering an acute hangover from the Perón era. Inflation is rampant, unemployment is rising and the economy is tangled up in government controls and regulations. The meat and railroad industries are in desperate straits, and the government seems convinced that only more state planning can set things right.

The Illia government's first important action, the nationalization of foreign-owned oil companies, is a good example of the kind of economics the president prefers. Last year the government cancelled the contracts signed in 1958 with 10 foreign petroleum firms by the regime of Arturo Frondizi. Dr. Frondizi was a leader of strong socialist convictions, and his agreement with the oil companies was viewed as heresy by many of his own followers. Yet within five years after the 1958 pact, Argentina for the first time became self-sufficient in oil and relieved itself of the burden of spending $300 million a year on oil imports.

By denouncing the Frondizi pact, Dr. Illia became a hero to the country's more rabid nationalists. But by placing the oil companies under inefficient, bureaucratic management, the president has seriously jeopardized the industry's outlook.

For one thing the government must now find a way to repay the millions of dollars spent on unsuccessful oil exploration by the foreign companies. Of the 10 firms involved, only two found deposits that can be worked economically.

Meanwhile, Dr. Illia has irritated the Argentine people by introducing meat rationing in this big beef-producing land. Terrible droughts in 1961 and 1962 seriously depleted the country's herds, from 44,000,000 head in 1962 to less than 40,000,000 today. This was bad news to a people who consume 200 pounds of beef per capita annually, and who rely on beef exports for 27% of their foreign revenue. Unemployment in the cattle industry is mounting; 4,000 packing plant workers were laid off in one week alone.

The government has instituted wholesale and retail price controls, abolished the free auctioning of cattle and proclaimed two meatless

President Arturo Illia.

days a week. Few observers in Buenos Aires believe the measures will put the meat industry back on its feet.

Argentina's absurd railroad system, which is so antiquated it verges on uselessness, runs an annual deficit of $700 million. Many other state-run enterprises are heavily in debt and the 1964 national budget, which does not include losses on such socialized enterprises, nevertheless will show a red-ink total of about $650 million. The government is now hoping to get a five-year plan under way later this year, but cynics in Buenos Aires claim the economy may collapse before the plan matures.

"Argentina has the knack of making trouble for itself," says a Buenos Aires newspaperman, adding, "Considering what we have to work with, this country is short on reasonable excuses."

Argentina, for instance, is not saddled with a large, inert Indian population as are some of the Andean countries, nor is it imprisoned by criss-crossing mountains. Except for the extreme northern and southern regions, the country has a temperate climate and good soil. Its capital, Buenos Aires, is the center of a metropolitan area that forms the largest city in the southern hemisphere. A busy port, Buenos Aires is also an essentially European city, civilized and sophisticated. The nation has one of the highest literacy rates in all of Latin America—90.3 per cent.

Stop-Gap Solutions

Why, then, so much trouble?

From the beginning, Argentines have been afflicted with short-sightedness, with a passion for stop-gap solutions to major problems and a quick return for every effort. The result has been that problems have not only lingered, but multiplied.

As they did throughout most of Latin America, the early Spaniards got Argentina off on the wrong foot by zealously digging in the mountains for gold and silver while ignoring the fertile central plains known as the pampas. The Spanish cow, brought along to supply the gold seekers with meat and milk, showed better sense. When a few of these tough, stringy beasts escaped, they wandered into the pampas and multiplied phenomenally. Still the Spanish government was not interested in cattle growing, so the industry which was to become the nation's most important was begun by the gauchos, nomadic cowboys proficient with the long knife, the lariat and the Indian *boleadoras*. The latter device, made of three stones on the end of thongs, could bring down a 650-pound steer on the run.

It was the gaucho, functioning as an early cattle herder, who made possible the *estancia*, the Argentina cattle-raising equivalent of that classic Latin American institution, the *hacienda*. To be profitable, land holdings had to cover large tracts and support many head of cattle. The absentee landlord became the rule, because the monotonous, primitive life of the *estancia* offered little allure. Thus the city population numbered among its prominent members the owners of huge ranches, and the rural population consisted mostly of landless, drifting cowhands.

In the early 19th century the first *saladero,* or meat salting plant, was erected in Argentina, and the country prospered as it shipped tons of salted meat throughout the Americas for use

Spain came in 1816.

The coast took over the economic life of the country increasingly, drawing men from the hitherto dominant interior. By the middle of the 19th century, however, the *saladero* days of the beef business were over. Slaves and seamen got tired of eating the leathery salt flesh (the poorest beggar in Europe had never been willing to eat the stuff), so the great land owners were forced to try something else. Unlike most areas

After the droughts, two meatless days a week.

as food for slaves and seamen. The *saladero* opened new sources of profit to the cattle owners, who had formerly sold only the hides and fats of the animals. The upsurge in this business solidified the prosperity and political unity of the coastal regions, and helped propel the entire country toward independence.

The creole leaders of Argentina handed the Spanish Vice Regalty at Buenos Aires its walking papers in 1810, and final independence from

of Latin America where animals graze, the pampas lent themselves very well to growing grains, so entrepreneurs turned to this source of income.

In the 1870s the cattle industry was revived. British investors brought good beef breeds into the country and fattened the new stock with alfalfa. *Frigerificos*—packing plants and floating iceboxes—boomed the Argentine cattle industry into the world markets.

The sheep (mostly grazed in the southern

barrens of Patagonia), cattle and cereal industries vied with each other for first place in the nation's economic life throughout the last half of the 19th century. They all helped provide Argentina with fame, fortune—and foreigners.

Argentina contains the largest percentage of foreigners in Latin America, and more of its people are direct descendants of Europeans than are those in any other Latin American country. The result is that almost all have white skin and a strong emotional link with Europe.

Rickety Railroads

All of this culminates in the capital city of Buenos Aires. One-third of the country's people crowd in and around the city. Many of them live in the *villas miserias,* Argentina's slum equivalent of Rio's *favelas* and Caracas' *ranchos* or *barrios.*

The bizarre railroad system contributes to the congestion around Buenos Aires and the remoteness of the interior. The railroad lines, rickety in any case, form a series of spokes going from the coast inland, neglecting connections between points in the interior. What's more, the tracks are of three different gauges, often making it impossible to re-route rolling stock from one line to another.

But Argentina is much more than Buenos Aires and the pampas. Over 2,000 miles long, if superimposed on the northern hemisphere, it would reach from Greenland to Greensboro, North Carolina.

The central plains, which run into the jungles of the Chaco on the north, extend southward into Patagonia, as mysterious a region as there is on the continent. Though Patagonia touches the sea on the east and comes close to it on the west, it is extremely arid. And it is the very barrenness of the Patagonian deserts that, while giving little, has historically attracted men.

Like a gaping vacuum, the lack of color, sound or life has drawn humans weary of civilization to expound the uncanny pull of the place. Charles Darwin wrote of the friendly,

child-like Indians of Tierra del Fuego (sailor Joshua Slocum found them anything but friendly) who were later slaughtered by immigrating sheep farmers. W. H. Hudson spent days in the calm of the desert, feeling civilization drained out of him by the vast void, in which the whiteness of a buzzard's belly acted like glaring color in a solid gray landscape.

Oil and coal have been found in Patagonia, but the area still holds little appeal for prospective settlers. In their opinion, the poets are welcome to it. It is the plains of the pampas that form the nation's bread basket and its heartland.

The dominant figure in the life of this dominant part of the country has been the man on horseback in all his various incarnations. The prototype of the Argentine hero is the gaucho. The *estanciero,* or ranch owner, followed. As the *estancias* grew in importance, number and size, and as Spanish centralized rule collapsed in the early 19th century, the *estanciero* kept Argentina from chaos by ruling his sprawling lands with considerable personal force. Local loyalties and power structures developed. When the advent of railroads and a strong federal government centralized control of Argentina, the leader swung down from his horse and mounted the political platform. One such *caudillo,* or chief, has profoundly influenced the nation since he first stepped upon the scene. His name is Juan Domingo Perón.

Oratorical Boleadoras

The colorful tradition of the original Argentine hero—the gaucho—echoed in Peron. Tough, brutal and armed with a demagog's oratorical *boleadoras,* he built a mystique similar to that acquired by the old-time gauchos with deeds of valor. But like many of the gauchos who left the bulk of slaughtered animals for the vultures and the sun, Perón was essentially a destroyer.

After training in a Fascist camp in Italy, Colonel Perón took office as vice president in 1944, only to be booted out a year later. But in the 1946 elections, thanks to his enormous popularity among the workers, he won the presidency with 52 per cent of the popular vote.

A man of great personal luster on the Latin model, Perón's dynamism, masculine vigor and military background assured him worshippers. And he had at his side a powerful proof of his

Argentina is gradually replacing its ancient rolling stock, but three different railroad gauges still make overland shipping a difficult business.

Paris Match

In exile in Madrid, Perón and wife, Isabelle

male appeal: Eva Duarte, a good-looking blond who was also a zealous and wily politician. Once a prostitute and then mistress to Perón before he married her, Evita was regarded by the Argentine people at the time of her death as the epitome of womanly virtue. Like a queen and angel, she officiated at the opening of hospitals, personally doled out money for the poor, and saw to it that her husband plastered Argentina with huge posters of her lovely face.

When she died of cancer in 1952, she was venerated as a saint, and the government that ousted her husband in 1955 secretly disposed of her remains lest her burial place be turned into a shrine by fanatical admirers.

When Perón took over in 1946, the outlook for Argentina was good. The war had done well by the country with its seemingly endless supply of food on the hoof and on the stalk. Foreign exchange reserves were high, and in the

following years starving Europe continued to provide a market for Argentina's grain, sheep, and cattle.

Perón's manipulation of food sales exemplifies his ability to turn a financial killing for the government and himself into a propaganda killing as well.

To "protect" the farmer after the war, Perón set up an agricultural clearing house called the Argentine Institute of Promotion and Exchange (IAPI). All goods were to be sold through this agency before resale abroad in order to protect the producer from world price fluctuations. Radical price shifts have been the plague of Latin America's one-product economies, but at that time the farmer was commanding very high prices for food. Perón bought the goods at low fixed prices and sold them for the most he could squeeze from his hungry customers abroad. He was praised by the people for defending the interests of the small farmer—and he made a healthy profit as well.

Perón dreamed of an industrialized Argentina. His first five-year plan (1947-51) changed the nation from an agricultural country dependent upon foreign markets to a manufacturing country catering to local consumers. His giveaway programs provided workers with wages and other benefits, the likes of which they had never seen before.

Expenditures for these grandiose schemes pulled the plug out of the government's reserve tank, draining 60 per cent of its substantial foreign exchange surplus. So the printing press was put to work and fresh paper money was used to pay the bills. The cost of living began to climb rapidly, and it hasn't stopped since.

Today the Argentine government must deal with a nation of spoiled children, and somehow it must employ needed reforms without alienating a populace that remembers the Perón economic orgy with wistfulness.

Perón's party and person are now outlaws in Argentina, although there was talk in mid-1964 that Perón might return. The Peronistas, even without Perón, continue to exert a major force in the country's political life. Compare the results of the two presidential elections which have been held since Perón's overthrow in 1955.

In 1958, Arturo Frondizi won the presidency as the candidate of the Intransigent Radical Civil Union (UCRI) with 45 per cent of the popular vote. Half his support came from Peronistas who had been instructed by their exiled leader to vote for Frondizi. If this support had been lacking, Frondizi would have lost.

Oscar Alende, running for the presidency in 1963 as the candidate of the same party, won only 16 per cent of the vote. Why? He had not courted Perón, and Perón's forces were told to cast blank ballots. Some 19 per cent of the voters cast blank ballots; if these votes had gone to Alende, he would have beat out Arturo Illia, the man who is now president.

In 1962, when Frondizi was president, Peronist candidates were allowed for the first—and so far the last—time to run for election in congressional and gubernatorial races. Returns in their favor were so large that elections in five provinces were annulled, Frondizi was overthrown by a military coup, and eventually all 1962 election results were voided.

The prelude to the 1963 elections was as turbulent and confusing as a large county fair. Every elective office in the land was to be filled. Parties split apart and alliances regrouped within days of the election.

The balloting itself went smoothly. In the race for the presidency, three groups commanded most of the attention and, eventually, most of the votes: The People's Radical Civil Union (UCRP), the Intransigent Radical Civil Union (UCRI), and the Peronistas. The UCRI supported pro-labor, pro-Perón policies, a stance which gave the party victory in 1958. The UCRP took an anti-Peronista position.

Arturo Illia of the UCRP, under an electoral college system, won the presidency with a scant 25 per cent of the popular vote.

Dr. Illia contrasts in every way with Perón. He is not a man winked about because of his boudoir activity, not a wheeler-dealer (one reason antic-weary Argentines settled on him), not a wooer of the military, and not a demagog arousing mobs of workers.

But these are negative attributes; positive ones are harder to find. He is inexperienced in politics and susceptible to questionable economic schemes and the yearnings of an extremely flag-proud people. It will be for his constituents, as much as for himself, to decide whether Argentina will continue to square off against itself, or whether it will achieve the good life its resources rate.

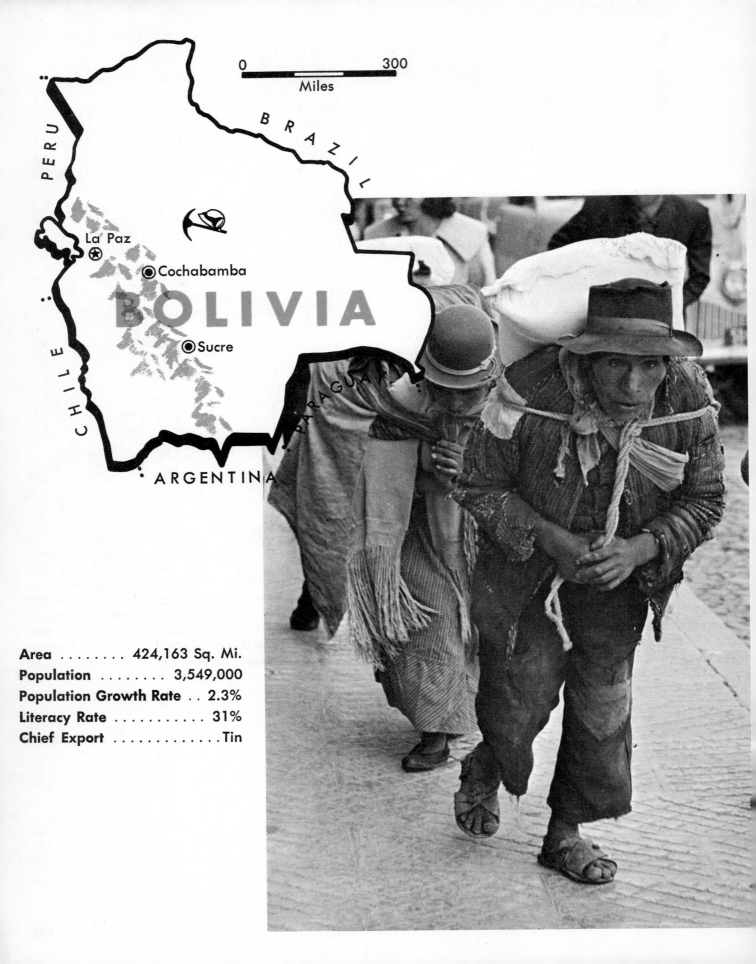

BRAZIL

PERU

La Paz

Cochabamba

BOLIVIA

Sucre

CHILE

PARAGUAY

ARGENTINA

0   300
Miles

Area . . . . 424,163 Sq. Mi.
Population 3,549,000
Population Growth Rate . . 2.3%
Literacy Rate 31%
Chief Export . . . . Tin

BOLIVIA

Taming the Wilderness—and the Miners

ON THE night of May 31, 1964—election night in Bolivia—one Bolivian and two American reporters crouched on the roof of an apartment house overlooking the *Plaza del Estudiante* in the capital city of La Paz. Government troops fanned out below and ordered pedestrians and motorists out of the area. From the vicinity of San Andres State University, less than a block away, came the crack of rifle fire, the occasional boom of exploding dynamite, and the thud of hurled cobblestones.

A group of radical students opposed to President Víctor Paz Estenssoro, who was re-elected that day to a third four-year term, were emphasizing their outrage by ripping up the streets and taking pot shots at the local constabulary. It was a very minor disturbance by Bolivian standards but there nevertheless were bullets pinging about and the bite of tear gas was in the air. The reporters on the apartment house roof were therefore startled to watch a young couple with three small children walk unperturbed across the well-lighted Plaza and on down the darkened street where the students were shooting it out with police and soldiers. The family proceeded to stroll through the crossfire without changing their leisurely pace.

"That's typically Bolivian," exclaimed the Bolivian newsman. "They are so used to demonstrations and shooting they have come to ignore danger. I am glad you were here to see such a sight for yourselves. Now perhaps you can understand Bolivia."

Unfortunately, it's not so easy to understand Bolivia, although such sights do help a visitor come to know it. After 179 revolutions,

it stands to reason the country might become nonchalant about civil strife, and indeed the nonchalance seems to pervade everything except politics.

Few things that move appear as abstracted as the Bolivian Indians who account for 70 per cent of the nation's population of 4,000,000. Residing mostly on the Altiplano, the vast upland plateau where the air is thin and the soil poor, the Indians live difficult, primitive lives—and die young. They alleviate their misery by chewing *coca* leaf, which dulls the edge of hunger and provides a narcotic respite from reality. A common sight on *El Prado,* the tree-lined boulevard in La Paz, is a slouching Indian plodding along, doped by *coca* and gazing about with the eyes of a dead man.

Yet, because of U.S. aid and a government that subscribes to the methods and goals of the Alliance for Progress, Bolivia is making progress. The radical tin miners are being brought under control, thousands of Indians are being moved from the Altiplano to the more fertile eastern lowlands, badly-needed roads are being built, and some 40 per cent of the children go to school (only 5 per cent of the children attended school before the 1952 revolution that destroyed the feudal oligarchy). In 1963 the economy expanded by 6.5 per cent and a similar improvement is looked for this year.

Although many obstacles and problems remain, the progress thus far, if it has not materially improved the lives of most Bolivians, has practically eliminated the Communists as a serious internal threat. Only three years ago the Reds held powerful government jobs and dominated the mine unions. Today they are

President
Victor Paz Estenssoro

Bolivian mine workers:
Short tempers and short lives.

without important influence anywhere in the country.

To make this kind of headway, the government has had help from many sources—especially from the United States which has poured well over $300 million into the country since the revolution. This amounts to more aid per capita than Uncle Sam has given to any other nation in Latin America. But money alone has not been the answer. The government, under tough, egocentric President Paz, has brought about social reforms that were not always popular. Bolivia's 30,000 miners emerged from the 1952 uprising as government pets, demanding and winning work benefits that would have bankrupted the country if Uncle Sam hadn't subsidized the national treasury.

Even today, with the Reds all but out of the labor movement and other radical union-

ists boxed in by the government, the traditionally anarchistic miners remain an unpredictable force in national life. And they are an especially important force in a country where tin accounts for 70 per cent of the foreign revenue.

The trouble with the miners dates back to 1952 when, after the revolution, the big, private mines owned by the Patiño, Hochschild and Aramayo interests were seized by the new government. Though production has improved in recent months, it had been running at an annual rate 45 per cent below the pre-revolution level. After the takeover, lax work practices became the rule and machinery was allowed to fall into disrepair.

In 1953, the deterioration was speeded by a law that set up "control obreros"—worker leaders—at the mines, with broad powers. Union meetings are held during the one-shift workday (most mines in other nations operate two or even three shifts a day). Output per man-day at the Bolivian mines has been running less than one ton, compared with the five or six tons that are considered normal in other tin-producing countries.

As a consequence, most of the nationalized mines have been producing tin at a cost per pound of close to 25 per cent above the price world consumers have been willing to pay—although in the last year the rise in world prices has narrowed this gap.

Triangular Plan

More than two years ago a so-called Triangular Plan was launched, under which the United States, the Inter-American Development Bank and West Germany were scheduled to provide about $37,750,000 over a three-year period to try to make Bolivia's mines profitable again. The idea was to rehabilitate the equipment, lay off about 5,000 surplus workers (the "featherbedding" at the mines verges on insanity), and return to management some of the rights that had been usurped by labor leaders.

The Triangular Plan is "behind schedule," in the euphemistic words of one American diplomat, because the leftist labor leaders have sabotaged it. But since his re-election, President Paz has taken steps to undercut the labor leaders' power and clear the way for the Plan's reforms.

President Paz himself has had a peculiar political development.

After he was called back from exile in Buenos Aires following the 1952 revolution, Paz served four years as president, stepping aside in 1956 for Hernán Siles Zuazo. From 1956 to 1960 Paz was ambassador to London, returning to seek the presidency again. His experience in England had mellowed him; he was no longer the man who, during his first administration, had set up five concentration camps where flaming torches were applied to the bare feet of his political enemies.

"In England," said President Paz, "I learned how a civilized people can live."

In 1961, Paz amended the constitution so that an incumbent chief executive could succeed himself. Most people thought at the time that the provision was to take effect only after Paz was out of office. But the president put a different interpretation on it and decided to seek re-election. Because the president controls the election machinery, his decision was in fact a decree that he would serve another four years.

Paz's many opponents within and without his own party boycotted the election. Some went on a brief and ineffective hunger strike. When the dust had settled, Paz was more powerful than ever, and Uncle Sam was inclined to overlook the fact that the Bolivian president was something less than a democrat. True democracy in Bolivia will take time.

To be poor and uneducated as most Bolivians are is, obviously, not to be free. Compulsory voting laws which exist in Bolivia, Chile and other Latin America countries are feeble, futile substitutes for an informed, participating citizenry. And poverty in Bolivia has geographical as well as sociological roots.

Bolivia is physically a vast prison in which its inhabitants are confined from the rest of the world, and within which its inhabitants are sealed off from each other. The country is landlocked; in the War of the Pacific (1879-1883), it lost the ports of what is now northern Chile and the Bolivian government is currently trying to get Chile to give at least one port—Arica—back. Chile, not surprisingly, has declined and the two countries have severed diplomatic relations.

Mountain Barricades

But even if it still possessed this opening to the sea, Bolivia would be relatively isolated. Barricaded from the Pacific by the 400-mile-wide wall of the Andes, the nation is all but cut off from its eastern and northern neighbors by the thick jungles of the Amazon basin. Linking the lowlands and the mountains are the *yungas*—valleys sliced into the sides of the Andes. These sub-tropical valleys are extremely fertile and, like much of the tropical lowlands, could produce useful crops facilely.

Bolivia, however, is largely an Indian country and the Indians are wedded physically and culturally to the high Andes. Gradually they are being enticed eastward, but it will be at least a decade and perhaps a generation before the Bolivian people begin to make the most of what they have.

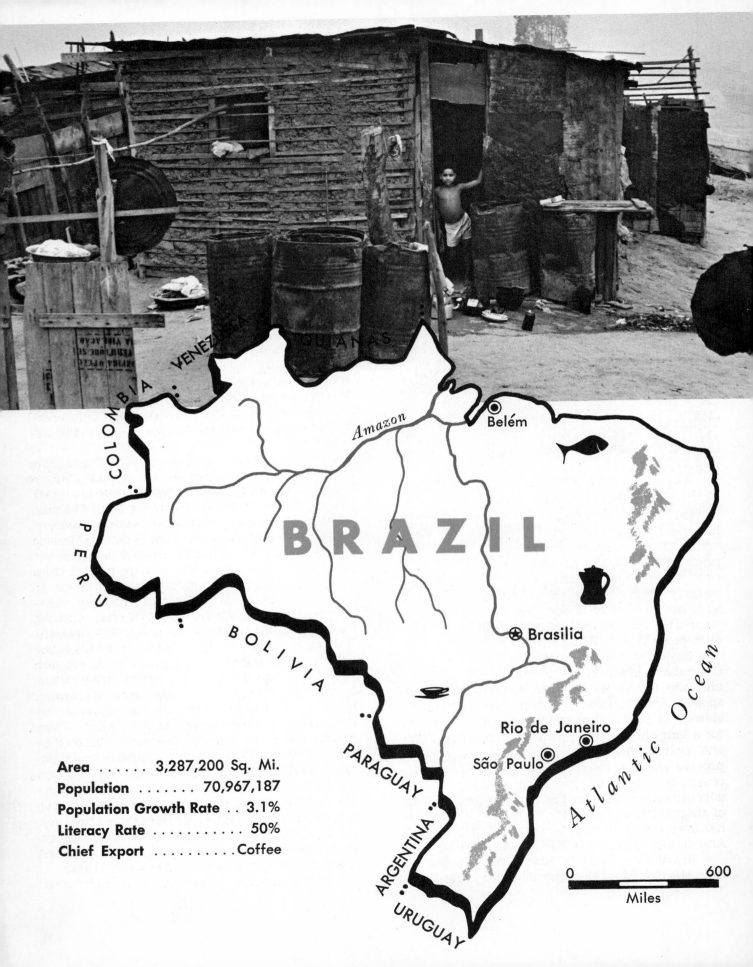

BRAZIL

Amazon

Belém

Brasilia

Rio de Janeiro

São Paulo

Atlantic Ocean

COLOMBIA

VENEZUELA

GUIANAS

PERU

BOLIVIA

PARAGUAY

ARGENTINA

URUGUAY

Area . . . . . . 3,287,200 Sq. Mi.
Population 70,967,187
Population Growth Rate . . 3.1%
Literacy Rate 50%
Chief Export . . . . Coffee

0   600
Miles

BRAZIL

The Army Holds the Line As a People Regroups

THE HILLS and harbor of Rio de Janeiro, cast in beauty by nature's hand, tend to accent rather than hide the city's remarkable man-made ugliness.

The slums in Rio have been described as among the worst in the world, as wretched even as the reeking hut-clutters of Asia. On the main thoroughfares the crystal air that wafts in from the sea is quickly polluted by the thick, black exhaust of growling diesel buses. And even on Copacabaña Beach, the famed crescent of white sand and oceanfront hotels, evening strollers along the famous mosaic-tiled walkways are frequently startled by scampering rats.

This ugliness-amid-beauty is not restricted to Rio nor, certainly, to Brazil. But it does symbolize the plight of a potentially rich nation that historically has been hobbled by decadent leadership. The structure of officialdom prior to the revolution last spring was wormy and rotten, and the country's new leaders were faced with the job, not of remodeling that structure, but of bulldozing much of it down and building anew.

Carlos Lacerda, governor of Guanabara State (Rio de Janeiro) and one of the nation's most outspoken politicians, recently declared: "I have heard many people for a long time ask why Brazil, which is so large and rich in resources, could not prosper and provide security for her people. Well, the main reason is that Brazil has been a victim of bad government. Brazil has been cursed by a system of stagnation and of corruption from which she has been trying to free herself for over 30 years. And finally Brazil has freed herself."

Brazil was freed in March 1964 not only from the demagogic deviltry of its deposed president, João (Jango) Goulart, but from the more serious danger of imminent Communist take-over. Goulart had been using the Reds until he was all but devoured by them. It was at this critical point that the army ousted Goulart in a revolution that was bloodless because it had the overwhelming support of the people. The new leaders named as president a man of character and prestige, General Humberto de Alencar Castelo Branco, who was to serve until January 31, 1966, when Goulart's term would have expired.

But in the summer of 1964 congress amended the constitution to extend Castelo Branco's term to March 15, 1967, while changing the date of presidential elections from October, 1965, to December, 1966. The move was aimed at giving the revolutionary regime more time to enact urgently needed reforms.

No reform is more needed than the government's present steps to slow down Brazil's runaway inflation. Under Goulart the cost of living had risen about 100 per cent a year, almost entirely because the government engaged in a reckless spending spree at a time when foreign revenues were declining. Goulart made up the difference by printing more paper money. When prices shot up as a result, Goulart attempted to assuage the working class—and gain their loyalty—with huge pay raises. Thus did inflation spiral.

But inflation, in a sense, was merely the most dramatic symptom of Brazil's political rot. Goulart, the army contends on the basis of persuasive evidence, was a master crook who set the moral tone for most of the bureaucracy.

It was because corruption was so widespread

that the army took punitive measures against the people who rode the gravy train under Goulart. Some politicians who lost their political rights were punished not for corruption, however, but for other reasons. Jânio Quadros, for instance, was deprived of his political rights for 10 years because, by resigning the presidency in 1961, he permitted then Vice President Goulart to take control of the government in the first place.

Former President Juscelino Kubitschek, the man who practically bankrupted the country by building the splashy city of Brasilia deep in the interior, lost his political rights because the revolutionary government was afraid he would be elected president again. Kubitschek is very popular with the masses who are impressed with his building projects. But in the event of his return to office, the army feared, he would again put the country back on the road to economic chaos with his ambitious development schemes.

Outspoken, Honest, Efficient

With so many prominent politicians removed from the scene, a man some observers think may well succeed Castelo Branco is Carlos Lacerda. And, whether he ever becomes president or not, Lacerda could be an important factor in the reshaping of Brazil. Despite his falling out with the revolutionary regime he is, like Castelo Branco, a conservative; moreover he has proven himself an honest and efficient administrator (he has established in his state one of the best school systems in Latin America) who is not afraid to speak out. His disagreement with the current administration seems to be based on methods rather than aims.

As the most outspoken opponent of the previous administration, Governor Lacerda kept up a drumfire of criticism against Goulart during the deposed president's two and a half years in power.

A former newspaperman—reporter, columnist and eventually editor—Lacerda has never hesitated to attack anyone who held the reins of power, no matter how unpopular or downright dangerous such tactics might be. In the early 1950s he kept up a slashing attack on Dictator Getulio Vargas until one night in 1954 gunmen took potshots at Lacerda, wounding him in the foot and killing an air force officer who stood along side him. Clues led police to the chief of Vargas' palace guard; shortly thereafter Vargas committed suicide.

Some Brazilians say that Lacerda's public attacks on Jânio Quadros, whom he accused of dictatorial designs, were instrumental in causing the unpredictable Quadros to resign only seven months after taking office. Thus, say the scorekeepers, Goulart was the third president of Brazil that Lacerda has been at least partially responsible for deposing.

In the midst of Goulart's anti-American campaign, Lacerda kept right on praising the U.S. despite the political risks of being pro-Yankee. In a speech in Rio before the revolution, for instance, he said: "It is easy to understand

Carlos Lacerda.

why those who live in fear and hatred loathe and dread the North American people and their civilization."

He said it was erroneous to describe that civilization as materialistic. "It was precisely idealism which molded it. It was not only with oil but also with its idealism that the United States unleashed in the world a powerful reaction against misery and injustice" and a longing for "social, cultural and economic progress."

If Lacerda is a tough, skilled political infighter at age 50, he's also something of an intellectual. He's an author of books. He's equally at home in Portuguese, Spanish and English. And he speaks knowledgeably on a variety of topics.

Example: A visitor to his palace office in Rio is treated to a lengthy lecture on the state of Brazilian agriculture.

Agricultural production increased only 4.5 per cent over the past 10 years, Lacerda says, failing to keep pace with a three per cent annual growth in population. "Our agriculture is backward because it has had to pay the bill for fast industrialization," he adds. Money that could have been used to modernize agriculture, he contends, instead went for industrialization.

Then he slips into a discussion of land reform. He's critical of those who see it simply as a job of breaking up large land holdings into small ones. He cites the tendency of U.S. farms

President Castelo Branco.

to grow larger—instead of smaller—as they grow more efficient.

For all his virtues as an administrator and deep thinker, Carlos Lacerda is regarded with some uneasiness by many Brazilians. One reason for this is the way he hounds his enemies. His assaults on the opposition are relentless if not ruthless. And the easy-going Brazilian tends to resent the politician who is always making the feathers fly. Also, Lacerda is too conservative for many of his countrymen.

In personality, Lacerda could hardly be more different from President Castelo Branco, the quiet-spoken soldier who is serving as interim chief executive. Castelo Branco, accord-

ing to U.S. diplomats in Rio, harbors no personal ambitions for himself and in fact opposed the amendment to extend his time in office by 14 months. He is a veteran of the Italian campaign in World War II and a long-time friend of the U.S.

In Castelo Branco, and indeed in the character of the Brazilian army, the nature of last spring's revolution is reflected. And, despite some of the excesses which inevitably follow any revolution, the new regime has tried to impress upon the Brazilian people—without resorting to the firing squad—how vital to a successful society is a respect for law. The regime has done this in two ways. It has enforced laws that previously were ignored (ranging from traffic regulations to tax statutes), and it has tried to make the law itself more respectable.

Interestingly, it is the army that by its mere presence behind the scenes is lending some measure of dignity to Brazilian politics. There are many reasons for the special status of the army in Brazilian life; the chief of these is that, in Castelo Branco's words, it is a "middle-class army." Unlike some other military establishments in South America, the top officers do not represent the country's aristocracy.

Pinching Cruzeiros

Castelo Branco himself has had to pinch *cruzeiros* all his life. And one of his fellow general officers is the son of the man who was valet to the late dictator, Getulio Vargas. The army is essentially a middle-class institution because wealthy young Brazilians don't fancy the low pay that military service offers. Too, the army has traditionally not been a gateway to political power. Moreover, the army has attracted young men from the middle class because it offers the prestige of a stable institution in a country that is forever tinkering with its political structure.

It is sometimes hard for an American to understand all this because it clashes with the stereotype. And the current ascendancy of the army seems almost the classic Marxist case of the "bourgeoisie" crushing the "people"—*i.e.* the Communists and thousands of plain liberals.

But the vagaries of Brazil's historical and cultural developments have endowed the army with vast respect. It is considered the guardian of civil rights and the 13,000-man officer corps

General Castelo Branco (left) conferred with fellow officers while his army tanks rolled into Rio. Goulart decided to leave quickly.

has a reputation for honesty.

Brazilian generals earn about $600 a month, enough to live comfortably in that country. But lower-ranking officers make considerably less. For the families of majors and colonels to make ends meet, it's often necessary for the wives to go to work. Because they are largely middle-class citizens, army officers mingle socially with middle-class civilians, thereby reducing any feeling that the military comprises a separate caste—as it does, for instance, in Argentina.

In a country the size of Brazil, there are bound to be strong regional ties much as there are in the United States. The army is able to transcend this regionalism, however, because its officers are moved frequently from post to post. They thus serve as an integrating influence in national life.

Fighting Illiteracy

Latin American nations are frequently criticized in the United States for spending too much money on their military establishments. Brazil spends 12 per cent of its annual budget on its army, which varies in size between 100,000 and 150,000 men, depending upon the state of the government's treasury. But the army, which is rated high in competence by American military men, is much more than a fighting force. It is also one of the nation's most important educational institutions.

More than half the conscripts taken into service for an eight-month period each year are totally illiterate. When their eight months are up, they have learned to read and write, and they also have been taught a trade.

The vocational training is keyed to the skills that Brazil's expanding economy sorely needs. In agricultural areas, the soldiers are released from duty every Thursday so they can work on farms on Fridays and Saturdays. Although there are frequent charges that rich men's sons have been able to buy their way out of the draft, such devious practices have little meaning. Out of 2,700,000 young men eligible for the draft each year, only 100,000 are taken—for budgetary reasons.

The army is more than twice as large as the navy and air force combined. But its influence can be traced more to its history than to its numbers. Although it might strike some as

small praise, there are few institutions in Latin America that have more consistently championed the rule of law over the years than has the Brazilian army.

End of an Empire

In 1889, when General Deodoro da Fonseca ended the Brazilian imperial era by kicking out Dom Pedro II, he almost immediately provided for the separation of the church and state and, two years later, gave the country a constitution modeled on the U.S. charter. As has been the custom in South America, the general gradually took for himself dictatorial powers. But even so, he opened the way for eventual popular participation in government.

In the 1930s the army, for a time, was able to promote social reforms and protect the right to vote under Getulio Vargas, who later became a dictator. During the late 1930s it was the army that crushed revolutionary movements by both the Communists and the *Integralistas*, or local Nazis. Finally, in 1945, Vargas refused to relinquish any of his dictatorial powers and the army threw him out. In 1950, Vargas was legally elected president again. And again he sought to establish authoritarian rule. The army was pressing him to resign when he took his life in 1954.

Interestingly, very few military men have become president of Brazil. And no military action has ever been taken that had as its first purpose the installation of an army officer as chief executive. On the other hand, many generals have run for president and were beaten in the elections without causing the military uprisings that would likely follow such an event in many Latin American countries. Four times in the past century the army has gone into neighboring countries to boot out dictators and establish, for a time, popular rule.

But history affords no example of the army's freedom-oriented tradition quite so dramatic as the action last spring that saved Brazil from sliding into Communist hands. Nor did the U.S. State Department have any doubt that that was about to happen.

"If the army hadn't moved when it did," declares one U.S. official, "Brazil wouldn't have been another Cuba. Brazil is 16 times the size of France, larger than the continental United States. It accounts for half the area of South

Belém—part of a nation's memories.   São Paulo—part of a nation's hope.

America, as well as half the population and half the industry. No, Brazil would not have been another Cuba. It would have been another China."

The problems facing Brazil, including badly needed reforms in almost every area of national life, are as big as the country itself. Nor is the smallest problem the fact that the Brazilian people have not yet learned to trust and guard their political institutions, and thus they frequently have been fooled by demagogs. But so long as the army remains, it will not be easy to subvert the country into communism. Brazil is indeed "occupied" by its own army, and that's not the best arrangement in the world. But before Brazilians can govern their country successfully, they must learn to govern themselves. And right now it is the army that is giving them the time they need.

Our Lady of Fatima Chapel, Brasilia.

COFFEE

The Market Doesn't Forgive
Too Much Output Too Late

IN 1962 and 1963, the worst drought in the modern history of Paraná and São Paulo states hit these two prime coffee-growing areas of Brazil. With the drought came waves of forest fires and ruinous frosts.

As a result of these calamities, the 26,000,-000 bags of coffee Brazil produced in "coffee year" 1963-64 (a "coffee year" runs from October 1 to September 30) plummeted to 11,000,-000 in "coffee year" 1964-65. Such a drop has wide implications because Brazil has traditionally accounted for more than 40 per cent of world coffee exports.

Twenty-four countries and territories in Latin America export coffee: Every republic except Argentina, Chile, and Uruguay, plus Guadalupe, Jamaica, Martinique, Puerto Rico, Surinam (Dutch Guiana) and Trinidad. In coffee year 1963-64, Brazil copped 40.1 per cent of the world market, Colombia 12.6 per cent, Venezuela 8 per cent, the Western Hemisphere as a whole 71.2 per cent. The importance to the economies of these countries of their coffee exports usually far exceeds their large chunk of the world market.

For Colombia with only 12.6 per cent of the world market, for instance, coffee accounted for 71 per cent of its foreign exchange earnings. Guatemala earned 62 per cent of its dollars from coffee, El Salvador 57 per cent, Brazil and Costa Rica each 53 per cent, Haiti 48 per cent.

Such heavy reliance on coffee is particularly hazardous, for the coffee backlash from crop fluctuations is slow in coming. A coffee tree does not begin to display sizable numbers of the bright cherries which contain two coffee beans each until it is three to five years old, and for another five to ten years the tree's yield increases. Thus if coffee is a good source of income in a given year and everyone starts planting more of it, only five years later will the extra coffee begin to flood the market, driving down coffee prices and dislocating national economies.

The recent history of Brazilian coffee dramatically illustrates the momentum of extreme reactions to coffee price changes. In 1953 and 1955, Brazil had catastrophic weather like that of 1963. The consumer felt the frosts in 1954, when he had to pay over a dollar a pound on the average for coffee: The highest post-war price to date. The 1955 bad weather gave prices another boost: The 98-cent average in 1956 was the second highest post-war price.

Coffee growers reacted by enthusiastically starting new seedlings in huge quantities. Five years later, mountains of green coffee beans begged to go to New York for roasting, but importers could pick and choose. Like a street full of competing gasoline stations, the Latin American neighbors began to cut each other's—and their own—throats by slashing prices. Nevertheless, coffee stockpiles mounted. The leg on which many of these countries had been placing most of their weight suddenly became very shaky, and economies and governments threatened to topple.

The buyer and seller reacted to this extreme situation in a more organized way than they had to other climactic moments in coffee's history. In 1962 they set up the machinery for the International Coffee Agreement, in which 36 coffee-producing and 23 coffee-consuming nations today are joined to regulate world coffee trade.

The Agreement brakes producers by setting maximum export quotas, and controls importers by setting a minimum price for green coffee. The Agreement is not altogether successful in policing its far-flung beat: Prices have fallen below the established minimum, reaching in August 1963 the lowest level since 1950.

But prices have climbed sharply since then. March green coffee prices reached their peak since 1957. They have tapered off slightly since, but consumer prices, slow to catch up, still climb.

More Coffee, Fewer Sippers

High prices seem bizarre when two factors are taken into account. Per capita consumption is falling in the United States, which drinks over half the world's coffee, and stocks of coffee in the United States are at one of their highest levels in history. But with the cold winds that blighted coffee crops in Paraná and São Paulo breathing down the necks of buyers, they continue to lay in supplies, and the price stays high as a result.

The choosiness of the U.S. coffee importer rather than scarcity of supplies drives the price up. Brand name coffee makers, seeking to keep the same flavor in order to keep the same consumers, insist on purchasing good quality green coffee beans, and shun Brazil's vast supply of older coffee. Brazil has perhaps 4,000,000 bags of coffee of the freshness and quality sought out of a total of 50,000,000 bags stockpiled from the crops of 1962-64.

The quantity of Brazil's coffee, not its quality, gives it the reins in world trade. Coffee is traditionally divided into two types: "Brazils" and "milds", and the milds are considered better. The best Latin American milds come from Colombia, Jamaica, and Costa Rica. All except the most expensive coffees blend Brazils with milds or with other Brazils.

The search for mildness and the better aroma and flavor which tend to accompany it dictate the location of coffee plantings. Fussy coffee trees dislike great heat, are even less fond of too much sun, and give up the ghost altogether if frost settles on them. Consequently coffee is grown primarily on tropical mountainsides, where the temperature stays mild (the best range: 65-75 degrees) and shade relieves the direct torch of the sun part of the day. The altitude range is wide—1500 to 6000 feet. The farther from the equator, the lower coffee must be grown to avoid frosts. On the other hand, the higher the trees within the range of possible altitudes, the milder the coffee. It's little wonder the best Colombian milds cost half again as much per pound as Brazils and blends.

At first glance a high price would seem disadvantageous to the U.S. citizen. Not necessarily so. If the price of green coffee drops 30 cents per pound, as it did between 1959 and 1963, the loss in revenue to Latin America equals all foreign aid to the area for a year. Since almost all imports into Latin America come from the United States, the U.S. stands to lose much export income from a drop in the buying power of coffee countries.

The bright, bean-containing cherries are stripped from coffee trees, the first leg in their journey to the cup.

Coffee, of course, generates many jobs in Latin America, where it employs 13,000,000 people. An outline of the steps in coffee production shows why so many are employed in bringing coffee to its drinkers.

Coffee lands are seeded by slips or by an unusual process wherein the top of an existing tree is plugged into the ground. It sprouts roots in a few months. Young coffee trees are kept to themselves in shaded groves. They are replanted twice, ending in their third, final, least shaded home at the age of 18 months. There they grow into tangled patches which are constantly pruned so that the pickers can make their way among the plants.

Each tree is picked several times a season, so that the bean-containing cherries will leave the tree when just ripe. Trees are picked by hand; no machine has yet been invented which can replace a skilled manual picker, who garners 100 to 125 pounds of cherries a day, which yield 25 to 30 pounds of beans, which in turn

reduce to 20 to 25 pounds when roasted. The beans are washed and dried, a several-week series of processes, some by hand, some by machine. On plantations which place a high value on the quality of their coffee, the good beans and the bad are then separated by hand. The green beans then go into bags, usually the 60-kilogram (132+ pounds) bags, which are the standard measure for coffee, and are shipped off to market.

Roasting is done in the country of the importer. A coffee's taste and aroma depend importantly on the roasting process, but even more on the science of tasting. Coffee tasting is among the most delicate operations in the world. Those who practice the art train from an early age to develop their palates and probosci. Their sensitive decisions influence the purchase and the purchase price of coffees.

Because most of the myriad steps between a small coffee tree and a bag full of green coffee beans can be done by hand—most *have* to

The trees are picked by hand several times a season.

Separated from the cherries, the beans are then washed.

be done by hand—coffee is an agricultural product which can be grown economically in small plots by individual land owners. Around Medellín in Colombia, home of the world's top coffees, some farmers eke out an existence on 25 acres. Cooperative machines for the washing and drying now serve communities where many small patches produce coffee.

On the other hand, since each tree yields only a pound of roasted coffee, and since the seedling-to-market road is such a long one and involves so much labor, and since one long process, the washing and drying, can best be done in quantity and by large machines, the prospects for one-family coffee farms are not good.

But the one-family coffee plantations where a single family owns a gigantic tract of land worked by many others probably will not continue either. There is growing agitation for agrarian reform on coffee lands.

The coffee industry presently faces a number of questions. The International Coffee Agreement has already increased the export quotas originally set: Should these quotas be increased further to compensate for Brazil's diminished crop? If export quotas jump, would an unhealthy step-up in coffee production result? Would this encourage coffee countries to continue to rely on one product?

Diversification to avoid the see-saw syndromes of one-product economies is desirable, and is being carried out in many countries, among them Brazil, Colombia, and Mexico. But diversification presents problems too, for usually coffee lands are turned to production of food products, which, distributed within the country, do not lure the foreign revenue necessary for development.

Coffee, then, is vitally important to the countries that grow it, perhaps even more important than it is to the bleary-eyed American who each morning reaches for the cup that primes the body and restores the soul.

The beans dry in broad, sunlit patios for four to eight days.

The man who rules upon a coffee's quality—the taster—considers the evidence.

Pan-American Coffee Bureau

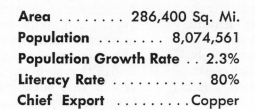

Area	286,400 Sq. Mi.
Population	8,074,561
Population Growth Rate	2.3%
Literacy Rate	80%
Chief Export	Copper

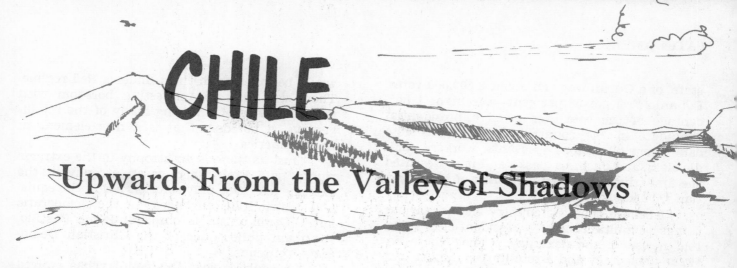

CHILE

Upward, From the Valley of Shadows

THE historic day started clear and warm, a harbinger of the South American spring that would soon lift the snow and rain from the beautiful mountains and valleys and lakes of Chile.

The country was nervous, but also strangely confident. "You will see," citizens of this proudly democratic republic repeated over and over. "There will be no trouble. This is Chile."

All morning on September 4, 1964, Chile's crucial election day, this patient people waited in long lines to cast their vote. The women vote separately from the men and, in the "Red *barrio*" of San Miguel, the women waited in line eight hours—and then they voted against communism 2 to 1.

In the town of Los Andes, 16 Catholic nuns left their house for the first time since taking their vows—to vote. In the Santiago suburbs, there was a carnival atmosphere. Both rich and poor voted in the same polling places. "Here there are no class prejudices," said one ragged old man as he walked into the Military School polling place in front of an elegantly dressed businessman.

This was the day that Chile was going to select as president in its moment of crisis either a Marxist, Dr. Salvador Allende, or Christian Democrat Eduardo Frei. Both promised revolution for the economically and socially troubled country.

But it was feared that Dr. Allende's revolution would lead to a one-party state dominated by his Socialist-Communist coalition, the FRAP, or Popular Action Front. Senator Frei's slogan, on the other hand, was "revolution in liberty."

By 4 p.m., the soldiers were drowsing against the buildings from boredom, and the first returns were beginning to come in. In Allende headquarters, Allende men started writing down the votes as they came over the radio.

About 10 blocks away, at Frei headquarters, a giant blackboard was jubilantly dropped out the front window, with scores kept up to date.

By 8 p.m., Frei was 400,000 votes ahead, and at 8:35 p.m. Salvador Allende emerged, his square, amiable face tight, from a meeting with his chiefs.

For 15 months he had sought the presidency, working day and night to bring the first socialist government to Chile. Now, while his aides wept, with a choked voice he told about 1,000 of his supporters outside his headquarters to accept his defeat "calmly and with dignity," as in the distance came the victorious shouts of "Frei si, viva, viva, viva Frei."

It had been the most widely watched election in Latin America in a decade or more, and some thought it would be the ideological turning point. Chile is the most democratic, one of the most cultured countries in Latin America. It considers itself European and looks down just a little on the "Indian" and "tropical" Latin countries. Chileans like to hear themselves called "the Englishmen of South America."

At this moment in 1964, with all Latin America at an ideological crossroads, torn by old fears and prides, poised between the old authoritarian dictatorships of the right and the possibility of new totalitarian dictatorships of the left, as in Cuba, Chile made its choice.

In the freest of elections, in an atmosphere of scrupulous legality and respect for the electoral niceties, the Chilean people overwhelmingly rejected the possibility of a one-party state, of a Cuban way. Of about 2,500,000 votes, Eduardo Frei got 56 per cent—the highest percentage of the vote ever given a presidential candidate in the country's history. His vote came from all sectors—peasants, workers, middle class, and business class—and it represented the first triumph in Latin America of the Christian Democrat philosophy.

"I believe that the country elected various things simultaneously," President-elect Frei told newsmen the next day. "They chose between democracy and a totalitarian danger, but it was not simply this. They don't want to keep living under the present modes. They have seen the present form as very limited. In one word, this country wants change, but it does not want to sacrifice liberty. However, liberty signifies little to those living in misery."

A Warning From Haya

The reasons for Eduardo Frei's outstanding victory at Chile's moment of decision are many, but one unmistakable element was fear of communism. A well-financed and well-organized campaign of anti-communism increased in temper every day during the last weeks of the campaign.

One day there was published in the papers a "letter from the Cuban mothers," warning the mothers of Chile against what communism would do—"send your sons to the *paredón*" (the wall). The next day brought a warning from Peruvian *Aprista* leader Victor Raúl Haya de la Torre, which particularly irked Allende, because he said, "I was invited to Haya's birthday party in 1960 and I was the same man then as now."

There were letters from former president Manuel Urrutia of Cuba, now estranged from Castro, and the night before the elections, Juana Castro, Fidel's sister, broadcast specially from Buenos Aires. The streets were filled with posters with pictures of Cuban peasants being shot by Castroites.

Allende was gradually driven to the wall by the campaign, whose charges he never answered fully. Nor did he ever fully repudiate the Cuban way, although he repeated over and over that Chile had "different realities" and therefore could have socialism in a different way.

But there was not only fear of communism, particularly on the part of the women, who were told daily on the radio that their children would be taken from them under a Red regime. There was also an interesting boredom with the whole idea of it among many of the intelligentsia—a boredom that is a new element in Latin America.

"Just as there is an atrophy in the extreme right," said Frei, "there is an atrophy in the extreme left. Our only solution lies in the equitable distribution advanced by the democratic left." Communism is obsolete, Jaime Castillo, the main philosopher of the Christian Democrats, contends.

"The fact is that this country has evolved socially and economically and arrived at a different solution in history. It is a new epoch, a new step, a new situation."

On the other hand, there was a distinct freshness about the ideas of Frei that was not lost on the people. There was the feeling of a new, untried way that incorporated all the things dear to Chileans—Christian ideals without direct church interference, economic planning, anti-communism with constructive alternatives, democracy and respect for the individual.

Dr. Salvador Allende.

Eduardo Frei.

Allende's meetings had the taste of the past, of Socialist meetings of the '30s. Frei's meetings, even during the campaign, had a feeling of newness, of jubilance.

There was, too, of course, the great promise of change—change for the barefoot peasant in his primitive cart lumbering across the countryside, change for the shantytown dwellers, change for the mother, and change for the child. And, for the large, sensible middle class of Chile ("We are pragmatists," says one Chilean scholar. "You will find few saints here), there was the common sense and justness of Eduardo Frei, a learned man who gives the impression of having suffered over his ideas.

"We are not nationalists," Frei will say. "We are always ready to listen. We ought to have a word in the world because we have our own personality. If we always look outside for blame, this too is a form of dependence. We must look for our own blame to find our own personality."

And behind these unusual words, behind the exemplary behavior of election day and the gigantic tolerance of the people is the unusual mixture of characteristics and contradictions that is Chile.

Chile, first of all, is in a hangover from feudalism. The peasantry is not racially divided as in other Latin American countries; they are white Europeans, a fact that shocks many observers at first glance.

In the giant *fundos* (big farms) of this long, thin country, many men still work as "renters" for two *escudos,* or 60 cents, a day. By contract, and not because he is sold with the land as was until recently the case in Peru, he works 6 days a week, 8 hours a day in winter, 12 in summer. He understands that the master orders and he obeys.

This might have gone on longer, except for the shortsightedness of the *fundo*-owners, almost all of whom now live in Santiago and haven't increased their production.

Last year alone agricultural output went down 11 per cent—it has been going down steadily for 20 years—and the people of Chile were, simply, hungry. This meant that the country, which is $2 billion in debt, had to import $100 million worth of food a year, adding to its severe economic problems.

A Worn-Out Frame

The Chilean peasant is a quiet and, as they say in Spanish, a "closed" man, unviolent, unexpressive. He lives in the shadows of two long mountain ranges (those shadows meet in his valleys) and of a system which has both protected him and used him for 400 years. But he has a deep feeling of patriotism. One Chilean peasant, unable to find a job, went to Argentina to work and, when asked about it by the Argentines, said quietly, "It is not Chile's fault that she cannot give me work."

The frame of Chile, however, is worn out. None of it—not social, not economic, not political—works anymore. It doesn't correspond to the reality inside the people. Peasants have been leaving the land and going to the cities, where they settle in the giant *callampas* ("mushrooms"), or shantytowns that ring the city.

Through the usual process of development —but strangely without the violence attendant upon this in other countries—they have arrived at a point where they have enough pride and security to want to be a part of society. An un-

Paul Conklin

New doors opening for a "closed" man.

shaven workman said, in the simple poetic language that the Latin American poor often use: "We don't have any way to arrive at a civilized life. We always have to be in the shadow of the mountains."

What confuses many observers in Chile is that, despite the rigid class system that has put these people outside of society, outside of a dignified life, there has been this real spirit of democracy and, in particular, a genuine respect for law.

Frei and the Christian Democrats, who get their inspiration from the Christian Democratic parties in Europe but are of much more revolutionary cut, explain this by saying that Chile has been a political democracy, but not an economic and social democracy. And the Christian Democrats, according to the scholars who have studied them, are exactly the angry products of this same structure.

"The oligarchy always used to absorb the middle classes," explained Dr. Eduardo Hamuy, the University of Chile's noted sociologist. "The mining bosses were absorbed, and the new entrepeneurs. The oligarchy never started a new enterprise, never initiated anything, but they always absorbed every group. They mixed socially and the new groups married into the circle of the elite. Even the family names changed in this process of absorption."

Then, after World War II, he continued, a new middle class began to grow, but now there was no room for them in the upper class inn. "They developed new industries, but now there was no more room for newcomers. Now they were not absorbed. It was an economic fact. The best businesses were monopolized by the old oligarchy and the first industrialists and there was no capacity to satisfy the aspirations of the new group. These people . . . are the leaders of the Christian Democrats."

"A Vigilance of Christian Values"

At the same time, new ideas were coming from Europe, particularly through the Roman Catholic Church. Influenced by the ideas of Jacques Maritain and the other modern Catholic philosophers, a new group of Jesuit priests began reforming the church in Chile at the same time that a group of young rebels, led by Eduardo Frei, were breaking away from the old church-related conservative party to form the Christian Democrats.

To Jaime Castillo and the Christian Democrats, the party philosophy has "universal roots, it is a vigilance of Christian values."

But it grew through savvy political methods that are now paying off. It organized and used many approaches of the Communists. First, ten years ago, the Christian Democrats captured the student federations (in almost all other Latin countries, these are strongholds of Communist strength). They got the teachers' associations and then they began to work inside the labor unions.

"One thing we did," says one of the founders, Enrique Matta, "is to confront the Marxists on their own ground."

Cells inside factories have now grown in influence. Students are wildly enthusiastic. They did not take vacations in 1964. Instead, for four months, they went to the rural areas and built 5,000 classrooms, taught 150,000 persons how to read and write and worked for community development and agrarian reform. Since 50 per cent of the population is under 21, this enthusiasm among the young is of singular importance.

To Dr. Hamuy and other scholars, the Chris-

tian Democrats represent a new kind of spiritually-inspired (their principles are taken from the social doctrines of the Roman Catholic Church) but technically-minded man in Latin America. "They are in the model of American entrepreneurs," says Dr. Hamuy, who is not a Christian Democrat. "They believe in introducing new business techniques and they believe in rationality in administration."

Partly for these reasons the Christian Democrats do not exploit nationalistic feelings, and tend to think rationally about things that are emotionally exploited in other countries.

"We are not conformists," says Frei, speaking of relations with the U.S. "One (conformity) is handing everything over to the United States and being always tied to what the United States dictates. The other is to deliver ourselves to the declaration 'anti-imperialist' which doesn't advance our defense or interests one step."

He said the day after his election that he hoped for the "best possible relations with the American people, whom I admire in an extraordinary degree."

"Sarcophagus of Ideas"

Frei will take some power away from the U.S.-owned copper mines because "we cannot have a foreign state within our state." He may put the production sector in the hands of the state. He will doubtless insist upon a more workable Organization of American States, which he calls a "sarcophagus of ideas," and for changes in the American system. He says he favors peaceful ways of bringing Cuba back into the hemispheric system.

For weeks after Frei's victory, the country was still living in the euphoria of election night. As the figures began to pile up for Frei, the Chileans took to the streets in Santiago in a wildly jubilant and immensely good-natured jam. They paraded down the middle of the streets, waving their torches, and banged out "Viva, viva, viva Frei" on the sides of their cars.

People waved flags and shouted songs and wore masks and blew through New Year's Eve noisemakers. The city reverberated to the victory. Then, at midnight, the good-natured and fatherly Chilean police told people quietly, "You'd better go home now, you must be tired."

That is Chile.

Bogotá

COLOMBIA

ECUADOR

BRAZIL

0   300
Miles

P E R U

Area . . . . 439,513 Sq. Mi.
Population 16,069,000
Population Growth Rate . . 2.9%
Literacy Rate 63%
Chief Exports . . . . . . Coffee, Oil

COLOMBIA

From Furious Politics, Curious Government

COLOMBIA is now wondering what in the world it takes to achieve meaningful political stability. In 1958, the country somewhat desperately decided on a coalition form of government in which the leading antagonistic parties, the Liberals and the Conservatives, would take turns running the nation. While moderates in both parties have succeeded in making this odd scheme work, "the System," as it is known in Colombia, is now threatened by extremists of the left and the right who have splintered off from the traditional parties.

The current political strife is particularly vexing because Colombia is making substantial strides in other, and one would think, more difficult areas. The bloody banditry that has ravaged the interior as the legacy of Colombia's 10-year civil war is at last coming under control. Only scattered bands of marauders now roam highlands where two years ago Colombian soldiers feared to set foot.

More importantly, the government has made notable progress in preparing for social reforms and economic development. Before the Alliance for Progress came into being, Colombia's enlightened although often slow-moving oligarchy had passed agrarian and tax reform laws. Colombians embraced the Alliance program: Colombia was the first Latin American country to have a 10-year plan for economic growth approved by the Alliance. In many ways the country is regarded as an Alliance "showcase." It is a political showcase, too, but more as a curiosity than as a likely model for other Latin countries.

Under "the System," until 1974 all government offices will be divided evenly between the Liberals and the Conservatives and the four-year presidential terms will be alternated between the two parties. In 1962 the transition of the presidency from Liberal Alberto Lleras Camargo to Conservative Guillermo León Valencia was accomplished smoothly enough. In practice this unique set-up has survived fairly well. But dissident elements at either end of the political spectrum have been growing in power because of mounting inflation and the hesitant pace of a government administering through compromise.

Colombia adopted this coalition government, called the National Front, after four years of dictatorship and a decade of civil fighting in which more than 200,000 people died. The civil strife erupted in 1948 after a popular Liberal leader was assassinated in the highland capital of Bogotá. *La violencia* pitted brother against brother, village against village. Weary of the bloodlust, Colombians turned in 1953 to General Gustavo Rojas Pinilla, who pledged to end the fighting. Rojas instead installed a dictatorship, which lasted until 1958 when he was deposed. By 1964, army patrols were mopping up the last of the mountain bandits.

Although officially barred from politicking, Rojas has been seeking to return to power. *Rojistas,* followers of the aging dictator, pose the greatest threat to the continuation of the National Front. The *Rojistas,* as well as the extremist groups of the left, are capitalizing on the soft spots arising from Colombia's rapid industrialization and urbanization in the postwar years. Unemployment in the summer of 1964 reached 10 per cent of the work force.

The softest spot of all is coffee, which ac-

In Colombia, dedicating Latin America's largest housing project, 1961.

counts for more than 70 per cent of the nation's exports. The Colombian economy suffered severely with the world-wide drop in coffee prices until the trend was sharply reversed late in 1963. A penny a pound drop in coffee prices means the loss of $6,000,000 in annual revenue for Colombia.

To lessen its dependence on the vagaries of the world coffee market, Colombia has been strenuously pushing agricultural diversification. The country's soil and climate are amenable to the cultivation of numerous crops and Alliance for Progress officials have been helping farmers grow tropical fiber crops such as yucca and kenaf, which are used in the manufacture of bags. A nationwide campaign to increase the production of cacao may make the country self-sufficient in that product within a few years.

Improved methods of breeding and feeding livestock are being introduced. Technical schools offer training in the use and maintenance of farm machinery. Agricultural credits are available to farmers and land distribution and colonization programs are making slow headway. But Colombia remains a land where one per cent of the landowners hold more than half the land

and much of the rest is split into small plots that provide a bare subsistence living for the owner.

In the far more ticklish field of monetary policy the government devalued the peso from 6.7 to 9 to the dollar in November 1962. Government operating costs have been cut sharply and through vigorous income tax measures the government now gets nearly half its revenue from personal and corporate incomes. Colombia has maintained a steady five per cent increase in the gross national product.

With no history of expropriation, Colombia is highly attractive to foreign investors. The country puts no strings on the repatriation of capital or profits by foreigners. International financing institutions have loaned Colombia more money than any other Latin American country. The World Bank, noted for the stringency of its requirements for loan projects, is financing a $45,000,000 loan for a hydroelectric plant to service Medellín, the country's leading industrial center over the last 60 years. The loan is for 35 years, the longest the Bank has ever granted. The Bank favored the Medellín project because it considered plans for the facility the best ever submitted to it by a power agency.

Colombia's vigorous business class has taken imaginative steps to make the country's light industry more self-supporting. Typical of such steps is the planning for a plant to produce polyester fiber, presently imported. The plant will give an added boost to the textile industry, which has grown rapidly in recent years. Colombia now ranks among the leading South American nations in textile production.

Improvement of the 2,000-mile railroad system is under way although Colombia's mountainous terrain makes railroad construction difficult and costly. Once completed the system will open rich timber reserves along the Pacific and Atlantic coasts. Colombia's flourishing timberlands and promising mineral deposits remain largely unexploited because of a lack of adequate transportation. Half the land is covered by forests.

Colombia is a country replete with contrasts that are reflected in the reaction of the people in various regions to economic challenges. If a man is ambitious, industrious, and confident he is taken for an *Antioqueño;* that is, he is probably from that mountain area with thin soil surrounding industrial Medellín.

The Happy-Go-Lucky Costeños

The coastal areas, conversely, are inhabited by purportedly happy-go-lucky Negroes known as *costeños.* Blessed with excellent ports on both the Atlantic and the Pacific, the coastal Colombian has been slow to take full advantage of his opportunities. The government is paying increased attention to the coast with special emphasis on improving the fishing industry. Inferior hotels in the coastal cities have hurt a tourist industry considered potentially lucrative because of the lovely beaches on both coasts.

Colombia has pioneered in programs of public health. Recently water supply and sewage system projects have been introduced in nearly 400 towns. In the town of Candelaria in the center of the Andes, for instance, a health program started six years ago today is a major testing ground for methods of public medical care.

But for all these signs of moving forward, large sectors of the population remain poor and

Guillermo León Valencia.

increasingly impatient. More than half the population makes its living off the land and it will take years before the new agrarian reforms will reach most of these peasants. The growing labor class, which has no voice in the government, is becoming restive. When coffee prices fell, President Valencia introduced austerity measures that riled the workers. So, to mollify the workers, the government in 1963 voted wage increases of 25 per cent, speeding up an inflationary trend. Corruption in government has further rocked the Valencia administration, which has lagged at implementing reform laws.

The difficulty in Colombia is that while it is forging ahead in many areas of social reform and economic development, it may not be moving fast enough for an expanding population with expanding expectations. The months before Colombia's 1966 presidential elections, when "the System" calls for a Liberal, will be critical. A political upheaval could well bring about a new era of dictatorship—and the destruction of the Colombian "showcase."

0 300
Miles

Pacific Ocean

COLOMBIA

Quito ⊛

ECUADOR

Guayaquil ◉

PERU

Area . . . . 106,508 Sq. Mi.
Population 4,596,000
Population Growth Rate . . 3.0%
Literacy Rate 64%
Chief Export . . . . Bananas

ECUADOR

Strange Interlude of the *Dictablanda*

THE favorite joke in Ecuador these days goes, "We don't have a *dictadura,* we have a *dictablanda.*" It's a nice play on Spanish words, for while *dictadura* means dictatorship, *dura* means tough and *blanda* means soft.

The subject of the joke is a four-man military junta that has run Ecuador since July 11, 1963. Though the foursome—the heads of the air force, army, navy, and military school—is indeed a dictatorship, it's a strange one for Latin America. The four strive to at least appear democratic, progressive, and liberal.

They drive around in their own cars, go to soccer games, change decrees when people complain, constantly inaugurate projects, and even "drink with the boys" in neighborhood bars. Their press chief says, without winking, that "this is the most perfect democracy in Latin America. In other countries, the military rules behind the scene. Here, they are in charge."

Of course, Ecuador today, a beautiful, chopped-up little country of 4,450,000 persons, is no democracy. But the people say things like, "After all, they're not as bad as the elected presidents," or "Things haven't gotten better, but they haven't gotten worse."

The man the junta forced out, Carlos Julio Arosemena, had embarrassed the country so much by his drinking there was little protest. The strange amalgam of political parties wasn't ready to take over in any responsible way. Outside of the old Conservative and Liberal organizations, the parties seemed like political clubs that got together just in time to run someone for office.

"When the junta came, there was a general feeling of uncertainty," says one U.S. diplomat.

"Arosemena had a philosophy of looking at Cuba with friendliness. There was a flight of capital. The *sucre* was devaluated. The Alliance for Progress wasn't moving at all."

The junta began early to assume political habits, like kissing babies. Recently on television, one junta member said they may have to stay in power a little longer than they thought, maybe four years; he added wistfully, "Well, the other fellows had four years. Are we any worse?"

The Alliance for Progress works with the junta now. "We do not have any iron clad rule," said Edward Castleman, deputy AID director in Quito. "We go case by case. It is a military junta and we're against that, but they're much more receptive to our programs than maybe an elected government would be."

In fact, the junta promised to develop the Alliance, and pushed through the Punta del Este reforms with a diligence that would startle some more democratic governments. But Ecuadoreans are well aware that the U.S. does not like dictatorships. Says one businessman in Quito, "This is a military dictatorship, and that keeps us from getting all the aid from the Alliance that we could get."

There is not, of course, any real constitutional freedom in Ecuador. Freedom of assembly is non-existent. When students tried to demonstrate in Central University in Quito early this year, the army moved in and the university closed. Student representation in the university government was reduced from 60 to 30 per cent before it opened again. There is freedom of the press, but newspapers are talked to, albeit gently, if they go too far. True, there are few political prisoners, and many are Communists. But the junta rules by decree, not by law or parliament, which it dissolved.

It is a paternalistic government, in keeping with the historically paternalistic structure of Ecuadorean society. Every Wednesday afternoon citizens are free to come to the white presidential palace, so pretty it resembles a Caribbean resort hotel, and tell the junta their needs. The air force chief is the most gregarious of the four, and is believed to be campaigning for the presidency, whenever that office is restored.

It is ironical that the Liberal Party, which fought hardest for years for constitutional government, is not complaining. Perhaps, explains former president Galo Plaza, one of the most respected democratic leaders in South America, this is "because they realize that the reactionaries want a return to constitutional government because they know nothing can get done."

Alfredo Muñoz López, leader of the Federation of Liberal Centers of Pichincha, the largest state, said, "We believe the junta is doing a practical job. All our relations with the junta are very cordial. In the beginning relations weren't so cordial, but now we realize we have to help them to do the work that will be effective."

Pedigree in the Highlands

But even he admits a fear that the Conservatives, who blocked reforms for years, would stymie change in a constitutional government. He indicated Liberals feel their best chance for structural change is through the junta.

On July 11, 1964, the junta passed the country's first land reform bill to mark its first year in office. Gradually it is abolishing the historic *huasipungo*, Indian servitude to the land. First, all state lands will be divided, then the big estates broken up. It affects blocks of land bigger than 400 acres in the mountains and 750 acres on the coast.

Tax and budget reforms have impressed U.S. officials. Formerly, different products had many taxes—beer alone had 35—which went directly to autonomous regional agencies which were more like little states. Now all taxes are paid into and dispersed from one central fund.

"The primary objective of the junta is the restructuring of the country," says Rear Admiral Ramón Castro Jijón, one of the ruling four, "establishing firm bases for new political statutes to constitute a new Ecuador, discarding the institutions that have grown old or have been corrupted, and, above all, the *caudillos*, who have converted the democracy of the republic into a caricature."

There is surprisingly little opposition to the junta. "They're better than the guys we've elected," say many Ecuadoreans. Galo Plaza traces this seeming acceptance of things to the Ecuadorean society that, in contrast to the political situation, has been fluid for some time.

An End to Huasipungo

"Why," he asks, "are the pressures in Peru, for instance, not present here? For one thing, in Lima you have this tremendous urban concentration in one place. Here we have two major cities—Quito and Guayaquil. In Peru you could never have a national airline as we have, without subsidies, going back and forth between two major cities.

"Here the old families live in the highlands. They have the pedigree, but the people with money are in Guayaquil—Lebanese and Indian merchants. When you have a society open at both ends, there's no way of creating pressures. In a list of 200 of the most powerful names in Ecuador, for instance, you'll find that 90 per cent of them are from the middle class. Almost none are known socially, so there's no target, like the oligarchy.

"The middle class has run things here for a long time. The oligarchy lives quietly in their valleys. Why, their children haven't even been going to the universities. At the same time, the children of many of their servants are going. Now the oligarchy's children are occupying lower jobs in the government and they find their servants' children have big jobs."

For illustration, he points to one junta member, the illegitimate son of an oligarchy family. Now the family has taken him back. "They've come down, he's gone up," says Mr. Plaza. "He's delighted."

Gonzalo Rubio, a noted sociologist with the National Planning Board, says there is a great coming and going of Indians and half-castes between the mountains and the coastal cities like Guayaquil which, while thriving, is surrounded by the worst slums in Ecuador. Guay-

Facing the Main Plaza in Quito is the Presidential Palace, an elegant structure that lacks nothing except a president. Surrounded by admirable scenery, Ecuadoreans acquire an appreciation of beauty at an early age.

Nowhere in Latin America is the church more conservative than in Ecuador.

aquil, however, in contrast to staid Quito, has been the more politically creative city.

Quito is an exceptionally beautiful and gentle city, ordered and stratified. Its setting is breathtaking, with green valleys and wooded mountainsides and white peaks all around. Hotel Quito, perhaps the most beautiful in Latin America, hangs on a cliff above the city.

Downtown is a series of almost oriental, checkered domes and European church spires. On the archbishop's palace appear the words: "You can as well glorify Babylon for its murals, Nineveh for its greatness, Athens for its literature, Constantinople for its empire. Quito conquers by the key of Christianity, and to this city belongs the discovery of the great Amazon River."

The church is the most conservative in Latin America. Several years ago the American Maryknoll priests, who are doing noteworthy work in the other Andean countries, angrily left Ecuador. "We simply could not work with the Ecuadorean church," one of them says.

Somewhere in all this is the explanation why, with the exception of Galo Plaza, Ecuador has had a series of strongmen as leaders who have done little for the country. Even after Plaza's excellent term of office, when he insisted on turning the government over to a freely elected president, Ecuador chose an old demagog, José María Velasco Ibarra.

Lately, however, the country's economic sit-uation has improved considerably. The *sucre* is sound. In the first three months of this year, foreign exchange was at an all-time high of $42,500,000. Per capita income increased from $119 in 1950 to $182 in 1962. Since 1950 there has been an annual increase of 5.47 per cent in the gross national product. Since 1962, CENDES, the government institute to promote industrial development, has spurred investments —about 80 per cent of them Ecuadorean—totaling $50,000,000, in 31 new industries, including plywood, refrigerators, and agricultural tools, since 1962, thus generating 8,000 new jobs. Runaway capital is coming back and other Latin American countries are now investing in Ecuador, whose economic rating had rested mainly upon its reputation as the world's leading banana grower.

The Alliance moves along steadily, but Ecuadoreans complain the aid comes too slowly. Americans complain that $70,000,000 in unspent loans is being wasted because Ecuadoreans lack experience in administering it. "Right now there is a big dam stopping everything," says an American official, "but one of these days the dam will break."

In contrast to some other Latin countries, Ecuador appears to be patient and non-violent. Right now it is showing a definite technical mentality and a concern for economic development, but there is no guarantee that even four men on horseback can ride herd indefinitely on a people grown weary of waiting.

PERU

ECUADOR COLOMBIA

BRAZIL

Pacific

Lima

Cuzco

BOLIVIA

Chile

0   300
Miles

Area . . . . 496,222 Sq. Mi.
Population 10,838,500
Population Growth Rate . . 2.2%
Literacy Rate 47%
Chief Exports . . . . . Fish, Cotton

Change and the Twilight of the *Criollo*

MANY THOUSANDS of feet above the sea stands a church some judge the most beautiful in Peru: *La Compañía de Jesus.* This rich and gracious monument to the Christian God rises on the spot where an Incan temple once graced the city of Cuzco, capital of the old Inca empire. In buildings attached to the church, the city had long maintained a modest university; but now, as more young people seek higher learning, the old quarters will no longer do and the university has recently been moved to larger buildings elsewhere in the city.

Thus the lovely church not only stands in the three worlds of Peru—the Indian, the Spanish and the modern—but it stands, too, in the midst of sudden change that is making those three worlds one. There is still a thick veneer of tradition—of traditional control of the economy by a small, aristocratic in-group, of traditional control of the culture by the old *criollo* way of life, of traditional control of politics by the old, shifting coalitions of aristocrats and workers.

Yet beneath this veneer everything is changing. New forces, unheralded and almost unnoticed, are coming to the fore. The country is beginning to move. And little more than two years after a military coup that seemed to bode no good for the nation's aspirations, the country has a freely-elected president who appears to be leading Peru into a new era of progress and democracy. Rumors of an imminent military takeover are persistent in Lima, but informed observers take little stock in them. President Fernando Belaúnde Terry, since his election in June, 1963, has convinced even most of his enemies that his program is sound,

honest, and very likely to be effective.

With a majority in congress generally opposing him, Belaúnde has managed to put through the country's first agrarian reform law, and he has made a beginning at revamping the tax system, building a marginal road to open up the lush jungle backlands and inaugurating a Peruvian Peace Corps. Too, he has instituted municipal elections for the first time in 42 years and he has started work on a variety of development programs financed by U.S. loans and U.S. grants.

Ostensibly against Belaúnde, but actually in agreement with him on many points, is the 40-year-old *Aprista* party, Peru's first reform party. The *Apristas,* formally known as the *Alianza Popular Revolucionaria Americana,* after fighting bitterly for change all those years and after seeing thousands of their people machine-gunned by Peru's series of dictators, are now faced with a popular reform president whose program calls for exactly the innovations that the *Apristas* had been dying for.

They have at times, with bitterness, opposed Belaúnde. But a few months ago they supported him and passed an agrarian reform measure aimed at dividing up all the big mountain *haciendas,* thereby changing the way of life of millions of Peruvian serfs, turning them into small landholders. The *Apristas,* however, did not agree to the bill before gaining an exemption for the big sugar and cotton plantations on the coast. It has long been an *Aprista* theory that these great holdings must not be chopped up because they can function economically only if they are big, and their well-being is essential to the nation's balance of trade.

Because of this stand, the other parties have accused the *Apristas* of growing old and conservative.

Criticism of Belaúnde, particularly from the left, is rife. He was supported by the Communists in the election, but has recently found it necessary to imprison Reds for agitation among the peasantry and to expel some top leftists in his own party, *Acción Popular*.

All of this represents a small turn to the right—not in programs but in an awareness that the Communists do not have the same interests as he does, an idea the U.S. State Department has been working hard to promote.

But the real importance of Belaúnde's administration is that a new class has come to power for the first time, the middle class composed of physicians, dentists, engineers, architects, and technicians who are no longer satisfied to let the oligarchy have its way, politically or socially.

The Imperfect Prefects

One of Belaúnde's prime beliefs is that the government must be decentralized. Until now all the departments, or states, have been completely dependent upon Lima, with no self-determination at all. They were ruled by prefects or sub-prefects appointed in Lima who took little interest in anything except collecting taxes to send to Lima.

Now, after last fall's municipal elections, every town in Peru has its own elected mayor and this innovation has had immediate repercussions. In the village of Pucará, for instance, the mayor was elected by the *campesino,* or peasant, vote, not the town vote. He immediately began calling regularly on the local American Peace Corps volunteer who lives with the *campesinos,* to ask him to help draw up a program to benefit the peasantry.

Everywhere in Peru there are new and interesting changes in the political balance of power. In Puno, for instance, two local brothers named Cáceres, who had been businessmen, organized a politically independent federation of *campesinos,* now numbering 80,000 members. These *campesinos* sent the Cáceres brothers to congress and captured nearly half the mayoralties in the municipal elections. If the vote is ever extended to illiterates, the *campesino* power will

grow enormously. But it will grow in any case as educational facilities are expanded.

In the booming fishmeal center of Chimbote, Mayor Guillermo Balcazar did an unorthodox thing recently. The city required 90 new school teachers to take care of its fast-growing population. The Ministry of Education, not known for its efficiency, sent only 20 teachers to Chimbote. So Balcazar did what no town had ever done in Peru; he went out and hired 45 teachers on his own, with the city paying the bill. By U.S. standards the action is hardly notable, but in Peru it was revolutionary. It shows how decentralization is changing the customs of

Fernando Belaúnde Terry.

the country, and how local governments are beginning to grasp not only power, but responsibility as well.

Most people still refer to the dominant culture in Lima (which to them means all of Peru) as *criollo*. This word means a number of things, but it mainly means a way of life dominated by the mestizos, or half-castes, and upper-class Lima residents. It means the "waltz *criollo*," the slow Latin waltz that they do in Lima. It means all the old niceties of a Lima that has long since ceased to be: Carved balconies, shy gentlewomen and dashing gentlemen, and certain ways of behavior as well as strict class differences.

Cuzco: Ancient ways persist in the mountains, but in Lima new values are bowing in.

But *criollismo* is already a thing of the past, although few people are really aware of it. Most sociologists now consider Lima a *cholo* city, an idea that would greatly shock the *criollos*.

Cholo is a term that can be used in many ways, but the broadest definition is "a citified Indian." It refers to the people from the mountains, to the Indians who have left their traditional culture and come down to the coast, looking for work and a better life. By upper-class *criollo* standards, the word is contemptuous. *Criollos* use *cholo* the way some Americans use the word "nigger." Yet *cholo* is a respectable word when used unemotionally.

Paul Doughty, a Cornell University anthropologist, is one who has traced the new *cholo* character of the city in several years of intensive study. "The city is 70 per cent *cholo*," he says. "It is becoming a *cholo* city, and the *cholos* aren't going to become *criollo* and they're not going to be Indians. They're going to be something new. They have a stake in both lives. The *cholo* is a transitional man, a marginal man."

The *cholo* is the Indian woman in western clothes who vends *anticuchos*, a meat delicacy, from her cart in the streets of Lima. It is the man selling shopping bags along the Jirón Unión, the maid, the new industrial worker, the waiter. They are alive and aggressive. They are bringing new values and a new vitality to an old and stratified society.

Peru's overall economic picture is bright. The budget is almost balanced, and exports and foreign reserves are climbing. Although prices have risen nine per cent in the last year, this is not serious inflation by Latin American standards.

Among Peru's strengths is a diversified list of exports; the country does not rise and fall with the price of a single product as so many of its neighboring countries do. It also has domestic savings that can be tapped, a well-developed commercial banking system and a growing class of resourceful entrepreneurs. On the debit side, Peru must begin to grow more of its own food; today the country buys $75,000,000 of foodstuffs abroad.

But the trend is up. Still hamstrung in many areas by a melancholy, impoverished Indian mentality and still facing many enormous problems, Peru is nevertheless rolling up its sleeves and getting to work. If it can keep its politics on an even keel, its prospects are good.

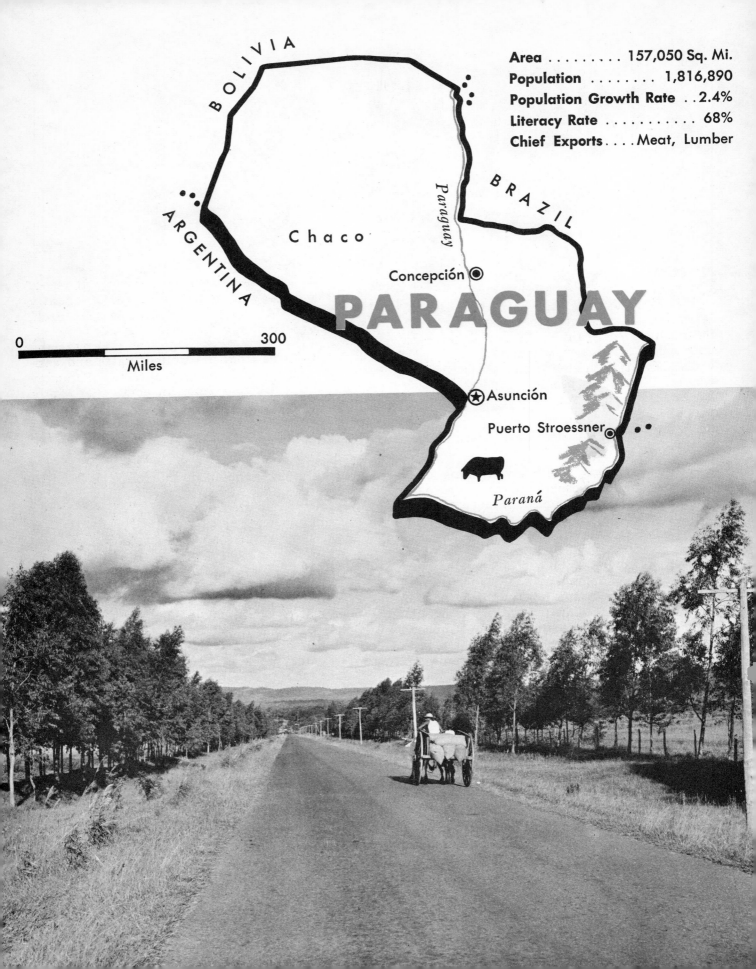

Area . . . . 157,050 Sq. Mi.
Population 1,816,890
Population Growth Rate . . 2.4%
Literacy Rate 68%
Chief Exports . . . . Meat, Lumber

BOLIVIA

ARGENTINA

BRAZIL

Chaco

Paraguay

Concepción

PARAGUAY

0   300

Miles

Asunción

Puerto Stroessner

Paraná

PARAGUAY

Under a Dictator, Short Steps Forward

GENERAL ALFREDO STROESSNER, president of Paraguay, is the latest in a long line of dictators that have oppressed this California-sized country since it became independent from Spain in 1811. But there are signs that Stroessner, though he runs the whole show, is enlightened enough to work for a better life for his people.

Not the least of the government's successes has been the nearly stable character of its currency in recent years, in contrast with most South American nations which have been experiencing soaring inflation. Living costs in Paraguay have risen only about five per cent in the last two years. Prices in Brazil, in contrast, are expected to rise at least 50 per cent this year, even though the military government there is making a major effort to restore integrity to the currency.

Nor is Paraguay protecting the *guaraní,* its monetary unit, by ignoring needed public improvements. The country recently inaugurated the long-talked-of road from Asunción, its capital, to the Bolivian border. The road is 475 miles long and cuts through the vast Chaco area, which contains some of the thickest, swampiest, most reptile-ridden jungle in the world.

A $30 million hydroelectric facility on the Acaray River near Puerto Stroessner is under construction; this project is aimed at opening up the undeveloped eastern part of the country adjoining Brazil. Several communities have sprung up along a new highway connecting Asunción with Puerto Stroessner; the new dam is expected to help make these towns grow fast.

In the grasslands of the south the chief industry is stock raising, and its outlook is bright. Exports of meat are currently at record levels—no small achievement for a country that has not always been able to feed itself, much less sell its farm output abroad.

But despite these signs of progress, and despite loans from the United States and various international lending agencies, Paraguay continues to suffer from an acute shortage of investment capital. In addition the country's development clock has been wound back by its history, which is notable chiefly for two disastrous wars. From 1864 to 1870 it was practically wiped out in a war against Argentina, Uruguay and Brazil. Paraguay not only lost the war, it lost 90 per cent of its male population. The country was eventually re-populated by foreign immigrants and by Brazilian soldiers who took up with the thousands of Paraguayan widows.

Paraguay also lost 55,000 square miles of territory to Brazil. In the Chaco War with Bolivia, 1932-1938, the Paraguayans won the 20,000 square miles of the Chaco, but the price was 60,000 Paraguayan men killed—more by disease and snake-bite than by the Bolivians.

The country was still reeling from the Chaco War when, in 1954, General Stroessner assumed power. The previous 15 years had been notable only for stagnation and crooked government. The government today is still crooked by American standards, but the country has at last begun to slog forward.

Compared to other Latin American nations, a high percentage of Paraguay's development projects have been started since the inception of the Alliance for Progress. In 1962, the country

GRAN HOTEL DEL I.P.S.

- UNA GRAN REALIZACION
- DIGNA DE UN GRAN GOBIERNO
- Y DE UNA GRAN INSTITUCION!

CONCEBIDA CON LOS AUSPICIOS
DEL EXMO. SR. PRESIDENTE DE LA
REPUBLICA GRAL. DE EJERCITO Don:
ALFREDO STROESSNER

GRA

Big Brother Stroessner.

established a secretariat for planning, and tax reforms were adopted. The government began a systematic redistribution of land in 1951, but it wasn't until last year that the measures were backed by a reasonably effective law. The Agrarian Statute provides for the breaking up and taxation of large estates, the merging of uneconomic small farms, and technical assistance and credit to farmers.

The Housing Institute set up in 1962 coordinates public housing programs for low-income families. The government has also embarked on a program to give most cities water systems within 10 years. It's too early to judge the success of these measures; what seems important to most Paraguayans is that the government is thinking about them—not about their freedom, or lack of it, but about their physical well-being.

Angry, But Not Too Angry

President Stroessner has made it a point in recent years to act the part of the genial, civilian politician. He permits an opposition party to hold a third of the seats in the legislature and to publish an angry—but not too angry—weekly newspaper. In 1963 he was re-elected to his second, full six-year term in a well-controlled election. Stroessner's enemies —tens of thousands of Paraguayans who find it healthier to live abroad—contend his police operate torture camps for political prisoners.

Such complaints are periodically filed with the Human Rights Commission of the United Nations. The complaints get nowhere because Stroessner won't let the U.N. group investigate them.

The Paraguayan is proud of the Indian element in the makeup of his country. Whereas the Indian occupies a lower place on the social and economic totem pole in neighboring nations, the Guaraní Indians native to Paraguay have so intermixed with the Spanish who colonized the land that racial distinctions have all but disappeared.

The Indians gave the country its name.

The Guaraní word *pararaguay* means "place with a great river." The great river referred to bears the name of the country in which it is a dominant delineator, source of wealth and means of communication.

The Paraguay River makes half of an elongated figure eight around the country. In the northeast it forms the border with Brazil for 200 miles; continuing southwest it splits the nation in two parts—on the southeast, the unusually, if latently, rich land where most of the population lives and where the city of Asunción is located, and on the northwest the marshy Chaco. Emerging at a point on the southwestern border, the Paraguay forms the border with Argentina for 200 miles, finally linking with the Paraná River which flows to the ocean 900 miles farther south.

The fertile eastern part of the country has long been shattered into uneconomic tiny farms, and the resulting poverty has caused large-scale migration to Asunción. That city is now almost hopelessly crowded and most of its inhabitants live in squalor. Only one-third of Asunción's population, for instance, is served by the municipal sewerage system and that system is the only one in Paraguay.

Hesitant Half-steps

For years the Spanish and Guaraní have combined their talents to produce one of South America's loveliest products: *nanduti* lace. Its name and its makers descend from the Guaraní; the style of lace-making itself, featuring circular construction, came to Paraguay with the Spanish conquistadors.

With a sub-tropical climate, fertile soil, and huge timber stands, Paraguay would seem suited to more than handicrafts. It can hardly prosper without a vast diversification of human skills and an efficient exploitation of natural resources. The country remains a dictatorship and social advances are slow in coming. But there are signs of progress, even though that progress is paced off in hesitant half-steps.

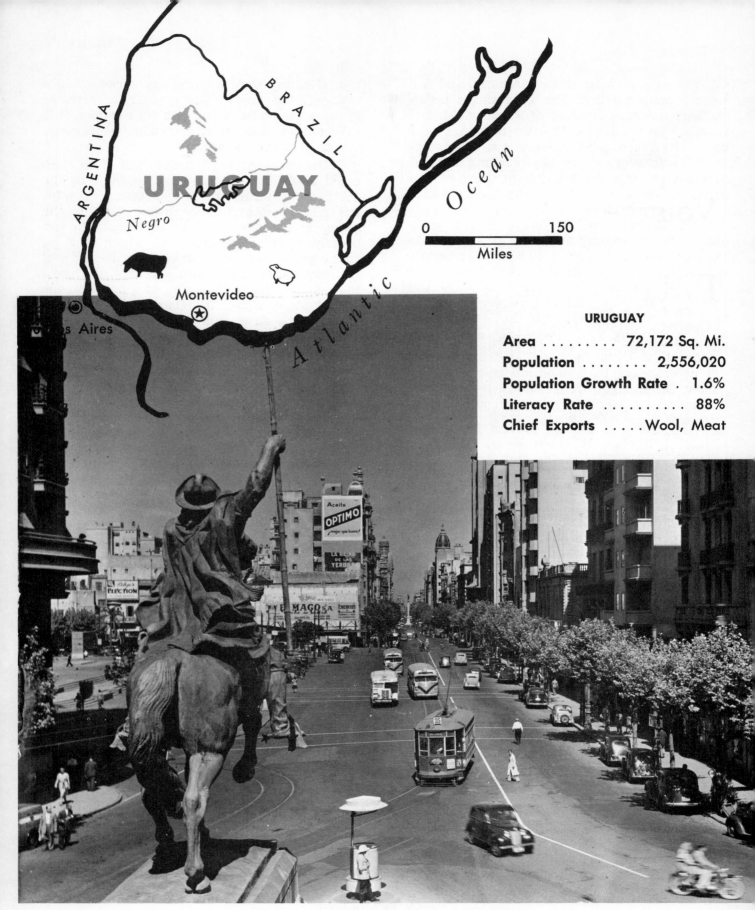

URUGUAY

Area	72,172 Sq. Mi.
Population	2,556,020
Population Growth Rate .	1.6%
Literacy Rate	88%
Chief Exports	Wool, Meat

Suddenly, beggars in the streets.

URUGUAY

Volatile Concoctions in a Liberal Laboratory

IT IS 13 miles from Carrasco Airport to downtown Montevideo, and most of the drive is made on a beautiful road next to the sea. Orange-tile rooftops glisten in the sun and well-tended lawns and sheltering palms remind the visitor that, while he is not in the tropics, he is nevertheless in a land unacquainted with snow. On all sides one senses a cleanliness and orderliness not common to the continent, and yet this first impression is deceiving. Uruguay in some ways is the most disorderly country in South America.

Since the early part of this century, when President José Batlle y Ordóñez began to move the country toward a government-regulated economy, Uruguay has been considered a showplace of welfare legislation and honest, democratic government. High value has been placed on popular rule, public education and economic security. Indeed, when compared with some of its South American sisters, in many ways the little republic has been an oasis of enlightenment. Unfortunately, for all the country's good intentions, the conspicuous lack of one virtue—moderation— has caused it many unnecessary problems.

Thanks to a political system that is unique in all the world, Uruguay seems unable to extricate itself from an economic morass that for years has kept the country near bankruptcy. Unemployment has continued to mount in 1964 and the value of the peso has plunged 40 per cent in the last year. Only high prices recently for wool and meat, the country's only important exports, have kept the economy going.

But the boost in foreign revenues is a temporary reprieve; factories are closing, the cost of living continues to climb, the government is practically broke, and beggars, once unknown in this country, are on the streets of Montevideo. And the worrisome thing is that even if Uruguayans suddenly reversed their thinking after 50 years of monumental boondoggling, it would be exceedingly difficult to adopt corrective measures. In its zest for representative government, the country has gradually destroyed the political tools with which to effect smoothly any basic changes.

Uruguay which, while the smallest of the South American republics, is nevertheless as big as all New England, is governed by a bicameral legislature and an executive that's not really an executive at all. Instead of a presidential or parliamentary system, Uruguay has a National Council of Government, a nine-member body that's supposed to do the job of one chief executive.

The four council members who were elected with the most votes take turns each year acting as council chairman and ceremonial president. This system was designed in 1951 to make it impossible for a dictatorship to emerge. In practice, the council functions as a third legislative body.

However unwieldy this setup is, it is pure efficiency when compared to a nearly anarchic party system. There are two main parties, the *Colorados* and the Nationalists (formerly the *Blancos*), as well as a scattering of minority parties, including a small Communist Party. The *Colorados* and the Nationalists are split into several factions which enjoy a legal status that makes them practically separate parties. Each faction is then split into sub-factions, and sub-factions within the same party often are more antagonistic to each other than they are to the other parties.

Uruguayans are not partial to compromise so the legislative machinery often breaks down completely.

But if the parties have no concept of unity they do possess a remarkable staying power. When the Nationalists whipped the *Colorados* in the 1958 election, it marked the first time they had been in control of the government in 93 years. The Nationalists tend to be more conservative than the *Colorados* but they don't dare press for the drastic economic reform measures that are needed. They are not anxious to be thrown out of office for another 93 years.

It is within this political framework that Uruguay's financial embarrassment must be viewed.

With a population of 3,000,000, the country's domestic market is small. It therefore must rely on exports to provide a decent standard of living for its people. But Uruguay is without mineral riches and its soil is suitable for growing little except grass. Livestock, therefore, is the country's economic base with wool alone accounting for 50 per cent of the foreign revenue. During the two world wars and the Korean War, Uruguay made huge profits selling wool and meat abroad. But between wars the country, largely because of the antediluvian operating practices of the livestock growers, has had trouble competing in world markets.

Faster Fattening

Uruguay today has fewer head of sheep and cattle than it had 70 years ago. It takes two to three years to fatten a steer for market in the United States. It takes four years in Uruguay, and the cattle are skinnier. Specialists from the University of Iowa are now trying to convince Uruguayan cattlemen that modern winter-feeding methods will make cattle fatter faster.

The country's utilities and other basic services are largely owned and operated by the government. There is a smattering of small manufacturing industries which Uruguayans got into reluctantly in the depression of the 1930s when they didn't have the money to buy what they needed abroad. Local manufacturers are protected by towering tariff walls and, since they face no external competition, they have declined to modernize their plants. Uruguayans are therefore rather inefficient manufacturers.

Billing itself as "the world's first welfare state," the nation takes great pains to see that its population is well insulated from economic reality. The government attempts to control prices by placing a ceiling on rents, by operating state-owned shops which sell goods at a loss, and by encouraging neighborhood vigilante squads that go around berating private merchants when they raise prices.

Foreign investment traditionally has been discouraged here. Fear of foreign economic control of the country, in fact, is what originally pushed the nation into government ownership of railroads, insurance companies, and other major services. This attitude has compounded the country's woes. Foreign-owned factories are closing at a rapid rate because of the profits squeeze. The foreign investor's costs are based on one value of the peso and his earnings, when withdrawn from the country, on another.

Moon-Lighting and Pensions

Significantly, Uruguayans don't get unemployed the way people elsewhere do; most of them hold two jobs and many work at three. Too, the system of unemployment benefits is so generous that workers can afford to be unconcerned when they are laid off; they collect between 25 per cent and 80 per cent of their take-home pay when they lose their jobs.

One incentive for working, however, is a pension system that is, well, typically Uruguayan. It works by points. A worker—whether he is in public or private employ—gets a point for each year of his age and another point for each year he has been working. With 90 points a fellow is entitled to retire with full pay based on his average wage of the previous five years, provided that not less than 30 points were accumulated on the job.

There is a provision entitling the 30-year worker to a six-month bonus when he calls it quits. If his 90 points include 36 years of work, he gets a bonus equal to 12 months' pay. If he's put in 40 years he gets a bonus of 18 months' pay.

Despite these incentives to stay on the job, it's not unusual for a Uruguayan to quit at age 50.

The pension system has two main drawbacks: It's helping to bankrupt the country and it is administered so inefficiently that it's customary for a retiree to wait three years for his first payment. According to one government official, some 20 per cent of all pension applicants die before they can collect anything.

But Uruguay is more than a big bungle. It is a land of friendly people, of tall prairie grass, of glittering beach resorts (such as Punta del Este), of gently rolling hills, and of winding rivers. The capital, Montevideo, is a handsome city, with modern office buildings and apartment houses standing in marked contrast to the ancient motor traffic. Because of import taxes, a new Chevrolet or Ford delivers in Uruguay for about $15,000 (although congressmen passed a law a few years ago entitling congressmen, and only congressmen, to buy a new car every two years without paying any import tax at all). Most autos are of pre-Pearl Harbor vintage, with Prohibition-era relics not uncommon.

A small country surrounded by big neighbors, Uruguay has historically supported international peace-keeping organizations. As a nation it will do almost anything if it can be convinced it is being "progressive" by doing it. But, unfortunately, this desire to be in the van of political pioneering and social engineering has been indulged in indiscriminately. And the cold breath of reality is now upon the republic.

Its choice seems clear. It can either free its economy and its people from the burden of a prodigal government, or it can go on spending and tinkering as usual, piling its meat and wool on the docks and hoping for some long and distant war.

Along with the gauchos, some fattening ideas from Iowa.

Monkmeyer

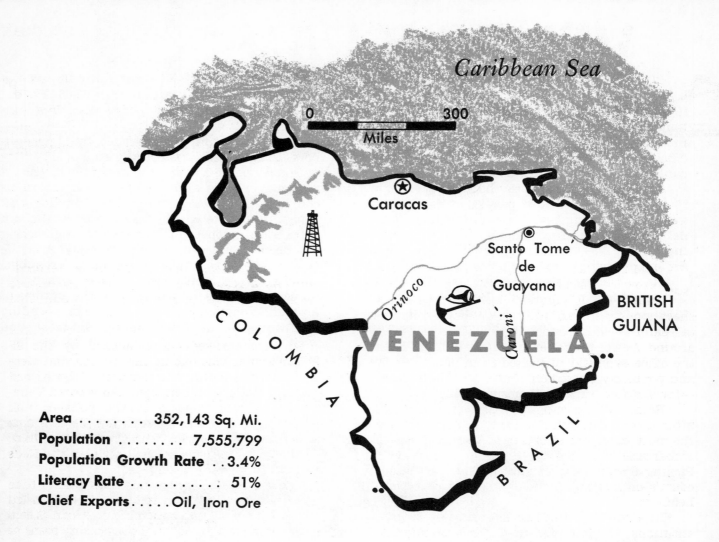

Caribbean Sea

0 ——————— 300
Miles

⭐ Caracas

Santo Tomé
de
Guayana

Orinoco

Caroní

COLOMBIA

VENEZUELA

BRITISH
GUIANA

BRAZIL

Area . . . . 352,143 Sq. Mi.
Population 7,555,799
Population Growth Rate . . 3.4%
Literacy Rate 51%
Chief Exports . . . . . Oil, Iron Ore

The steel plant at Santo Tomé de Guayana: Civilization comes to the interior.

VENEZUELA

Deep in the Bush, the Promise of Santo Tomé

ON MARCH 11, 1964, the dignitaries in the crowded senate chamber in Caracas watched in emotion-charged silence. A short, stout man carefully removed an ornamental band from around his neck and placed it around that of the taller man next to him. Thus the office of president passed from one honestly and popularly elected chief executive to another —for the first time in Venezuela's history.

Rómulo Betancourt, who left office that day after serving his full five-year term, had foiled the most strenuous efforts of the Communists to embarrass him and to discredit his regime. Picking up the reins of government was Betancourt's old colleague and fellow reformer, Raúl Leoni.

In a country that has known some 30 constitutions, 60 attempted revolutions, 20 successful overthrows of government and some of the harshest dictators in Latin America in its 135 years of independence, it was not surprising that Betancourt's term of office was marked by outbreaks of violence. But that he succeeded in parrying or beating back the worst his enemies could do is indeed surprising.

Even though Venezuela has shown it can support democratic institutions, the country remains almost under siege. Communist guerrillas infest the Falcón Mountains in the north and make-believe students mouthing the Red line regularly raise a ruckus on university campuses in Caracas. The guerrillas frequently toss bombs at communications installations and at the oil pipe lines that are the arteries of the nation's economy.

Nor is the U.S. Embassy taking any chances. A couple of years ago the top floor of the Embassy building was blown off by a terrorist bomb. As a result, security restrictions require visitors to apply for passes before being admitted into Embassy offices.

Interestingly, the Communist terrorism has so far boomeranged—as evidenced by the 95 per cent voter turnout in the presidential elections after the FALN, the terrorist-leftist Armed Forces of National Liberation, had warned Venezuelans to stay away from the polls or risk getting shot. But inasmuch as few Venezuelans seem interested in what the Communists have to say, bomb-throwing is the only way the Reds are able to get any attention.

Thus far, the country has been able to take the terrorist activities in stride and, while it led the fight in the Organization of American States to condemn Castro's Cuba for supplying arms to local Reds, Venezuela's chief concern is to diversify an economy that now rests almost entirely upon oil.

This aim at diversification is symbolized by a new city in east-central Venezuela called Santo Tomé de Guayana. The unusual nature of the city suggests that the country may be on its way to matching in the economic sphere the progress it has made in the political.

Santo Tomé is, first of all, a "designed" city. Starting almost from scratch, planning specialists from Harvard and the Massachusetts Institute of Technology set out to create a new city as beautiful as it is efficient. Its growth has been fantastic. In 1950, the population of three hamlets now absorbed by Santo Tomé was about 4,000. Today there are 70,000 in the city and the total is expected to zoom to 10 times that number within a few years.

Venezuelans queue up to vote: Some people don't scare.

Santo Tomé is the focal point in a plan to open up for development the great Guayana region, a sparsely populated area (see map) that accounts for roughly one-fourth of Venezuela's land mass and contains one of the most important concentrations of mineral resources in the Western Hemisphere.

"In a few years the Guayana will be the Ruhr of Latin America," confidently predicts a long-time American businessman in Venezuela.

It could be. The area is overflowing in natural resources. There are mountains of iron ore, deposits of gold, industrial diamonds, kaolin (clay for brick-making), manganese, titanium, and bauxite. In the southern and eastern regions

of Guayana, there are forests from which timber and pulp can be drawn. And the entire area is blessed with an excellent route to the sea. A channel dredged by a subsidiary of U.S. Steel enables all but the very largest ships to sail 175 miles from the Atlantic Ocean to Santo Tomé, at the confluence of the Orinoco and Caroní rivers.

Like so many areas in Latin America, the Guayana has long held immense promise that never has paid off in economic progress. Until quite recently, these resources were almost untouched. The reasons for this are very plain in Venezuela: A lack of capital, a scarcity of technical skills, and an almost incredible lack of initiative. Even today, with the Guayana project well under way, the government finds it difficult to get enough well-qualified Venezuelans personally interested and involved in the venture.

Still, the demands for industrial development continue to grow, and a close-up look at the Guayana project suggests some possible answers.

Vulnerable to Fluctuations

Although—thanks to its bountiful petroleum fields—Venezuela has achieved a higher economic level than most of its neighbors, it is still vulnerable to fluctuations in the world demand and supply of oil. Moreover, oil resources are exhaustible. So there is good reason for the government to seek a more diversified economy. Add to this the compelling fact that Venezuela's population growth rate of 3.1 per cent a year is among the highest in the world and it becomes clear why the government attaches some urgency to making the Guayana venture a success.

Guiding the Guayana development program is the *Corporación Venezolana de Guayana* (CVG), a public authority set up in 1960. Its president is Colonel Rafael Alfonzo Ravard, a gentleman who effectively combines the talents of engineer, philosopher and cosmopolite.

The most dramatic project in the Guayana today is the Guri Dam on the Caroní River, a hydroelectric installation that is designed to generate up to 6,000,000 kilowatts when it's completed. Its main function will be to supply power needed in the Guayana to process cheaply the 1.5 billion tons of high-grade iron ore that lie in huge chunks about the countryside. The first stage of the dam is due to be finished in 1968. The government already has in operation the second largest steel plant in South America, but the lack of trained manpower and some unusual Latin problems have combined to keep the plant's operation at only 25 per cent of its 750,00 ingot-ton capacity.

The reluctance of young, bright Venezuelans to participate in the Guayana adventure does not stem from laziness or a distaste for excitement. Latin Americans, contrary to popular myth, are an energetic lot, but they have a hard time extricating themselves from traditions that seem bizarre.

One such tradition was explained to a visiting American reporter at a dinner party in Puerto Ordaz, one of the settlements being incorporated into the new city. A young man from Caracas who spent four years at a university in the United States and who holds down a big job at the government's Orinoco steel plant made these remarks in the presence of his associates and his wife:

"If my mother and my wife have an argument, I automatically take the side of my mother. She loves me more than my wife does and I love her more than I love my wife. In Venezuela we remain very close to our mothers all our lives. My mother lives in Caracas and she doesn't like my living so far away from her. I don't like it either. If I lose my job at the steel plant, I will be happy to go back to Caracas where I will be near my mother."

If the best educated young people are not stampeding to the Guayana, great numbers of uneducated and unemployed people are. As they have around Caracas and other cities, these hapless folk have created slums on the outskirts of town, building shacks out of cast-off materials and somehow surviving outside the area's money economy. Training such people to work in the big steel plant is difficult and often impossible.

An Energetic Executive

Running the steel plant is the job of Charles Petry, an energetic executive who works for Koppers of Pittsburgh, the U.S. company that's teaching the Venezuelans the steel business. Mr. Petry attributes the plant's low operating figure to the normal shake-down period any new steel plant goes through. The Orinoco plant is only two years old. Too, there have been some labor union troubles, caused in large part by internal union politics.

But after touring the mills and machine shops, which rise incongruously on a 600-acre site on an empty plain, one perceives some of the problems that Mr. Petry and his aides are understandably reluctant to discuss. Acting as guide on such tours is Miguel A. (Mike) Figueroa, assistant to the steel plant's public-relations director.

At the open hearth furnaces were a couple of Yankee steel hands who, after being laid off in the States, decided to teach furnace tending to the Venezuelans. Tommie Turner, 51, who used to squint into furnaces for the Colorado Fuel & Iron Co. in Buffalo, had only praise for the learning ability of Latin Americans, contending they learn faster than apprentices in the United States because they take more pride in their work. He was seconded by Robert Campbell, 52, who came to the Guayana after U.S. Steel decided to close its ancient steel works in Donora, Pennsylvania.

Mr. Figueroa, the public relations man, agreed.

"In the blooming mill and in the mill where we make reinforcing rods everything is run by Venezuelans," said Mr. Figueroa proudly. "Our workers in those places understand their jobs so well they no longer require foreign supervision."

The reinforcing-rod workers were going about their business with apparent efficiency. A team in an overhead control booth was guiding the glowing rods down a track which passed them through a machine that shaped them. The rods, at this stage, were about 30 feet long and as hot as steel can get without melting. Suddenly one of the rods was misdirected by the fellow at master control. One end of the thing —it looked like an orange neon serpent—flew into the air and whipped about wildly. It ended by wrapping itself around the shaping machine.

Men and Machines

Someone set off a siren and a pushcart with a fire extinguisher came rushing up. As it turned out, the workers in the immediate area soon had everything under control.

"Somebody did something wrong," remarked Mr. Figueroa.

A few minutes later, Mr. Figueroa was in the blooming mill explaining how blooms— chunks of steel—were made into pipe. He had no sooner started when a bloom didn't feed into the right slot and the huge pipe-shaping machine caught fire. This conflagration also was soon under control.

An American engineer, asked later about the competence of Venezuelan steel workers, observed: "Well, they are very intelligent and they have their hearts in their work. But not being used to machinery they tend to be overly-fascinated by it. New workers like to flip switches just to see what will happen. We've

had a time around here with people pressing emergency buttons just for fun."

This touch of romanticism, of course, is not peculiar to Venezuela. It is one of several unusual traits that combine to make up the singular Latin American personality. Another trait is an enormous class-consciousness—except for the extremely sophisticated and the extremely poor. The extremely sophisticated are able to take a detached view of Latin American affairs, and the extremely poor don't really care.

This class-consciousness, which is creating problems for the Guayana development project, is so fundamental a Latin American attitude that it resists friendly discussion. Time and again in conversations in Venezuela, the lower class is referred to as "the stupid people." It is said not in intentional disparagement, but as the best description of people who—doesn't everyone know?—are nothing if they aren't stupid.

Keeping Up With Jones

In an attempt to keep slums out of the new city of Santo Tomé, the least expensive apartment houses were built in the middle of a neighborhood containing more expensive units. The theory is that when the poor people see how nicely their richer neighbors keep up their property, the poor people will want to do the same. This has caused some grumbling on the part of better-off residents who don't mind being emulated, but would rather be emulated from afar.

"It's not good that the man who lives right next door should be beneath me," declared one Venezuelan specialist. "He has his place, but it is not next to me."

No one is more aware of the social problems involved in the development of the Guayana than Colonel Ravard. "If anyone can change the customs, or at least modernize the customs, of the Venezuelans it is Ravard," remarked an American businessman who has known the CVG president for years.

The Guayana project symbolizes the diversified development Venezuela now seeks. And it emphasizes Venezuela's need to encourage more modern attitudes in its people before it can sustain a broad-based, industrial economy.

VENEZUELA

Caribbean Sea

0   300
Miles

Georgetown

New Amsterdam

McKenzie

Paramaribo

BRITISH

SURINAM

FRENCH

Cayenne

GUIANA

GUIANA

THE GUIANAS

Reds and Race Riots in a British Colony

IT WAS the kind of remark Latin Americans have an opinion about.

"Today the United States is practically sovereign on this continent, and its fiat is law upon the subjects to which it confines its interposition."

So said Secretary of State Richard Olney in a stiff note to Britain four weeks after he took office in the Grover Cleveland Administration in 1895. President Cleveland, patriotically flaunting the 1823 Monroe Doctrine, had stepped squarely into a South American territorial dispute involving land claimed by Venezuela and the British colony of Guiana. The long-smoldering territorial controversy had worsened when gold, including a 509-ounce nugget, was discovered in the contested area. Britain had steadfastly refused to arbitrate the dispute but after Cleveland's near-ultimatum the British decided to reach a political settlement with Venezuela rather than chance a clash with the United States over a far-away patch of jungle.

But, except for Grover Cleveland's intervention in Britain's colonial affairs in 1895, the United States took little interest in British Guiana until recent years. Since 1953 the emergence of Cheddi B. Jagan, an avowed Marxist and suspected Communist, as the most dynamic politician in the Minnesota-sized colony on South America's northeast shoulder has stirred anxiety in Washington. United States worry that the colony would slip into the Communist fold has had an important bearing on Britain's reluctance to grant the colony the independence it so avidly desires.

Projected by the slogan-spouting Jagan into Cold War entanglements, British Guiana contrasts sharply with the other two foreign-run Guianas, Dutch Guiana (Surinam) and French Guiana.

A hot, drab, unpromising land, French Guiana is an overseas department of France, constitutionally, at least, as French as Paris. Except for a brief turn-of-the-century gold rush, its hinterland is largely unexplored. Its citizens, chiefly languid creoles, live along the coast. Offshore waters teem with shrimp and other fish but, lacking canning, freezing, and port facilities, the French import fish from overseas.

In Surinam to the west, typical Dutch industriousness has fashioned a more solid economy than in French Guiana. Nearly four times as large as the Netherlands, Surinam is considered part of the Dutch kingdom overseas. The sugar industry has waned in the last few decades and rice-growing has become Surinam's leading industry. Surinam has considerable autonomy, including its own flag and national anthem. Its rich racial mix embraces Creoles, Hindus, Javanese, African Negroes, Chinese, Europeans, and indigenous Indians. Unlike British Guiana, Surinam's race relations have been untroubled and little agitation for independence has arisen.

Culturally different from the rest of South America, the three Guianas ("Guiana" means "land of the waters" and applies broadly to the territory between the Orinoco and Amazon Rivers, including parts of Venezuela and Brazil) were all but ignored by the Spanish and Portuguese during their exploration and settlement of the continent. Hampered by

Cheddi and Janet and "The Red House."

British Guiana

Area	83,000 Sq. Mi.
Population	590,140
Population growth rate	2.3%
Literacy rate	80%
Chief Exports	Sugar, Bauxite

Surinam

Area	55,167 Sq. Mi.
Population	325,000
Population growth rate	3.7%
Literacy rate	90%
Chief Export	Bauxite

French Guiana

Area	35,000 Sq. Mi.
Population	32,905
Population growth rate	0.5%
Literacy rate	95%
Chief Exports	Gold, Timber

heavy forest and impassable rivers in the interior and finding little gold, the Spaniards left the area to British, French, and Dutch colonizers. The three Guianas periodically changed hands through purchase, war, and political conditions in Europe. In 1667 the British ceded Surinam to the Dutch in exchange for what is today New York City. In 1814 the British acquired from the Dutch the area now constituting British Guiana.

First Elections

When Britain began breaking up its empire after World War II, the British decided to grant some measure of home rule to Guiana as the initial step in a gradual advancement toward independence. The first popular elections in the colony were held in April 1953. Winning 18 of the 24 legislative seats was the three-year-old People's Progressive Party (PPP) headed by Cheddi Jagan, who became premier.

The son of an East Indian supervisor of a sugar plantation, Jagan had studied at Howard University in Washington, D.C., and later earned a degree in dental surgery at Northwestern University. It was during his years at Northwestern that Jagan met and married Janet Rosenberg, a nurse at a Chicago area hospital and a member of the Young Communist League. Returning to British Guiana, Jagan became more heavily involved in politics than in dentistry.

Stridently Marxist, Cheddi and Janet helped form the PPP, gave key party posts to equally outspoken left-wingers. Janet even campaigned for the PPP while pregnant, peppering her fiery speeches with provocative, made-in-Moscow catch-phrases. In London, the government of Winston Churchill looked aghast at the political ferment in its once-docile colony. When left-wingers began talking about declaring the colony independent and raising a militia, the Churchill government sent troops, ousted Jagan after six months in office, and suspended the colony's constitution. A British government report said the PPP was "completely under the control of a Communist clique."

Abandoning its brief fling at limited home rule for the colony, Britain held the reins of government more closely until 1961 when it again gave the colony a measure of self-rule. In elections four years earlier Jagan had won one of 14 elective seats on the legislative council (the British governor appointed six others). Since 1957, the handsome, articulate dentist played down his Marxist leanings and sought to rebuild the PPP, weakened in 1955 when Negro leader Forbes Burnham, an Oxford-educated lawyer, broke with Jagan over communism and formed a new political party, the People's National Congress.

The sundering of the PPP inserted a new and dangerous element in Guianan politics—race. Most of the Negroes trailed Burnham out of the PPP; most of the East Indians stayed behind with their charismatic leader, Jagan. In the 1961 elections both Jagan and Burnham injected racial appeals into their campaigns. The racial amity that had existed in British Guiana for more than a century began to disappear.

The Negroes had arrived first in the colony, brought from Africa as slave labor to work on British-owned sugar estates and to drain coastal soil for ports. Emancipated in 1834, the Negroes forsook the sugar plantations for the towns, where they became civil servants, teachers and policemen. To replace the Negroes the British imported indentured laborers from India. The Indians, when their terms of service were completed, often stayed on in the colony, chiefly as cane cutters or small merchants in the urban areas.

UF's Free-Enterprise Platform

Thus, the Negroes came to settle primarily in Georgetown, the capital, or the smaller towns of New Amsterdam and Mackenzie, site of the largest bauxite resources in the world. The East Indians, except for some shopkeepers, lived mainly in the rural areas.

The East Indians, who are reproducing faster than the Negroes, now constitute about half the population and outnumber the Negroes by about 100,000. Nevertheless, the number of Negroes and East Indians of voting age is at present approximately equal. In the 1961 elections Jagan's PPP won 42.7 per cent of the vote and Burnham's PNC 41 per cent. A new third party, the United Force (UF), captured the remainder of the ballots. Led by Peter D'Aguiar, a wealthy Portuguese brewer, the UF campaigned on a strongly free-enterprise platform promising close ties with the West. The elections were conducted on a constituency basis with the

Amid bursting tear-gas bombs, the races riot in Georgetown.

PPP winning 20 seats, the PNC 11, and the UF 4.

Jagan, in his second turn as premier, immediately called for independence. Britain, despite some misgivings over Jagan's Marxism and against the wishes of Washington, seemed ready to grant it.

In his first budget the new premier ordered some needed austerity measures, including increased taxes on consumer goods and a compulsory savings plan. The budgetary innovations, however, hit primarily the Negro population in the cities. Egged on by the opposition parties, the unions called a general strike. The business community, also opposed to Jagan's moves, backed up the unions. The five-day strike culminated in a wild riot in Georgetown that left six dead, $30,000,000 damage, and 20 per cent of the capital ruined by arsonists' torches. Jagan, for all his railing against "imperialists," was forced to appeal to Britain for troops to put down the rioters. The premier later set aside the harsher fiscal measures in the budget.

Citing the disorders, Britain called off a British Guiana independence conference scheduled for May 1962. In October 1962 the conference was held but ended in a deadlock between Jagan and the two opposition parties. The premier wanted independence before elections. Burnham and D'Aguiar called for elections first—and on a proportional representation basis, which they believed would end the PPP's majority in the legislature.

Jagan refused to say whether he was a Communist but in 1962 he began diverting the colony's traditional Western-oriented trade to Cuba, Russia, and other Communist countries. More Guianans were sent to Communist countries for schooling. Communist-line educational material began turning up in the colony's schools. The PPP set up a trading company, the Guiana Import-Export Corporation (called "Gimpex"), to get around the lack of British consent for government trade with the Communists. Jagan, an open admirer of Cuba's Fidel Castro, said communism "will win everywhere."

Suspected Power Grab

In 1963 the PPP-dominated Parliament sought approval for a bill requiring government supervision of all union elections. Suspecting Jagan of an attempt to grab power in the unions, 50,000 union members went on strike. The 80-day walkout shut down the sugar mills, bauxite mills, railroads, and airports and brought the colony's economy to a standstill. Again Jagan was obliged to ask Britain for troops. Again he backed down, scrapping the controversial bill.

Blocked by the strike from any possible takeover of the hostile unions, Jagan tried an end run with a sugar workers union, the Guiana Agricultural Workers Union (GAWU), he had established in opposition to the 20-year-old Manpower Citizens Association (MPA). When the sugar producers refused to recognize the pro-

Jagan union or hold representational elections, the GAWU went on strike. The strikers fired unharvested cane fields, attacked MPA workers who stayed on the job. Although composed largely of East Indians, the MPA was run chiefly by Negroes. The clash between the unions led to large-scale defections of East Indians to the GAWU.

The union struggle rapidly turned into a racial one. Negroes ruined the shops of East Indian merchants in the cities. Rural villages, hitherto untouched by the racial trouble, were partitioned into Negro and East Indian sections.

No Formula Forthcoming

By the time the 24-week strike was settled in July 1964, the death toll had reached 159 and the sugar-bauxite economy was sorely set back as business activity and new investment declined. For the third time in three years of rule, Cheddi Jagan had to ask for the help of the British to put down disturbances he was at least in part responsible for. The British governor of the colony invoked a state of emergency, further diminishing Jagan's authority.

The British government, still hopeful of granting the colony independence, sought in vain for a formula that might solve British Guiana's mounting racial difficulties and reverse the trend to the left. In April 1964 the British Parliament approved a plan to hold elections on the basis of proportional representation before freeing the colony. The British set no date for independence.

Britain still hopes for a reconciliation between Jagan and Burnham. The Negro leader, who calls himself a "leftwing-democratic-socialist," is ideologically closer to Jagan than to D'Aguiar. Personal ambition is believed nearly as responsible as ideological disaffection for his withdrawal from the PPP nine years ago.

But the East Indians and Negroes today are split along geographic, economic, and political as well as racial lines. Jagan, well aware that in a few years the East Indians will have a clear majority of voters, has said, "Time is on our side."

Caribbean Sea

HAITI

DOMINICAN REPUBLIC

Santo Domingo

0 — 150
Miles

Area . . . . 18,816 Sq. Mi.
Population 3,013,525
Population Growth Rate . . 3.5%
Literacy Rate 64%
Chief Export . . . . Sugar

NO HAY PLAZA "VACANTE"

"No Jobs"—The factory is new, the unemployment problem isn't.

DOMINICAN REPUBLIC

'A Kind of Collective Madness'

THREE years after the bloody reign of Rafael Leonidas Trujillo Molina came to an appropriately bloody end, the Dominican Republic is still experimenting with self-rule. The Dominicans weathered one coup and one attempt by Trujillo's brothers to reimpose the old dictatorship. They even elected a president in the country's first free election in 38 years. But he managed to stay in office for only seven months before the army succeeded in its second attempt at casting out civilian leaders it opposed.

"We Dominicans," lamented the Santo Domingo daily *El Caribe* during a May 1964 transport strike, "seem to be suffering from a kind of collective madness."

El Caribe may have been justifiably overwrought. The end of the 31-year Trujillo era had not magically turned the Dominican Republic into the Promised Land overnight. The military, the Communists, Trujillo's henchmen and relatives, and assorted political novices all sought to fill the vacuum left when Trujillo was shot to death in an ambush May 30, 1961. The military came out on top as the military so often does in Latin America and now rules through a three-man civilian tribunal.

So, the Dominican Republic reverted to a dictatorship 28 months after Trujillo died. True, it is a dictatorship with a difference. Gone are the secret police, the concentration camps, the torture chambers that were Trujillo's chief sport. Gone, too, is the incredible domination of the economy by Trujillo monopolies.

The triumvirate's leader, Donald Reid Cabral, a wealthy importer of Scottish ancestry, has provided his country with an efficient, economy-minded administration. Cabral's imposition of needed austerity measures provoked the May 1964 strike, which he quickly broke up. The government has offered hefty tax exemptions to lure foreign investment, enacted strong income tax measures, and continued the breakup of the big estates once owned by the Trujillo family. Cabral and his colleagues have promised to hold elections in 1965.

Surprisingly enough, Trujillo, for all the savagery of his long reign, fashioned considerable economic progress, particularly in the cities. He created a light industry and protected it from foreign competition. He built roads, schools, hospitals, and port facilities.

True, Trujillo had selfish reasons for his country's economic advances. He and his followers owned 60 per cent of the industry and 50 per cent of the arable land. The Dominican Republic was Trujillo's *hacienda* and what benefited the country benefited its squire. Estimates of the Trujillo family's fortune range from $200,000,000 to $1 billion.

The countryside suffered under Trujillo since bigger profits could be gleaned from the industrial monopolies than from agriculture, which embraces 80 per cent of the population. The Dominican Republic's rich, black soil, however, kept the country's larders fairly well stocked with such staples as bananas, rice, corn, cassava, beans, and sweet potatoes. Sugar is the country's biggest foreign exchange earner, amounting to half the export volume. Coffee and cacao also are major exports.

Despite the official neglect of the peasants under Trujillo, the government did overcome two difficulties that had plagued the country

Trujillo's $2,000,000, 316-foot personal yacht:
The late dictator took his country for a ride.

Building a sewage system in Santo Domingo:
The channels of power are less constant.

throughout its history. Trujillo's well-trained army protected the Dominican people from any aggression by next-door neighbor Haiti and the dictator repaid the country's sizable foreign debt by 1947.

Before Trujillo, the Dominican Republic suffered periodically from attacks by Haiti and from fiscal irresponsibility of the various dictators who constantly succeeded one another in Santo Domingo. In 1821 the Dominicans declared their independence after more than three centuries of Spanish rule only to fall before invaders from Haiti. The Dominicans threw off the Haitian yoke in 1844 when Haiti was torn by revolution.

In the next 72 years, the Dominican Republic averaged one revolution every 15 months and a new president every 20 months. The political instability and the expenses of warding off Haitian incursions drove the Dominicans deeply into the debt of American and European creditors.

In 1916 the United States landed Marines at Santo Domingo after the Dominican Republic refused American demands for supervision of its finances. The Marines departed in 1924, leaving as one of their legacies a disciplined army. Among the soldiers was Rafael Trujillo, an ambitious, energetic officer whom the Marines rapidly promoted through the ranks. In 1930 when the Dominican president tried to prolong his rule unconstitutionally, he was overthrown and Trujillo was elected president.

Warships to Santo Domingo

The United States again attempted to direct the country's destiny after Trujillo's overthrow.

When two brothers of the slain dictator attempted to re-establish the Trujillo rule in November 1961, the United States sent warships to lay off Santo Domingo. Two months later, at American urging, the Organization of American States (OAS) dropped economic sanctions imposed on the country after Trujillo tried to kill President Romulo Betancourt of Venezuela. The Kennedy Administration increased tenfold the country's quota for sugar sales in the United States. Washington exuberantly talked of turning the Dominican Republic into a "showcase for democracy," free of rightist or Communist dictatorship.

When an air force general tried to grab control of the country in January 1962, Washington made known its opposition. The Kennedy Administration presented the new civilian government with a $25,000,000 grant for public works projects.

Most of the politicians in power, however, were hand-me-downs from the Trujillo days. With Trujillo, his family, and his cronies gone, few capable administrators remained in the country.

Putting the Kibosh on Bosch

So, when Juan Bosch, a poet, novelist, and political science teacher who had stayed in exile for 25 years, was elected president in December 1962, the Kennedy Administration pulled out all stops to help the government. Top American personnel were sent to train the Dominicans in public administration, finance, and agriculture. U.S. per capita aid to the Dominicans was triple the amount dispensed throughout the rest of Latin America.

But Bosch turned out to be an inefficient, although well-meaning, executive. In his election campaign, he had made pie-in-the-sky promises. In office he found he was unable to carry them out as his ill-trained bureaucracy struggled along from day to day.

Too, Bosch thought the best way to control the Communists was to allow them to organize openly. Bosch's policy toward the Communists alienated the business class and the army. In September 1963, seven months after he took office, Bosch was forced out by army officers. A disappointed Washington immediately halted most of its Dominican aid programs.

The Dominican Republic, three years after the death of Rafael Trujillo, remains an empty showcase.

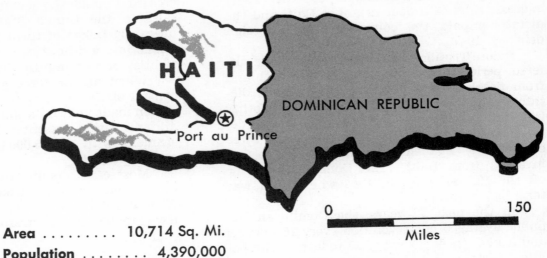

Caribbean Sea

HAITI

DOMINICAN REPUBLIC

Port au Prince

0   150
Miles

Area . . . . 10,714 Sq. Mi.
Population 4,390,000
Population Growth Rate   2.1%
Literacy Rate 10%
Chief Exports . . . . Coffee, Sugar

Death at a moment's notice.

HAITI

Squalor Plus a Real Live Bogeyman

THE words of Christopher Columbus echo with bitter irony today. It was December 1492 and Columbus in sailing the waters of the Caribbean Sea had landed at the island of Hispaniola, then called by the native Arawak Indians "the mother of all lands." "So lovable, so tractable, so peaceable are these people . . . there is not in the world a better nation nor a better land," Columbus wrote.

Within a generation the indigenous Indian population of the island was all but exterminated, dying in battle or from the hardships of slavery under their new masters from Spain. The sad ironies persist to this day in Haiti, which occupies the western third of mountainous, wind-swept Hispaniola.

The first Latin American nation to achieve independence, Haiti has known only one prolonged period of freedom from bloodshed and dictatorship—and that was during a 19-year occupation by United States Marines. Once the most lucrative of France's overseas possessions, Haiti today has the lowest per capita income in Latin America. The $38,000,000 of goods exported by the land in 1962 was $4,-000,000 less than the value of its exports as a French colony in 1788.

The United States has lavished more than $100,000,000 on the country in the postwar years. All Haiti has to show for this largess is a small dam, some repatched roads, and a lessening of the incidence of tropical yaws. Much of the American foreign aid was wasted or disappeared into the bottomless pockets of Haitian politicians and their cronies.

The cruel regime of Dr. Francois Duvalier, who had raised such high hopes in Washington when he took over the presidency in 1957, has made little effort to lift Haiti out of its lethargy and misery. Nine of every 10 Haitians are illiterate but the Duvalier government makes only a nominal attempt to aid education. The tourist trade a few years ago was an $8,000,000 business. Duvalier has let it dissipate. Haiti badly needs private investment but its floundering economy discourages foreign capital.

Duvalier's harsh rule and unconcern for Haiti's social and economic advancement is nothing new to Latin America's most densely packed country. Haiti's troubles can be traced to its birth, when the slaves, brought from Africa to work the profitable sugar, cotton, and tobacco plantations, turned against their French rulers. France had taken over the land from Spain in 1697 when the Spaniards lost interest after Haiti's gold mines were exhausted.

Haiti's rebellious Negroes were inspired by the French Revolution and their bloodthirstiness rivaled that of the rampaging commoners in Paris. By the time Haiti declared its independence in 1804 few white men were left in the country. The Negroes, associating plantation life with French rule, flocked from the sugar cane fields, which fell into disuse. The elaborate French-built irrigation system for the sugar fields was left untended and eventually rotted. The death or expulsion of most of the remaining Frenchmen left the newborn nation with neither technical knowledge nor capital. The first Haitian rulers, trying to revive agricultural production, doled out to peasants small, uneconomical parcels of land that today barely provide a subsistence income.

The first flush of unrestrained freedom brought clashes between Haiti's liberated Ne-

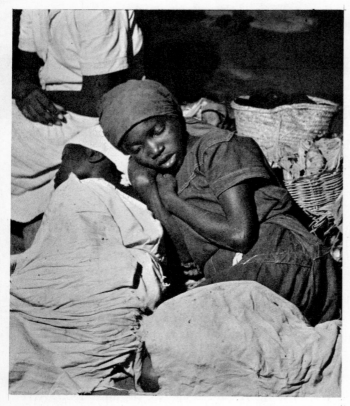

Monkmeyer

Asleep in the streets of Petionville.

groes and its mulattoes, most of whom had been freedmen under French colonial rule. Although a minority, the better-educated, French-oriented mulattoes held the reins of government from 1820 to 1843 and again during the U.S. occupation.

The U.S. Marines landed in Haiti in 1915 when the country was wracked by political and fiscal chaos. From 1843 to 1915, 23 men ruled the nation, all but five of them being overthrown by revolution. The last was hacked to pieces by a mob after his government had ordered the massacre of 160 opponents of his rule. The United States, anxious about American banking and railway investments in the country, sent in the Marines the next day.

Until 1934 Haiti remained under the protection of the United States. The American rule, hated as it was by the Haitians, brought fiscal responsibility and political stability, schools, roads, and considerable improvement in health standards.

Once the Americans had left, Haiti reverted to its old ways. The army put one dictator in power in 1946, threw him out four years later, and then ousted the second man in December 1956. In the next eight months, six governments took office, one lasting just 19 days. Finally, elections in September 1957 brought to power Francois Duvalier, a soft-spoken, American-educated physician affectionately called "Papa Doc" for his work in combating infectious diseases among the Haitian peasantry. U.S. officials were relieved at Duvalier's election, hopeful that the owl-eyed physician would lead Haiti out of its political and economic wilderness.

Duvalier, however, quickly slipped into the pattern of his predecessors, introducing a few new twists of his own. He fostered racial prejudice, egging on the Negroes against the wealthy mulatto elite. To end the military's control over political change, he constantly shuffled commanders and created a 10,000-member armed militia that has grown twice as large as the regular army.

Besides the militia, Duvalier's rule is buttressed by the shadowy activities of the *ton ton macoute,* a creole word meaning bogeyman. The *ton ton macoute* serves as enforcer and informer for Duvalier, quickly dispatches opponents of the regime, and shakes down businessmen for "contributions."

Cruel Reprisals

The latest of Haiti's many dictatorships has proved one of the most oppressive. The press is controlled. Opponents of Duvalier disappear from the streets. The occasional insurrections or invasions from abroad only bring cruel reprisals against relatives of the rebels.

The United States has alternated between stopping economic aid for Duvalier and continuing it on the ground that the Haitian people are desperately in need of it. But the aid seldom seems to reach the 80 per cent of the population trying to scratch out a living on land that is badly eroded. Only one-third of Haiti's land is cultivable; 43 per cent of it is sterile and unusable for growing crops.

"Pulling out of Haiti altogether would leave no hope of influencing the government," one American official said after the Kennedy Administration twice suspended, then resumed, aid. "And no people in the world needs help more."

Watching over the bogeyman in the homburg.

Ariel's Tomorrow

IN ITS report of the soccer riots in Peru a few months ago—riots in which almost 300 persons were killed and hundreds more injured —an American newspaper noted certain historical and psychological characteristics of the Peruvian people which tended to explain such extraordinary and senseless carnage. General frustration, protracted and acute, born of old military defeats, poverty and the feeling of helplessness of the large Indian population, provided ample powder for the explosion. A referee's ruling against Peru's soccer team was only the hammer.

Parts of the story were reprinted in the Lima press, along with editorials castigating the reporter who wrote it. By that time, perhaps luckily, the reporter was in La Paz, Bolivia, a city with a large Peruvian community. At a dinner party one night the reporter showed the story to a number of Peruvian businessmen. The article was passed around the table and each guest read it without comment.

Finally, after a few moments of uncomfortable silence, one Peruvian gentleman removed his glasses, folded his hands under his chin, and locked the reporter in a hard stare. "Your facts are insulting," he said.

The future of Latin America depends at least partly on how willing its leaders are to accept "insulting facts." Too often in the past, Latin Americans have ascribed their troubles to external influences, especially to greedy, heavy-handed Uncle Sam. They are reluctant to admit that U.S. investors and U.S. markets have made a massive and indispensable contribution to Latin economies.

That contribution is being vastly augmented these days by Uncle Sam's role in the Alliance for Progress. The Alliance will continue to be criticized, of course, because Latin America isn't going to be turned into a bustling, prosperous Western Europe in one decade or three.

But billions of dollars and thousands of specialists from the States have helped get the job started. They are helping Latin Americans rebuild their societies, not after the U.S. model, but along more socialistic lines. And it may be as futile for American conservatives to protest this trend as it is for American liberals to berate the artificiality of so many Latin "democracies." In the end it is up to Latin America to find its own way.

Meantime, the Communists are having troubles with each other because they are split into Soviet, Chinese, and Castroite camps. And they are having trouble with the Latin personality which, while hardly the same in every country, is everywhere hard to stuff into a Marxist mold. The Reds can be counted on to continue their adventures but they face a formidable task.

José Enrique Rodó, the Uruguayan philosopher, once wrote an essay called *Ariel*, which has been termed the "Bible of Latin American youth." In it the U.S. is symbolized by Caliban, a low-minded character who thinks only about material gain. The hero is Ariel who possesses a sensitive, spiritual nature and serves as an ideal Latin rationalization of Latin-ness. Rodó expropriated both spirits from Shakespeare's play, *The Tempest*.

For all the "insulting facts" that it takes to make a book about Latin America or any other place, it would take a genuine Caliban to discount an ancient culture that listens so attentively to the human heart. It is a culture that, in the short run, has managed to contain the Communists while, in the long run, surviving the worst it could do to it itself. It has, in fact, withstood everything except prosperity. When prosperity finally comes, can Latin America endure it?

Probably. Ariel is nothing if not resilient.

γ